D1476611

Collecting
INDIAN KNIVES

Identification & Values

by
Lar Hothem

ISBN 0-89689-059-7

TABLE OF CONTENTS

Mohawk Indian chieftain, Chief Newhouse, Canada. Leather sheath is at belt or sash, and knife is held in the left hand. Note trade silver brooches across chest.
Photo courtesy Public Archives Canada

A Sioux couple using small knives to strip the outer bark from red willow saplings. The inner bark is combined with tobacco to form a smoking mixture.
Photo courtesy South Dakota State Historical Society

Indian women preparing dogmeat for a feast.
Photo courtesy South Dakota State Historical Society.

ACKNOWLEDGEMENTS

Respectfully thanked are all those who contributed in some way to the completion of this book. Well over four hundred photographs were received, and the book would not have been possible without this generous assistance. Those who contributed photographs are hereby thanked, and their names appear in the photo credits.

Such photos are especially welcome, as these help make the book coverage go beyond state or region to provide a sort of national overlook of prehistoric and later knife types. Charles D. Meyer, Florida, did many professional-grade drawings for the chapter on "scientific" blade types, and I think you will agree that science and art have been combined in a beautiful way.

Gary Fogelman, Pennsylvania, Editor-Publisher of *Indian-Artifact Magazine,* provided support, photos and during a visit asked some hard questions about just what is or isn't an early chipped blade. As usual, my wife, Sue McClurg Hothem, provided a wide range of support, including crucial instructions on using a word-processor and printer.

Photo Acknowledgements:

Cliff Morris	California	Tom Hendrix	Alabama
P. A. Everhart	Alabama	Howard Popkie	Canada
Eugene Heflin	Oregon	Randall Olsen	Utah
Robert Swope, Jr.	Virginia	Jim & Teresa Dresslar	Indiana
R.G. Roberts	Missouri	Scott K. Silsby	Virginia
Gerald Riepl	Kansas	W.R. Eckles	Nebraska
William Lea	N. Carolina	Mert Cowley	Wisconsin
Gary Fogelman	Pennsylvania	Bob & Gerry Rosberg	Illinois
Dwain Rogers	Texas	Wayne Parker	Texas
A. W. Beinlich Jr.	Alabama	Bob Griswold	New Jersey
Rodney Peck	N. Carolina	John Alward	Michigan
Richard Warren	Missouri		
Jack Hall	Georgia		
Stephen Porcelli	Virginia		
Robert Calvert	Canada		
Ben Thompson	Missouri		
John Geyer	Michigan		
Marguerite Kernaghan	Colorado		
Col. Floyd B. Lyerla	Kansas		
W.J. Creighton	Arizona		
Tom Noeding	New Mexico		
Arnold Moore	Missouri		
Private Collections	Ohio		
Ernest Cowles	Washington		
Canfield & Company	New Mexico		
David G. Shirley	Michigan		
Pat Mahan	Texas		
Jim Cressey	California		
John Byrd	Montana		
Paul Nusbaum	Ohio		

Also thanked:
The South Dakota State Historical Society
Public Archives Canada
Hudson's Bay Company, Canada

INTRODUCTION

When mankind came out of Asia across the Bering Straits into what is now Alaska, useful tools also arrived. These hardy and adventurous people brought fire, for cooking and warmth. Another tool was language, and many hundred dialects were formed from that first system of voice communication. Beautifully chipped points helped secure game, and several kinds of knives were used for butchering and processing animals, and skinning them for hides and furs.

In the last few years much has been written about American Indian artifacts. The field is a favorite today, as an examination of any well-stocked bookstore will attest. Foremost are the chipped pieces (flint, obsidian), and projectile points are fairly well known. Serious collectors can name many point types (**Atl-atl** point or arrowhead) from their geographic region.

This leaves knives or blades, and a study is long overdue. No book exists with a focus just on North American prehistoric and historic Indian knives, so there has been no reference source, no intellectual springboard into the field. Little has been organized in the amateur archeological publications or recognized in the professional journals.

Information existed, for the most part, but has not been assembled into a single package. Likewise, very little has ever been done on historic and trade-era White-made knives, and there were many types in many regions.

The problem, if indeed it can be called that, has been two-fold. The large "true" blades (without basal cultural signatures like stemming or notching, usually diagnostic) often have far more similarities than differences. There is not a whole lot to study, because the blades are so much alike. While one could explain in detail what a knife was like, much less could be said about the age, whether Paleo, Archaic, whatever. With unhafted knives, most important differences — like their hafted counterparts — occur in the basal area.

The second consideration is that the hundreds of "named" or widely recognized chipped artifacts that have solid basal features are generally considered to be projectile points or "spears", whatever the type or size. The possibility that they may have served entirely or usually or occasionally as knives, as cutting tools, is rarely seriously considered.

This book will examine in depth the possibility, even probability, that very many of the hafted artifacts are indeed knives. The reader is simply asked to make up his or her own mind on the matter, especially after examining as many authentic examples as possible. There is little difficulty with some other Indian Knives described and pictured, for these are historic pieces long known to be knives and no more.

Overall, the book is an exploration of Indian cutting instruments, personal tools for specific tasks, or if ceremonial for community purposes. It is also a collector's guide to what is available, for how much, and with as much extra knife-related information as possible. No examples known to be fraudulent are pictured, unless so-described and presented for information-only purposes. Modern reproductions are included to show how many of the prehistoric blades might have been hafted, what these handles might have looked like. No prehistoric blades known to have been illegally excavated or taken from closed lands are pictured.

Dollar values for most specimens pictured are based on a combination of personal evaluation and recent market figures. They have validity in that this is how certain involved and concerned people value the knives as prehistoric or historic Native American artworks. The numbers are not prices, because for the most part the artifacts shown are not for sale, but are valued personal treasures from a now-faded lifeway.

Chapter entries are time-oriented, covering 14,000 plus years of American Indian knife-making. The astute reader will perhaps see some resemblances from which comparisons can be made. We will always wonder, however, exactly how a prized blade was used, who made it, where and when. While we may understand the generalities, the specific and unique story for each blade may never be told.

APPROACH

For a factual book, one of the hardest tasks is to decide what to use — what could be left out, what should be included, what should be emphasized. Usually the simplest approach is best, the shortest word-distance between any number of points, or here, knives. Such efforts tend to make sense and be easier to read and remember.

The first choice was to present chipped blades on a U.S. regional basis. This would be better done by a number of knowledegable persons, one from each geographic area, a committee project. Such books should one day be done. The second choice, followed here, was simply to go with the time factor, early to late, oldest presented first, starting at the beginning as we understand it today.

The author is fully aware that there are different names for, and ages of, prehistoric periods in various regions. There has even been some professional disagreement about which chipped artifact goes precisely where on the time scale. Such discussions are left for those who wish to pursue, and prove, them. What, after all, is the real importance in placing a blade late in the late Paleo or early in the early Archaic, especially if there was little difference in the overall long-ago lifeway?

This said, there can still be much learned by positioning certain early knives in broad time frames, trying to gain a perspective, make comparisons. Knives from New England can be different from California, Canada from Mexico, Louisiana from North Dakota, and so forth. And there can be similarities, as with a number of the Paleo knives, where a single type persists in one form for an area of thousands of miles.

Finally, this book is respectfully dedicated to responsible and informed collectors, those people young and old who have done the most to find and preserve the chipped prehistoric artifacts. They, more than any other group, have saved the past so it can be enjoyed and studied today.

CHAPTER I

KNIFE OR POINT — The Importance

This book is not intended to be an anti-point review of prehistoric pieces, but a pro-knife exploration of existing possibilities. The one bias, if that is the word, held by the author and freely admitted is that many points are really knives. This does make some differences. There are three ramifications here that probably involve a reinterpretation of accepted thoughts. These are also meant as an accolade to the early makers who were fully praiseworthy. And there are some matters of interest for today's collectors.

Interpreting Prehistory

If we are going to accept that many early chipped artifacts considered points are really knives — and a number of collectors are going in this direction — then a few other things follow. Some of these ideas go strongly against established thought, but in the opinion of a growing number of Amerind students, this is the more correct route.

If in fact a very high percentage of the "points" picked up today are really blades, many of them from the rich and highly active period of the Archaic, knives are as common as points in today's collections. This indicates prehistoric peoples may have spent less time on the hunt and more time processing felled game.

Early Indians may have been less concerned with hunting and killing animals than obtaining skins and furs for clothing, and bone and antler for tools after the animals were brought in, not to mention huge quantities of food. Village life may have been far more busy than formerly supposed, highly intensive, with more interaction and interdependence than we now believe. Even though transitional hunting or gathering camps may have played a part, the peoples of the Archaic may been far more settled than has been thought. The presence of so many knives (not points) on the village sites suggests the hut was at least as important as the hunt.

All this hints that early peoples may have eaten rather better and had more clothing of all kinds, good leathers, fine furs. And if knowledge about game-getting techniques of historic Indians has a bearing on how their ancestors operated, far more than projectiles were used. In addition to points of bone and antler (now disappeared) for certain animals, game large and small was obtained using deadfalls, snares, pits, traps, stockades, drives and the like. And if the evidence from early settlers means anything, there was an incredible quantity of wild food supplies almost everywhere in North American, hinting that making a living was rather easy most of the time. Perhaps a huge number of chipped projectile points really wasn't needed, so they were never made.

If a typical hunter made and maintained ten or so game-getting devices, he multiplied his game-getting ability many times. So in a number of ways, prehistoric hunting may have been quite different than what we think and far more effective than the way it is portrayed today. In short, the way we think of American Indians in time periods like the Archaic may be very wrong. And we may have to give the early Indians far more credit than we have so far.

AFTON knife, 1-7/8 x 4-5/8 in. long, well made of a light pink flint. This piece was found in southcentral Johnson County, Missouri. It was a creek find. $55
Photo courtesy Richard L. Warren Collection, Missouri

Excellent example of a large and early blade, late Paleo or early Archaic. Just the outlines of hafting (blade cannot be called stemmed) can be seen for one-half inch on base edges. Material is a mottled black flint, and piece is nearly 4-1/2 in. long. $60
Hothem collection

Indian Tool Design

Very simply said, and what collectors and others who study prehistoric utilitarian artifacts must remember, the Indians knew what they were doing. Their points killed, their knives cut up that kill. And what might seem to the average person to be just an old Indian stone usually turns out to be a very well designed piece of art. After all, if is no small thing to make a tool and have it considered an attractive thing of great beauty thousands of years later. Yet it was routine for the Indians, as countless millions of such artifacts prove.

1

To Collectors

As art items, knives should not be judged as are points. Certainly large hafted blades may seem more attractive if they are symmetrical. But many knives were made and used as asymmetrical blades, and so should not be penalized (either in aesthetic or monetary value) because they are not larger mirror images of points. These are two different classes and the same criteria should not be applied to overall shapes. While factors of size, material, chipping, condition and so forth remain all-important, shape should not be penalized if that is the way an artifact is **supposed** to be.

The matter, too, of missing parts is very important. To be discussed later is the technique of fracture-chipping the shoulder tips on certain blades. When done by ancient or modern accident, true damage, the knife can fairly be down-graded to whatever degree the loss seems to indicate.

But when shoulder-end or edge-removal was purposefully done, this is added craftmanship, prehistoric work. This should not detract but add to inherent value of any kind. The same should be considered for tip-fluting, again when done by the user, and the collector alone must decide on this for individual specimens.

For these reasons, it is important whether the artifacts are points or blades, for it will help us understand both ancient times and the piece itself.

CHAPTER II

U. S. BLADES — Named Types

Most of the over-500 named chipped artifact types in the country — Texas alone has in excess of 100 — came from two sources. By far the largest is the "official" list, those designated by scientists, many who have carefully excavated sites and determined the probable age of the artifacts found. The smaller grouping consists of names created by collectors and other students of Amerind lifeways in different regions of the country. At times, similar knives have been given dissimilar names.

Here is a random selection of known prehistoric artifact types, with professional-quality drawings by C. H. Meyer, Florida. Each was done on a 1:1 scale, actual size, and authentic private collection specimens were drawn in each case. These are presented in the chapter with provenance, without further comment. The author believes that these fifty CH-V depictions are all likely to be knives. lh

The type name (after Bell, Perino, OAS) is given first, followed by the origin (where found) and the material used. To better visualize the full-size specimens, remember that flint has a glossy surface, while chert is dull. The last caption section includes brief reasons why the particular piece is quite likely a knife as opposed to a point.

1. **Abasolo,** Smith Co., TX, grainy reddish-brown Ogalalla chert. Too broad for point, excellent for knife.
2. **Adena,** Simpson Co., KY, charcoal grey flint. Lack of tip, upper knife-like edges.
3. **Afton,** Taney Co., MO, mottled grey Jefferson City chert. Pentagonal-like right side, irregular left, unequal shouldering, width.
4. **Dalton,** Boone Co., MO, off-white Burlington chert. Basal size, obvious resharpening for haft size, thickness, length.
5. **Kinney,** Smith Co., TX, grainy black chert. Excurvate left edge, basal width, straightish right edge.
6. **Lerma,** Smith Co., TX, mottled grey-tan flint. Thick for point, long edges, side irregularities.
7. **Marcos,** Taney Co., MO. grey-red oolitic chert. Large for point, strong hafting, slightly different shouldering.
8. **Marshall,** Stone Co., MO, reddish-brown flint. Excurvate right edge, irregular left, edge damage, off-set tip, differing shoulders.
9. **Meserve,** Pike Co., MO, grey-white chert. Very heavily resharpened, indicating edge-use, or knife.
10. **Montell,** Smith Co., TX, red-brown flint. Tip slightly offset, very sturdy bifurcated base.
11. **Motley,** Smith Co., TX, grey flint. Right edge longer, differing shoulders, large for point.
12. **Osceola,** Pike Co., MO, white and tan Burlington chert. Good length and strong, wide-notched base, the perfect knife.
13. **Pedernales,** Smith Co., TX, grey-white mottled chert. Unimportant tip, missing shoulder, fairly wide base.
14. **San Patrice,** McIntosh Co., OK, brown flint. Very wide notching for size, overall width, slight serrations.
15. **Scottsbluff,** Texas Co., OK, grey-white rippled flint. Width and length and sturdy base suggest at least occasional knife use.
16. **Snyder,** Taney Co., MO, light tan flint. Irregular edges, differing shoulders, non-tip, great width.
17. **Standlee,** Taney, Co., MO, off-white chert. Pentagonal outline, strong size, wide and sturdy stem.
18. **Alberta,** Williams Co., ND, grainy grey chert. Poor tip, pressure retouching on right edge, large stem, overall size.
19. **Ashtabula,** Oneida Co., NY, charcoal grey flint. Wide notches on this specimen (generally more stem-like), overall knife appearance, offset tip.
20. **Copena,** Limestone Co., AL, tan chert. Large stem, excurvate/straightish edging, dulled tip.
21. **Ensor,** Stone Co., MO, grainy tan chert. Irregular edging, unbalanced shouldering, unimportant tip.
22. **Frazier,** Smith Co., TX, grey flint. Upper right edge retouch, percussioned left, width, relatively large base.
23. **Greenbriar,** Stone Co., MO, yellowish-tan chert. Beveled edges, wide sturdy base, dull tip.
24. **LeCroy,** Washington Co., VA, grey flint. Chipped-back length for wide base, angled blade, blunt tip.
25. **Decatur,** Washington Co., VA, grey translucent flint. Wide base, many of the type beveled and fracture-chipped base, irregular edge-line.
26. **Hardin,** Pike Co., MO, uniform light grey flint. Size, wide base, serrations, near-pentagonal outline.
27. **Castroville,** Stone Co., MO, dark grey flint with white inclusions. Wide base, excurvate-incurvate edges, angled tip.

U.S. BLADES - NAMED TYPES

28. **Palmillas,** Taney Co., MO, grey chert. Blade offset slightly to left, unequal edging, angled baseline.

29. **Pandora,** Limestone Co., AL, tan chert. Size, basal width, careful retouch on left blade edge above mid-section.

30. **Kirk Corner-Notch,** Washington Co., VA, sugar quartz. Tip and blade angled to left, wide base, distant notches.

31. **Shumla,** Smith Co., TX, light tan flint. Long stem, unequal shoulders, tip not truly pointed.

32. **Big Sandy,** Stone Co., MO, tan flint. Wide base, distant notches, tip and blade angled to right.

33. **Searcy,** Benton Co., AR, dark reddish-brown chert. Serrated blade edges more worn on left than right, poss. resharpening since shorter than average.

34. **Godar,** Pike Co., MO, cream-white chert. Basal strength, wide notches, and large notches.

35. **Beaver Lake,** Union Co., IL, mottled light and dark grey flint. Ear damage typical of twisting use, edge retouch.

36. **Wadlow,** Pike Co., MO, off-white Burlington chert. Length, unequal edging, basal width, tip offset to right.

37. **Sedalia,** Pike Co., MO, light tan Burlington chert. Length, general knife form, basal width, slender blunt tip.

38. **Etley,** Pike Co., MO, off-white Burlington chert. Size, wide base, differing shoulders, tip offset to right, overall configuration.

39. **Pelican,** Smith Co., TX, white chert. Basal width, blade width, unequal shouldering, edge-tip-edge angle almost 90 degrees.

40. **Big Creek,** Franklin Co., MO, tan chert. Wide base, knife-like tip, very excurvate edging, deep notching.

41. **Ledbetter,** Taney Co., MO, grey-brown oolitic chert. Size, upper right edge retouch, unequal shouldering, varied edging.

42. **Rice Side-Notch,** Taney Co., MO, white flint. Size, basal width, blade angled to left, overall configuration.

43. **Smith,** Taney Co., MO, off-white Burlington chert. There are at least seven reasons why this is a blade or knife.

44. **Waubesa,** Calhoun Co., IL, off-white Burlington chert. Stem width and length, overall size, unimportant tip, unequal shouldering.

45. **St. Charles,** Pike Co., MO, black flint. Basal size, very unequal edges, overall configuration, differing shoulders.

46. **Ponchartrain,** Union Co., IL, cream-colored chert. Length, rounded tip with "chip-down", edge retouch lower left and right.

47. **Benton,** Pike Co., MO, black flint. Size, length, wide stem, blade angled slightly to left, more retouch left edge than right.

48. **Dickson,** Pike Co., MO, brown chert. Long stem, differing shoulders, rounded tip, overall length.

49. **Cupp,** Benton Co., AR, off-white chert. Large notches, sturdy base, blade angled to left, differing shoulders.

50. **Rice Lobed,** Benton Co., AR, light tan chert. Irregular basal ends and shouldering, short for type, beveled edging.

U.S. BLADES - NAMED TYPES

ABASOLO, grainy, reddish brown,
Ogalella Chert
Smith Co., TX

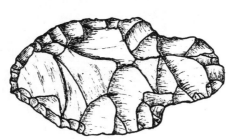

ADENA
Charcoal Grey Flint
Simpson Co. KY

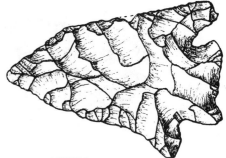

AFTON
Mottled gray Jefferson City Chert
Taney Co., MO

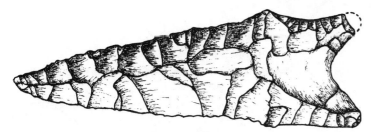

DALTON
Off-white Burlington Chert
Boone Co., MO

KINNEY
Grainy Black Chert
Smith Co., TX

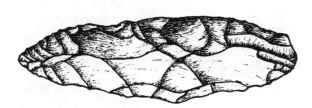

LERMA
Mottled Grey-Tan Flint
Smith Co., TX

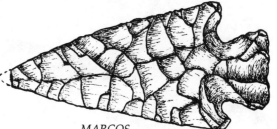

MARCOS
Grey-Red Oolitic Chert
Taney Co., MO

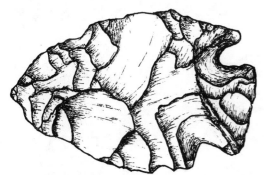

MARSHALL
Reddish Brown Flint
Stone Co., MO

MESERVE
Grey-White Chert
Pike Co., MO

MONTELL
Red-Brown Flint
Smith Co., Tx

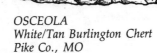

OSCEOLA
White/Tan Burlington Chert
Pike Co., MO

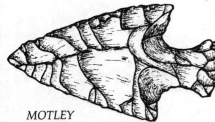

MOTLEY
Grey Flint
Smith Co., TX

PEDERNALES
Grey-White Mottled Chert
Smith Co., TX

U.S. BLADES - NAMED TYPES

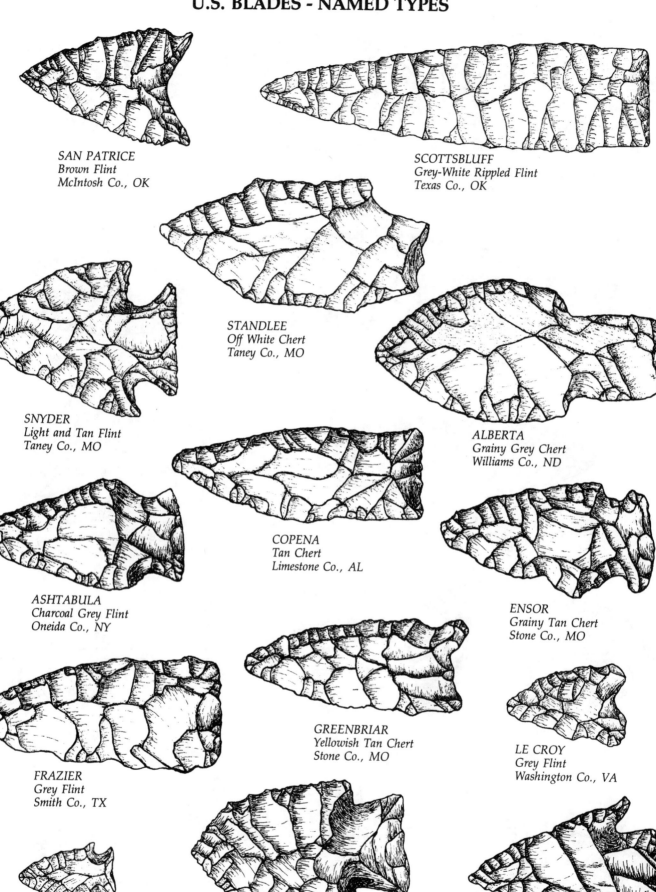

SAN PATRICE
Brown Flint
McIntosh Co., OK

SCOTTSBLUFF
Grey-White Rippled Flint
Texas Co., OK

STANDLEE
Off White Chert
Taney Co., MO

SNYDER
Light and Tan Flint
Taney Co., MO

ALBERTA
Grainy Grey Chert
Williams Co., ND

COPENA
Tan Chert
Limestone Co., AL

ASHTABULA
Charcoal Grey Flint
Oneida Co., NY

ENSOR
Grainy Tan Chert
Stone Co., MO

GREENBRIAR
Yellowish Tan Chert
Stone Co., MO

LE CROY
Grey Flint
Washington Co., VA

FRAZIER
Grey Flint
Smith Co., TX

DECATUR
Grey Translucent Flint
Washington Co., VA

HARDIN
Uniform Light Grey Flint
Pike Co., MO

CASTROVILLE
Dark Grey Flint Blotched w/White
Stone Co., MO

U.S. BLADES - NAMED TYPES

PALMILLAS
Grey Chert
Taney Co., MO

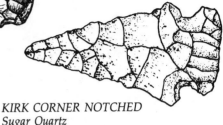

PANDORA
Tan Chert
Limestone Co., AL

KIRK CORNER NOTCHED
Sugar Quartz
Washington Co., VA

BIG SANDY
Tan Flint
Stone Co., MO

SHUMLA
Light Tan Flint
Smith Co., TX

SEARCY
Dark Reddish Brown Chert
Benton Co., AR

BEAVER LAKE
Mottled Light/Dark Grey Flint
Union Co., IL

GODAR
Creamy White Chert
Pike Co., MO

WADLOW
Burlington Chert - Off White
Pike Co., MO

SEDALIA
Light Tan Burlington Chert
Pike Co., MO

ETLEY
Off White Burlington Chert
Pike Co., MO

PELICAN
White Chert
Smith Co., TX

BIG CREEK
Tan Chert
Franklin Co., MO

U.S. BLADES - NAMED TYPES

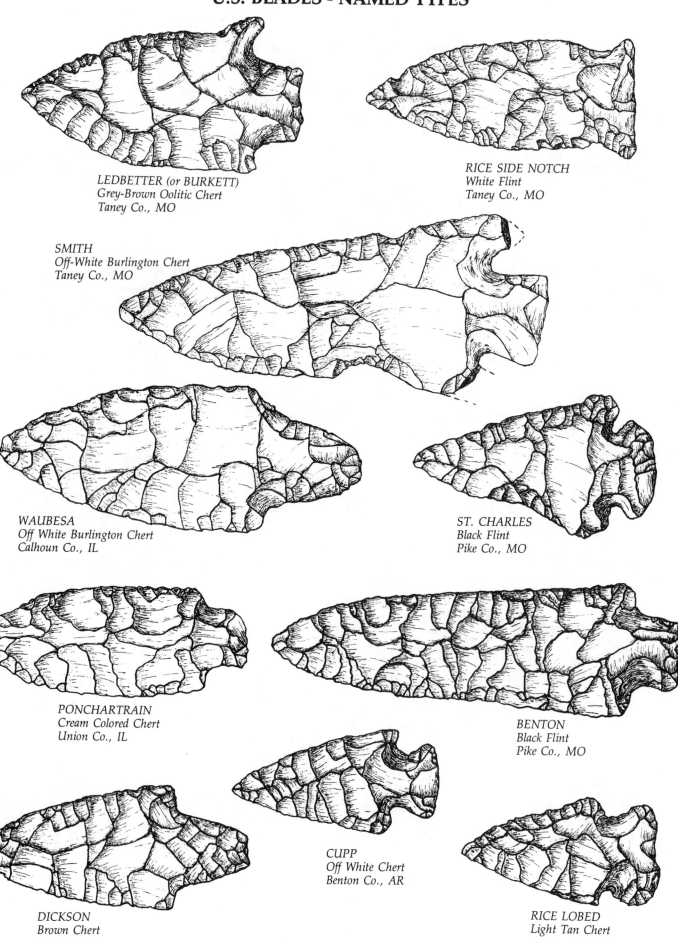

LEDBETTER (or BURKETT)
Grey-Brown Oolitic Chert
Taney Co., MO

RICE SIDE NOTCH
White Flint
Taney Co., MO

SMITH
Off-White Burlington Chert
Taney Co., MO

WAUBESA
Off White Burlington Chert
Calhoun Co., IL

ST. CHARLES
Black Flint
Pike Co., MO

PONCHARTRAIN
Cream Colored Chert
Union Co., IL

BENTON
Black Flint
Pike Co., MO

DICKSON
Brown Chert
Pike Co., IL

CUPP
Off White Chert
Benton Co., AR

RICE LOBED
Light Tan Chert
Benton Co., AR

CHAPTER III

KNIVES INTO TOOLS

Prehistoric knives had utility in directions other than and beyond use as knives. There are two major classes of salvaged blades, and one that is a distinct and different form. There are many other minor tool classes of course, all having in common the fact that they began as blades, or in some cases. large points. Additionally, the three classes all have hafted bases wholly or largely intact.

Hafted Scrapers

These are notched or stemmed forms that have no tips, and with a slightly concave edge located near the original midsection, or in fact wherever a break occurred on the blade. It is widely believed that these are damaged artifacts that were nearly useless as blades, but still entirely useful as another tool, a scraper. Most rechipping creates a slightly concave edge that is flush with one face, bevel-chipped away from the opposite face. In this sense, beveling was used from Paleo times into Contact times.

Their use as scrapers is inferred by several things. First, they look like scrapers. And, the edge curvature and beveling are almost identical to the common "thumb nail" or flake endscraper found in all early Indian cultures. Finally, the short sturdy edges often have moderate use-polish on hafted scrapers. It would seem the edge lost efficiency when heavily worn, and it was rechipped.

Not all scrapers were made from a blade that was broken near the haft, and some students believe that some hafted scrapers were purpose-made when needed. Be that as it may, some scrapers were made on nearly complete blades, and only a small region where the tip once was is employed as the actual scraper edges. For these examples, it is obvious that the form is scraper-knife, a multi-use tool, with two knife edges and a scraper tip. Handy.

A closely related hafted type, fewer in numbers, has the working edge that is not flush with one face, but centered. It is not chipped just from one side, but is chipped from both faces and is equi-distant from each. It too has a straightish to excurvated edge.

For years collectors called these "blunts" or "stunners" thinking they were projectile tips used to avoid drastic damage to birds and small game. In all probability most of them are specialized knives with one main working edge instead of two or more. Very large examples, often without hafting (unhafted) may be referred to as "choppers". Again, microscopic edge-study should provide telling evidence of use for any one example. It is also likely that some examples may have been scrapers (a few have well-polished edges) capable of being used from two directions.

Hafted Shapers

Found in all prehistoric periods, these have largely intact bases and a single or double working edge. But they differ from hafted scrapers in how the edge-face was formed. Instead of being chipped at the probable knife break area, it was ground down, a technique first encountered in Paleo Uniface blades. This gives a smooth edge face, and a sharp and very strong edge.

While hafted shapers may have indeed been used as were other scrapers, it is the author's opinion that they were used as wood-working tools. It would have taken much longer to grind down an edge than chip one, so there would have been a solid and important reason for the extra work. Chisel-like edges would have left smooth marks on wood, not the tiny ridges produced by a chipped edge.

Beyond these observations, much more study needs to be done on this little-known tool type made from knives. This includes various experiments with different materials, wood, bone and the like. But the collector should know that these are not just broken blades. The flat face or angled surface (still fairly flat) can be seen and felt; it is the proof of a complete and different artifact, no longer knife but tool.

Drills

Designed for hole-making, drills can be almost any length, though most are between 1 and 3 inches. Drills for the most part, hafted or not, have symmetrical bases. If the base is asymmetrical and suitable for finger-turning or pushing, they may be termed perforators. If the shaft is rather tapered and wider than a drill, the artifact may be a reamer, not used to make holes, but to enlarge them.

Whatever the long, slender artifact types, drills and reamers and some perforators often seem to have begun life as knives, born as something else. Drills originally made as drills may indeed be a rarity. Many drills have basal hafting identical to hafted knives on any given site, with wide shoulders chipped down to fit the drill configuration.

It would seem that knives were used as knives until efficiency lessened, whereupon they continued as fully efficient drills. This way, double use could be made of better flints, without the wastage involved (the lost, useless flakes) in making a drill in the first place. Even unhafted drills tend to be a bit shorter than the longer knives in any given prehistoric culture. The very long late Paleo drills correspond nicely to the lengths of lanceolate blades or points of the time.

KNIVES INTO TOOLS

Of course a few ceremonial-type drills or hairpins are known, but these are not drills the average collector will come across. Basal thinning and/or grinding on many drill bases — especially the between-notches region — indicate a knife origin. The drill shaft base, in fact, is often the blade stem or the area between the notches, entirely unchanged.

Theories move in waves, like fads, and a current theory is that some drills are worn-out knives, no more, simply the end result of endless resharpening. This is not so. Most drills are not a knife naturally resharpened to a column, but a purpose-chipped piece, this work done only after the knife was critically long for width. Most 4-sided drills had a knife ancestor, but 3-sided drills present more of a problem, and some of these could have been purpose-made.

Beyond the three classes mentioned, knives also continued as other minor tool forms. In a few cases, when the blade broke near or at the haft, the upper portion was what could best be salvaged, which may explain some unhafted rills. More often, and noticeably so, a blade or point will have a flattish base or stem bottom, where the original blade break occurred.

In a few rare cases, and on absolutely authentic specimens, there is a patina disturbance in the notches. This indicates the piece was salvaged, not by the original user, but by a much later person. Often when a tip portion was reworked, the basal chipping was sometimes not as well done as one would expect, in comparison with the rest of the blade.

Prehistoric knives, hafted or unhafted, once knife-use became secondary or impossible, seemed to have served as basic raw material for other tools. All this is in keeping with Amerind conservation of energy and natural resources and focus on purpose. These ideas are not so primitive after all.

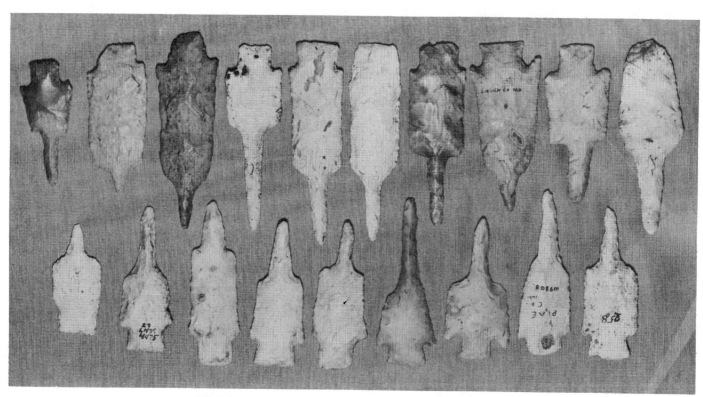

REWORKED KNIVES, several types. These were knives that have been rechipped into drills or perforators without being removed from the handle. They were probably broken and resharpened without rehafting. All are from MO and IL. $75-250
Photo courtesy Ben W. Thompson, Missouri

ARCHAIC blade, 5 in. long, forward portion worn down and tool reduced to a perforator or drill. It retains good balance and is a fine example of prehistoric salvage. While the base appears Paleo lanceolate, the design may well have continued into the Archaic. From Clay Co., AR. $150
Photo courtesy Arnold Moore Collection, Missouri

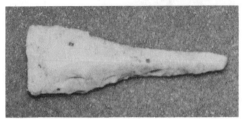

DRILL, 1 x 3 in., large for type, from Clay Co., AR. The large basal area suggests a reworked knife, as was so often done, and the tip appears broken or angle-dulled from use. This may be a late prehistoric artifact. $60
Photo courtesy Arnold Moore Collection, Missouri

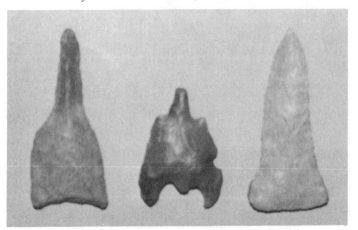

Retouched blades or blade fragments, worked into other tools. Right example is 2-1/4 in. long. Material, l. to r., is: Brown flint, clear agate, and, white flint. Values each... $15
Photo courtesy Gerald Riepl Collection, Kansas

Salvaged ARCHAIC KNIFE, 1-1/2 x 2-1/8 inches. This broken blade was later reworked into a shaft-scraper (top edge) and graver (tip) with one tip side fracture-chipped. In mottled flint with two tan shades. $5
Private collection

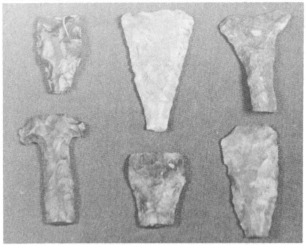

DRILL BASES, top center example 1-3/4 in. long, mainly Archaic period. All have been formed from artifacts that were originally knives. Specimen at top right and lower left still show evidence of notching in the original knife. Values for such incomplete pieces are mainly instructional.
Private collection

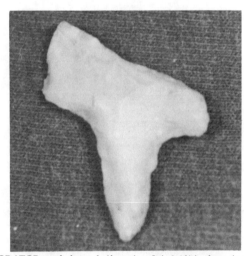

PERFORATOR, made from a knife section. It is 1-1/4 in. long, in pale grey flint, with shaft about 5/8 in. long. (If the piece had a symmetrical base it would be a drill.) Such "remakes" are quite common. $10
Private collection

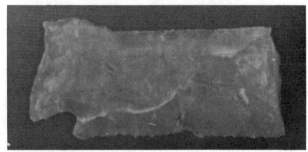

An interesting salvage job. This large Archaic corner-notch was damaged in use, and a new edge formed by chipping and grinding. Shown at top, it is steeply beveled, perhaps as a spokeshave. $12
Hothem collection

11

KNIVES INTO TOOLS

Knife blades and perforators or drills, gem quality from the Columbia River, lengths 2 - 4 inches. Material is flint, jasper and agate, and all chipping is excellent.   *Range, $30-90*
Photo by Ray Pace Associates; courtesy Cliff Morris Collection

HARAHEY KNIFE, with drill on one end. Of dark agate material, a surface find from the Robertson site, Neo-Indian period. This is a rare artifact.
3-1/4''   *$175*
Photo courtesy Wayne Parker Collection, Texas

HARAHEY KNIFE, Alibates flint, one end converted to a drill point. Panhandle Plains Aspect site, Hutchinson Co., TX. This is a rare piece.$200
Photo courtesy Wayne Parker Collection, Texas   *3-1/2''*

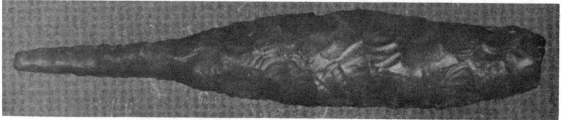

DRILL CONVERTED FROM KNIFE, dark Edwards Plateau Chert. Surface find on the Llano Estacado, near Playa Lake. Time period is unknown.
5-3/4''   *$150*
Photo courtesy Wayne Parker Collection, Texas

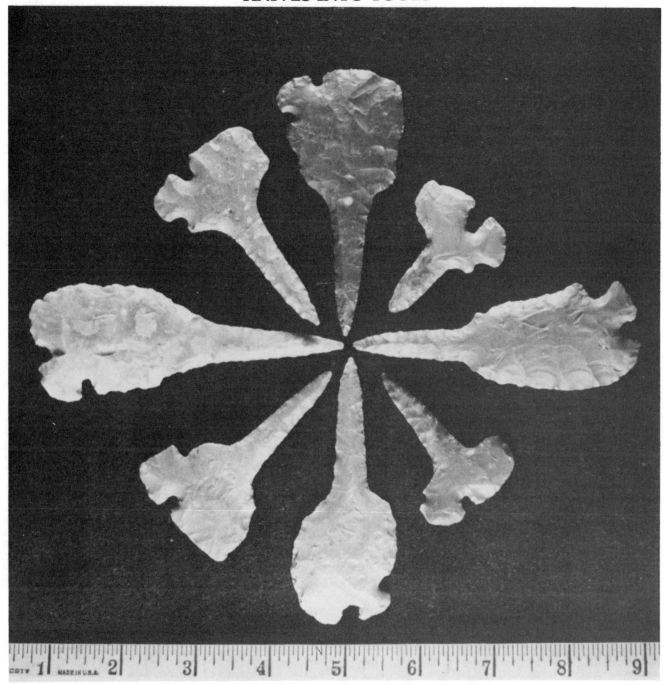

Very rare pieces, these are corner-tang drills, likely made from much larger corner-tang knives. Size is 2-1/2 to 4 in., and materials are black, tan and grey chert. All are from Bell and Coryell Counties, Texas. Values, each...
$250-$350

Photo courtesy D. Rogers Collection, Houston, Texas

CHAPTER IV

INDIAN KNIFE FACTS

Presented here in condensed form is some basic information about Amerind knives. The prehistoric section is generally presented first, followed by the historic section. This chapter alone will give a very good idea of the importance of knives to the native inhabitants of the Americas.

OBSIDIAN BLADES, North America, Upper, a STOCKTON CURVE, serrated edges; these were held between the fingers in claw fashion for fighting by northern California Indians. Ca. 1820-1870.
Lower, ceremonial curved blade from Columbia River area in western Washington state. 9''. Values. . .   *Museum Quality*
Photo courtesy Bernard Lueck Collection, California

At the Lindenmeier site, north of Fort Collins, Colorado, many of the diagnostic Folsom points were recoverable (sometimes even with the basal/facial fluting) but with blunt tips. The rarest knives found were the channel flute-flakes themselves, struck off during the fluting process. These then continued in service as small, uni-faced knives. A few other knives were well-made but without distinctive features. Large leaf-shaped artifacts flaked on both faces seem to have been combination knive-scrapers. The Lindenmeier site is ca. 7500 BC or 9500 BP.

On Santa Rosa Island, off the coast of California, microlithic blades of flint were found in large numbers in burials. They averaged less than an inch in length. It is thought that the bladelets were used as drills to make shell beads.

The Williamson site in Virginia has produced some Paleo knife forms. These — as elsewhere in the Midwest — were larger than fluted points, had some basal fluting, and totally lacked any grinding of the lower sides and base bottom.

The Canadian Sub-Arctic mocroblade and core is thought to have developed around 5000 BC. This technology was probably directly transferred from similar practices in Siberia, USSR.

At Illinois' Koster site in the 4000-year-old Horizon 4 (a temporary hunting camp) the hunters had shown an interesting pattern. Instead of carrying or dragging back the entire deer carcass, they field-dressed it, bringing back only the best portions. In other words, knives were a part of their hunting tool-kit. It was also found that as groups lived at Koster longer (for example, 6000 BC compared to 2000 BC) their tools became more numerous and specialized. Author's note: Extending this reasoning, and perhaps dealing mainly with Archaic times, one might expect to find more knife forms in the late Archaic than in early Archaic times, this both in number and types.

The Basketmakers of the western Southwest used chert for chipped tools, and the finer grades were more widely used. Obsidian, when available, was preferred. The more distant the source, the more carefully the material was worked and more often reused, "stretching" a scarce resource. Knives tended to be multi-purpose, different edges being used for cutting or scraping. Many Basketmaker knives had thin, sharply angled blade edges.

At the Iyatayet site in Alaska's Cape Denbigh in Morton Sound some interesting small knives have been recovered that may be at least 8000 years old. Such tiny blades, called "microliths", were struck from parent cores and then flaked very delicately in a diagonal direction. There may be 16 ribbon-like flake scars per inch. Such tiny blades — like the Eastern U.S. Hopewell bladelets — would no doubt have had bone or antler hafts or handles. Some flaked Denbigh-like bladelets were not further worked to any extent and had the cutting edge on one side or end.

KNIFE FACTS

Plainview points (somewhat like unfluted Clovis types, age ca. 7000 BC) have been recovered from a site at Great Bear Lake in Canada's Northwest Territories. Among other artifacts recovered were ovoid knives.

The skeleton of a butchered imperial mammoth was excavated at Santa Isabel Iztapan, Mexico, in 1952. Along with a Scottsbluff-like spear point were several scrapers, a triangular scraper-knife and a core-struck bladelet of obsidian. The obverse of this knife had three flat surfaces showing the scars of previous blades struck off. These artifacts were all under 3 in. in length. Another specimen found with another skeleton nearby was a broken knife tip or base with excurvate edges. The site was dated geologically at about 9500 BC.

Evidence from California's Mesilla complex — a stone **Atl-atl** hook and two broken weights — suggests use of this lance-throwing instrument around 3000 BC. (Information from elsewhere suggests use several thousand years earlier.)

Sites on the north flank of the Alaska Range in Alaska, dated at 9000 BC, have produced some instructive artifacts. These include large bifaced knives and much smaller tools that resemble projectile points but on the basis of edge-wear are considered knives. The base of the latter are not stemmed or notched, and are slightly off-center, making one edge a bit longer than the other.

In the California region, there was heavy trade in obsidian for knives, spears and projectile points. One route was from the Great Basin west to Sierra Miwok Indians, then to the Plains Miwok. Salt followed the same exchange pattern.

Animal bones, such as those of the whitetail deer, bear the marks of flint butchering knives at the Koster site in Illinois. Similar late-Woodland bones were found in Chesser Cave, southeastern Ohio, and at many other early sites.

Crescent-shaped blades are found in the West's Great Basin region, either as isolated surface finds or as concentrations of up to two dozen artifacts on what may be camp or kill-sites. At least three types are known, but many have a long and a short straight side, perhaps a work-down from larger pieces. The knife ends are sharply angled in the same direction, toward the straight or concave edges. Most examples appear to have all edges suitable for knife or scraper use, and these artifacts may or may not have been hafted. Time-wise, they are Paleo, because they are occasionally found with very early points.

At the Reagan site in Vermont, just short of the Canadian border, certain knife forms included flakes with chipped edges, and examples chipped nicely on both surfaces; these somewhat resembled projectile points in outline. In addition a few of the extra-wide "points", basal-fluted, may in fact be hafted knives, all from Paleo times.

Microliths or miniature bladed tools made from long, thin spalls, were known across North America and from the Arctic into Central America. Used as-is or further retouched, two prehistoric peoples made extensive use of them. One of course was the Hopewell people, ca. 500 BC - AD 700. And the Poverty Point Indians in Louisianna used this diagnostic blade, beginning around 1500 BC.

A very early knife-like artifact form was discovered in the early 1960's near Medicine Hat, Alberta, Canada. In a gravel deposit, stones were found that had been chipped to form a knife-like edge. The flaking appeared to be intelligently directed, and not the result of natural processes. C-14 dating produced an age range of 30-36,000 years.

Knives found at Mexico's Tamaulipas site and associated with slender duo-tipped Lerma points (ca. 9000 years BP) were mainly of three types. One was a curved half-moon shaped variety. Oval blades chipped on both faces by percussion only were found, plus a knife variety with squared bases.

At the Browns Valley site, Minnesota, an early burial was discovered in 1933. Four projectile points of the Paleo Lanceolate type were found, and two had oblique parallel flaking. Two larger objects, well over 3 in. long, were knives with asymmetrical shapes and chipping that was not as regular as on the points. The burial was possibly ca. 8000 BP.

Known historic accounts indicate that knife blades were sometimes fastened to handles with some kind of natural glue or cement, probably with additional thong or sinew lashings. Various authorities describe this glue as being made from many different materials, including: Sturgeon (a fish), salmon heads, pine gum or pitch, tar, boiled-down turpentine, asphaltum, deer's hooves, chokeberry pitch, salmon skin, bone marrow, and many others.

Prior to actual trade with Whites for iron knives and other superior-material tools, Northwest Coastal Indians may have learned about metal in a unique way. They likely discovered iron spikes and other ship-fittings on Japanese and Russian ships, wrecked in the dangerous waters of the Alaskan Coast.

While American Indians never made true utilitarian swords, except for extra-long flint or obsidian ceremonial blades, some great blades of iron were used by California's Yurok in the mid-1800's. They may have been copies of the naval cutlass of the 1700's. Some Texas Indians made copies of short swords, chipping them in flint. The whole idea of super-sized blades was so exotic that when eastern Midwest Indians encountered soldiers with swords, the Indians referred to them ever after as the "Long Knives".

KNIFE FACTS

Canada's Han, Kutchin and Tutchone Indians had large iron fighting knives with blades that were both fluted and duo-edged. These may have been obtained from Russian traders. California's Luisenyo Indians had a tribal scepter with a long flat handle and an obsidian knife-like blade at one flared end. Overall, it was about 25 in. long, and undoubtedly ceremonial in use.

The Tubatulabal Indians of southcentral California used two types of knives for dressing game. To skin and cut up the carcass, a large knife without a handle was used. A smaller knife with a handle was used for other cutting tasks.

The all-purpose semi-lunar **Ulu** was formerly made from slate or stone, usually with a wooden handle. (Elsewhere the form was chipped in flint.) Later examples were used for tasks such as filleting salmon, and were made from available metals like discarded saw blades. These blades seem to be quite old, and the Old Copper people of the western Great Lakes region had versions pounded from copper ca. 6000 BC.

Everyone has heard about Indian "scalping knives." Actually, there is no such thing as a special knife type, and large steel camp knives and typical sheath knives get the blame. The average historic Indian knife never scalped anything except an occasional run-away imagination.

An excellent Canadian knife of a Tahltan Indian (perhaps made by the coastal Tlingit) had a metal trade blade and a bone handle that was wrapped. The handle end had the head of a mythical creature with eyes and mouth inlaid with abalone shell.

In Canada, some historic Indians used spears on land, first driving woodland caribou into stockades or impoundments. The animals were then killed with bow and arrows or were speared at short range. Knives undoubtedly were also used upon occasion.

In the early 1900's, California Chimariko Indians imported blades in red and black obsidian. They especially valued red obsidian. At the time, short blades were valued at $10, while blades two feet or more in length were valued at $50. The historic Pomo of the same state made knives from chert and obsidian. These were attached to a special handle and were used like axes or hatchets.

The Pomo learned to "read" obsidian by color and origin. The best chipping grades were made into small projectile points, while those with mediocre fracturing qualities were made into larger knives or razors. Some California tribes made "Scarfication" knives, for ceremonial or decorative skin cuts that left scars. By most accounts, good obsidian is less difficult to chip than is good flint.

Coastal Miwok Indians in California made special use of obsidian blades. A long knife was used as an amulet for hunting, and an all-purpose utility knife was made of green chalcedony. Butchering knives were made of black obsidian, this material traded from the Wappo.

The Canadian historic Naskapi and Chippewa did indeed use true spears for specialized occasions, such as taking migrating Barren Ground caribou. Canoes caught the animals in rivers and lakes, and they were dispatched with antler or bone-tipped spears or lances. Later, trade-iron tips were used. Sometimes, moose were also speared when trapped in deep snow. Such spears or lances did not have barbed heads and could be used repeatedly. Another specialized use of spears was in the surprise attack against an unsuspecting target, as when Chippawas went against an Eskimo village in AD 1771. The Chippawas had guns, but did not use them.

In Canada, in historic times, an important use for small straight-edged pocket knives was in making **babiche**. This was tanned moosehide, cut into long thin strips after the hide was placed on a peeled log. These strips were later used for lacing snowshoes or braided together to make rope.

Many trees other than maple produce an edible sap that can be made into syrup or sugar. Canada's Metis Indians in the Fort Resolution area learned to do this in the late 1800's, cutting the bark of birch trees. The tip of a large butcher-type knife could be used, carefully guided with both hands to scour the trunk.

Kaska Indians of British Columbia and the Yukon had a number of multi-purpose knives of all sizes, the size depending on the purpose. Handles were made from horns of the mountain goat. Large obsidian blades to the California Tolowa were considered valuable for several reasons. One was prestige. The other is that actual purchases or trades could be made with them, so they were also a form of money.

A decorative knife sheath of the Tahltan Indians of British Columbia, Canada, was worn around the neck. It was part of the dress for ceremonies and dances. One example is of caribou hide covered in blue trade cloth with red trim, the beadwork done in concentric circles.

Semi-lunar knives had a curved blade and handle attached to the back. They were used in historic times for special purposes, and this was a blade that could both cut and scrape. Use in some northern areas was restricted to beaver and caribou hides, because the rounded shape reduced damage to furs and hides for clothing. The blade was held flat and angled, used with a pushing or pulling action.

Coastal Miwok Indians had tribal curing doctors or healers. The kit of one contained two dozen items, including: Obsidian hide scraper, skinning knife, and two obsidian biface blades for cutting a patient. These were wrapped in buckskin.

KNIFE FACTS

In Canadian Northwest Territories, one unusual way of carrying iron trade knives in ornate Indian-made sheaths was practiced by both men and women. They were hung on a short cord around the neck, with the sheath and blade dropping down the center of the chest, in the manner of a large pendant.

A prime beaver pelt in the early 1700's was equal in value to two crooked knives. One trade gun was worth 13 pelts, so a crooked knife was valued at the time at about 25 per gun.

Eastern Miwok of California shaped their bows with a knife made from an obsidian flake set in the leg bone of a deer. It was employed in a scraping fashion. The Eastern Miwok also tattooed young adults of both sexes using ashes for color. An obsidian or flint pointed tool was used.

Pit River Indians of northeastern California (so-called for pits they dug to take the deer) had major resources of obsidian for knives, points and tools. The material came from Glass Mountain and Little Glass Mountain in the Medicine Lake region. The Karok of California prized the large obsidian blades for wealth and ceremonial purposes. For butchering game, small obsidian knives were used, these with wooden handles.

A chief of the Nikolai Indians used a metal knife with voluted handle tangs as a spear to kill bears. The long shaft of the spear was wrapped with leather stripes at regular intervals. This helped reinforce the shaft and provided a non-slip grip.

Some Eskimos had a very different way of cutting meat while eating. Instead of pre-cutting it into mouth-sized pieces, they picked up meat and grasped part in the teeth. Then, using a sharp knife, they cut the meat just beyond the lips. They were very skilled at this, and early explorers did not mention any missing noses.

Possession of trade weapons such as muskets and metal knives gave one Amerind group a real or perceived advantage over nearby groups that lacked them. This generated an attitude of fear in those who did not have these trade goods, and great efforts were made to also acquire them. Such inter-group changes often took place many years before Whites themselves arrived.

One California artifact type, the Stockton serrated, received microscopic study. It was determined that sometimes these ''points'' were also used for slicing and whittling, or, more as knives.

French explorers in the early 1800's were surprised at how sharp the Indians of Arkansas' Ouachita Mountains kept their knives. The secret was a special stone which they used to hone their blades. Cut into slabs, the stone is available today as Soft (multi-purpose), Hard (finishing), and Black (razor-edge). The last two grades not only hone, but polish as well.

CHAPTER V

KNIFE VALUE FACTORS

NOTCHED-BASE DOVETAIL, just under 4 in. long, of blue and cream Coshocton County flint. Serrated and beveled, this 9000-year-old piece has small specks and pinpoints of brown organic material indicating long exposure to the elements. Personal find by the Author, Ohio, 11 Apr. 1985.

$400

Lar Hothem collection

There are many factors that determine what any one prehistoric blade is "worth." These vary according to geographic region, with Canadian pieces valued-favored there, Florida knives in that state, and so forth. Collectors usually prefer items made or used relatively close to where they live, being somewhat familiar with materials, styles and the prehistoric story. Another reason, too, is that when one is thus familiar with authentic specimens, fakes are easier to identify.

Here are nine basic knife value determinants for the prehistoric era, chipped blades, and a final single observation. These are not the ten commandments of ultimate knife acquisitions, but the buyer (and seller) would be wise to consider all of them. Collectors also place different emphasis on such matters, so there can be no one-to-ten ranking of importance. And, there is always that one piece that may prove any such statements wrong.

Symmetrics

For point collectors, symmetrics is all-important and both edges, even both faces, must closely resemble if not almost mirror one another. Notches and shoulders and stems need to be carefully balanced. Not so with knife collectors, except when stemmed or notched, for many do not have such basal features. Most true knives will indicate a small or drastic asymmetry (depending of course on type; **Dovetails** for instance usually are exquisitely balanced, with two primary cutting edges) whether by original design, use-wear or damage.

And the concept of symmetry is further demolished by such blades as the High Plains **Cody** and the Western **Corner Tang,** which are valued for their unique angular appearance, not to mention rarity. The fine concept of balance in an early blade must also relate to how it was used, and how well the design has lasted as an art form.

Size

At one time, years ago, the bigness of a blade was its beauty. No more. Fifty years ago, great knives (some of them actually old and authentic) could be had for $1.50 an inch, sold like yard goods. It is true that other factors being equal a larger blade is worth more than a smaller blade because one simply gets more for the money. But size is far from value in that huge natural slabs of flint or obsidian are of value only as raw material, no more.

Also, many early knives were always small to begin with, made that way, so type or name may be far more attractive and important than mere size. Size is always something the collector must learn to second-rate and put into perspective, and fit this factor in with other artistic (value) considerations.

Material

No matter how well a knife was done, material can override almost anything else. Good flint (glossy, fine-grained) is preferred over chert (dull, large-grained) because it chipped very well and made more attractive artifacts. Good obsidian in scarce shades (red, red and black) is more valued due to color and absence of impurities. But, this in itself does not always denote quality material, because a colorful chert

VALUE FACTORS

may have been difficult to work with, resulting in an inferior artifact.

The best grades of material — including Onondaga, New York; Flintridge, Ohio; Knife River (Lange agate), Dakotas and Montana; Glass Buttes, Oregon — were both widely used in prehistoric times and attractive today. The best lasts, and these materials chipped well both by precussion and pressure methods.

The very best grades have delicate yet strong colors, and are translucent. Held to a strong light source, the rays come through, not just on the edges, but over at least half the piece. This is one sign of gem quality, the material not just of knives but of jewelry and optics and art. Certain Amerind groups, like the Hopewell, seem to have selected such materials with this attractiveness in mind. Patina, in some materials and developed over thousands of years, often clouds an interior of even greater beauty.

Type

Some of the half-thousand "named" points and blades have always appealed to collectors, like the symmetrical notched Archaic "Dove," for they are indeed what everyone thinks an Indian knife should resemble. With more awareness, very special blades like the **Fracture-base** and **Pentagonal** became popular. About all that can be said for type as a value factor is that some collectors specialize in some types. Other collectors diversify, seeking a broad base of prehistoric artifacts.

Configuration

This is a fancy word for "shape" and simply means the overall design of the knife. This includes the presence of hafting (notches, or stem) which generally adds more to value. This is because many knives are expected to have the obvious knife-attachment places, and it looks (to some collectors) more Indian-like.

Undeniably, hafting preparation includes more prehistoric work, and the appearance at least of a more finished piece. Nothing, by the way, bothers a collector more than the suggestion (often only a faint hint) that the piece was meant to be further chipped in the basal region or elsewhere, but never was. Such pieces are termed "unfinished," whether they really are or not.

The configuration of a knife can be very practical for early use, but be somewhat unattractive — too thick in the "wrong" places, have angles that seem impossible to explain today, one shoulder too large, etc. — to the collector. Slowly the insistence on balanced blades seems to be fading, as collectors realize that some knives are in-balance for use by being out-of-balance in appearance. Yet some knives follow the ancient use-first principle and seem misshapen to modern eyes, and no amount of apology or explanation will change this.

Workstyle

Whatever the shape in three dimensions, workstyle covers the surface treatment of the artifact. This is the chipping, from rough block to preform to finished piece. While some blades were formed entirely by rough percussion flaking, most are a combination of percussion and pressure, giving a well-done look, a "polish" to the piece. Generally large flakes were taken off by direct or indirect percussion, and small or thin by pressure.

How well all this was done constitutes workstyle. Poorly done chipping gives an unskilled or didn't-care overview to the knife, a loss of attention that means a loss in value now. Collectors are not only a keen-eyed lot, but cognizant of what is good and what is even better.

Condition

This is one of the most important value considerations, and it is the difference between how the Indian made it and how the collector finds it. Condition involves at least six ways a prehistoric chipped knife was/can be damaged. And it should be well noted that any damage whatsoever detracts from aesthetic and monetary value, the exact extent depending on the individual.

The first way is use-signs, like well-worn, unrechipped edges, especially on one side of an otherwise symmetrical blade, or greater or lesser degrees of wear. This also includes large edge-breaks, obviously the result of use for a task that overwhelmed the edge-capability.

Second, accidental breakage is a detraction, and this generally involves the tip, base or shoulders. Simply, as above, too much force was used on some part of the blade, with obvious results. Why this ancient damage was in some cases not repaired on any one piece can be problematical.

Third, ceremonial breakage was a fairly common practice in some prehistoric periods, whether by fire or blows. Sometimes the pieces, as in **caches** or as grave goods, are close together, but sometimes all the pieces are never found. Many collectors have a few such pieces.

Fourth, there are numerous knives, whole or in part, that evidence fire-damage. This is not ceremonial or the controversial heat-tempering of material for enhanced chipping, but good pieces that seem to have been placed in the way of harm. This could have been too close to a campfire or the burning down of a dwelling.

But, all or part of the knife has the standard damage signs: Surface patina (usually on only one part or face) or heat discolorations; severe flaking with crystalline sub-structure (heat-fractured), spalling, and "pot-lid" blow-outs. This happened when heat reached a microscopic pocket of water, causing a miniature steam explosion. Some blades were so fragmented and massively damaged by heat that they are nearly unrecognizable as once being part of an artifact.

Fifth, agricultural equipment, in use for well over a century in most parts of the country, has accounted for plow-hits and disc-strikes and chemical changes. These are recent breaks, and most collectors can recognize the sharp recent edges, the uncharacteristic fractures.

Sixth, there is collector damage. This ranges from the long-ago practice of wiring artifacts to display boards to gluing them to frames to grinding off the backs to make them easier to mount. However, this type of damage has mostly stopped as collectors become more enlightened. Still, good pieces are kept in boxes where they regularly receive hurtful clashes, and accidental dropping on a hard surface still causes total damage. "Show and tell" at classrooms across the country has accounted for many such casualties.

Aesthetics

Another big word, this involves all of the preceding and how well everything "works" together. This really means is the piece just another Indian artifact or a true prehistoric artwork of whatever size? It also means a knowledgeable collector must do a quick summary of all or most of the foregoing and reach a decision. At shows, this can be done within minutes, at auctions it often must be done in seconds as bids increase. Such decisions of course mean that the piece is always mentally weighed against the price.

Provenance

Also spelled "provenience", the literal meaning is the place of origin. It means that and more to collectors, who also want a history on a knife, documented as much as possible. This is important to a collector for several reasons. This helps preclude the possibility that a certain artifact is fake. It also, hopefully, will give an unbroken "pedigree" to add further to authenticity. And there is the possibility that the piece can be tied to one or more well-known, highly reputable collections. The present stature of the collector adds or detracts from the validity of a blade, especially if it is a highly unusual example. Provenance can be good or bad, depending.

Bad provenance means a piece came from a dealer or collector semi-widely known to have questionable artifacts, and to trade heavily in such items. It also reflects to an extent on those who knowingly or unknowingly deal in such pieces from time to time. So-so provenance is typical, with little or no documentation, especially in regard to minor knives or blades found recently and yet unmarked. While present-day collectors probably record their finds or acquisitions better than did the long-ago collectors, they are more likely to keep the facts in notebooks or file cards or even computers.

Actually, it is a good idea to carefully mark the piece itself with india ink or pen, so that as much information as possible is placed on the less-good blade side. This way, the facts can never become separated from the find or acquisition. All too often, notebooks and artifacts become separated over time, no matter how carefully maker and owner sought to keep the two together. Good provenance has when and where it was acquired, by whom. Excellent provenance has this, plus where it has been all the years since the original acquisition.

Such a history may be a museum tag, markings on the blade, the collector's record book, appearance of blades in a specialized publication (such as this one, invaluable years from now), valid recollections of oldsters with a prize find kept in the family, and so forth. Good provenance is very much a plus in valuation.

Atmosphere

Psychological workings also apply. Value often involves how much one simply likes the knife or the person offering it. Other factors involve the surroundings, how much money one has that day, whether the weather is good, and so forth. There are other, highly personal variables, and all collectors know them. There are many measures for judging a prehistoric blade. Some are basic and must be observed if the collector expects to acquire artifacts that are not only worthwhile in themselves, but add to a sound and valid assemblage. When this is well-done, the sure result is a collection that produces admiration and inspires trust. And this is true today, tomorrow and a century from now.

Copper Knives

Good prehistoric blades have several characteristics, and large size is one of them. Blade configuration is important, with some collectors preferring certain types, so also with the manner of hafting. Much admired are copper knives with a complete metal haft, in the style of rat-tail, flat-extended or hollow-socket. This gives an indication of what the handle was like, and one does not need to guess as much as with notched or short-stemmed blades.

Flint or obsidian value factors do not much relate to copper, except in condition and provenance. Native copper reacts to soil chemicals, and most artifacts show the ravages of time. Very early Old Copper examples will have generally more and deeper pitting than, say, much-later Hopewell goods. However the latter tended (for Cult of the Dead ceremonies and burials) to pound, break or burn the copper artifacts.

VALUE FACTORS

Most copper develops a greenish patina of varying thickness, one sign of authenticity, and knives should never be cleaned or polished to remove this. Provenance is also important. Scientifically, it helps identify long-ago trade routes, and the extent of such exchanges. For the collector, it means some assurance that the piece is good, and not a recent creation that has been artificially patinated.

Also to beware of with prehistoric copper are knives that have missing sections, either early use-damage or more recent accident. Especially with copper, corroded areas may not just be surface problems, but may extend completely through a thin section; this mars both artifact and value.

Trade Era

White-made knives for Indian use overwhelm this field although some skilled Indians made their own blades. Many trade knives are found without handles, these having deteriorated, and the remaining metal is usually heavily rusted, thinned or pitted. The more the environmental damage to the blade, the lower the value.

Some examples were not lost on historic sites but were somehow acquired and saved while the knives were still in good condition. This includes the Eastern Woodlands knives and those of the Plains Indians, plus many examples from colder parts of North America, Canada and Alaska. Unbroken blades of fair size are excellent, and staining is tolerated but not massive rust that eats deeply into the metal and disfigures it and the knife-lines. Light pitting is satisfactory so long as the metal is not seriously weakened.

A few trade-era knives can be traced to the maker by stamped marks (provenance, again) but except for surface-found examples, the main interest is in the sheaths. Partly, this is because historic Indian knives were usually hard-used and the blade so resharpened that it is unimpressive today. Be that as it may, if there are good "papers" with such a blade, it can be highly valued as an Indian-associated historic item, not just a knife.

Any sheath provided with the blade was to protect the edge and prevent loss or accidents. The larger and more ornate the sheath, the greater the mystique and value. Condition is very important, not so much the blade but the blade covering. A collector's dream here is an original knife in fine condition and a well-made highly decorated sheath in mint condition.

While there are indeed established value factors for American Indian knives (one even being a combination of material and rarity as with Central American jade knives) of at least equal importance is how the collector weights or considers each factor. Even beyond such considerations is how such individual decisions are applied to any one knife form. As collectors know, such complications are what help set this field apart and add to interest and pleasure.

CHAPTER VI

FAKE AND QUESTIONABLE KNIVES

A very interesting and instructive photo. Left, fine Archaic blade, black flint, with one edge rechipped to form the excurvate edge, prehistoric salvage, fully authentic. $30
Right, broken knife salvaged RECENTLY by crude rechipping of the break area to form a new edge. Compare the smoothness of original work compared to the modern fake edge. Value...   *Instructional only*
Hotem collection

Too often, the author receives a letter like this one: ''A friend of mine bought some flint artifacts from _____. Three experienced collectors saw them on different occasions and each pronounced them fake even before they knew where he had obtained them. My friend paid over $500. Is there anything he can do?'' Unless one wants to go the legal route, there really is not much to be done.

Some collectors have left the early Indian knife field because, as one said, ''Everything's fake anymore''. But this could be said about almost any collecting field, from marbles to mirrors, stamps to statues. While there are far more authentic (old, Indian-made) chipped knives than modern-made knives in collections, many specimens available for casual acquisition may well be fake.

For example, probably at least half the Indian artifacts (including, or especially, knives) available for sale at the average U.S. flea market are not authentic and old. This is because most flea markets do not screen dealers and the average flea market visitor knows little about prehistoric blades — except that a large slab of chipped flint at a low price seems to be a good buy. Many of the knives are impressive, 5 to 12 in. long, usually notched or stemmed. Many are made of a tan or grey flint, diamond-sawed, then chipped in a drill press or by hand.

They may be displayed with other fraudulent Indian pieces, axes, slate ornaments, ''Southwest style'' silver or turquoise, even (believe it or not) fake pottery. Or, the bad blades may be mixed with good Indian material. Or, the blades may be good, all except for the largest and most expensive one.

Generally, the fakes and fakers can be lumped into three categories. The first ''improves'' a damaged artifact by restoration (supplying the missing portion) or rechipping, making the piece shorter or narrower or restoring a balance the piece perhaps never had. Unhafted authentic blades may have notches put in, or suddenly become a long-stemmed beauty or slowly change from a plain blade into a super-long drill.

The second category of fakers can chip flint reasonable well and they turn out fair copies of a few to dozens of point types. Often the material and size and chipping styles are remarkably similar, something else to look out for. Even intermediate collectors know enough to steer clear, because if a piece is not surely a fake, it is at least highly questionable. And questionable (maybe good, maybe not, with characteristics pointing both ways) means a piece is not to be collected. Here not having a lot of money can be a blessing, meaning that the collector must buy more carefully, hopefully eliminating questionable pieces.

The third category of faking are the true experts who can chip as well as did the Indians, often better. These people are highly trained, experienced in types and workstyles and materials, knowing which knife type ought to have certain features. Such experts, if they are indeed simply making modern copies of ancient artworks, should not hesitate to ''sign'' their works in a permanent way. Records should be kept listing basic data such as amount sold for, to whom, when and where. Some of these people are true if unoriginal artists, and one wonders why most refuse to mark their blades. One man said he'd like to sign his pieces, but does not because buyers don't want the signature. As to the reason why a buyer would not want proof on the piece of modern manufacture, well, that doesn't require a whole lot of thought.

Fake knives tend to be made in styles and types collectors want. **Hopewell** (Woodland), **Dovetail** (Archaic), **Clovis** (Paleo) are all favorites, and fake examples have been around for many years. Lately, attention has been given to such knife families as **Fractured-base,** these existing in dozens of styles. In short, if collectors want it, the type will suddenly appear, as if by magic. Even the large ceremonial blades of the West Coast sneak across the border from Mexico, where there are abundant obsidian sources and some of the modern chippers may even be of Mexican-Indian ancestry, hence, authentic Indian-made.

Condensed, here are some things to beware of:

1. Knife made from the wrong material for the blade type, one not usually used.

2. Patina change. Some materials have one look when fresh from the ground, another when thousands of years old.

3. Patina disturbance. A difference in surface coloration/texture when areas have been reworked recently.

4. Lack of finishing touches — such as basal grinding — when such should be present for the type or period.

5. Differences in chipping patterns at crucial areas, especially the base and tip.

6. A difference in edge sharpness that cannot be accounted for by prehistoric use.

7. Knives made in unusual or fanciful styles that are not true to type or somehow not quite right.

8. Signs (surface deposits) that indicate a blade has been artificially patinated or aged.

9. Be very careful with blades that have no damage of any sort.

10. Even the presence of ''old'' finder marks and fine script does not necessarily mean true age. Just as the knife can be fake, so can the inscription. Or, how about a fake inscription on an authentic blade?

For historic, trade-era pieces, the knives themselves are not usually faked. This is because large numbers of old knives still exist, so there is no need to recreate them. Since these were White-made goods, both Indians and pioneers often used identical blades. And they were often used for the same purposes, so even wear-patterns may be similar.

A good knife in a good sheath should fit perfectly, from long periods of having been in place, especially in the handle wear-spots depressed in the leather sheath. Remember that the knife can be too short or too narrow for the existing sheath (due to resharpening). But, wishful thinking aside, it can never be too wide or too long. And Indians (as with their flint blades) sometimes resharpened until a wide blade was reduced almost to the backing.

Historic Indian knife sheaths are being reproduced, and several have been seen at recent antiques shows. Beadwork is totally intact, sinew is present, the leather pale and Indian-tanned. But, everything is new. Some of the examples are Indian-made, and they are not old. Usually such examples do not have a knife present, and prices have been in the $125 - $250 range. At one of these shows, an authentic old Sioux sheath was also offered, without the blade, and the price was $400.

Some things are being done to combat fakes. Articles and editorials appear in publications specializing in Amerind topics, warning readers to take care. A number of amateur archeological societies do not permit fraudulent specimens to be shown or offered for sale, except as clearly-marked educational displays. Such organizations also have a fraudulent artifact committee, designated by the more positive term, ''authentication committee''.

In some publications, display or classified ads. are ''pulled'' if reasonable complaints are received from reader-buyers. In short, there is a guerrilla war going on that the general public knows nothing about. It is between the modern makers and those who prefer the real thing, between those who knowingly sell new pieces as old and those who want nothing to do with modern recreations. It is between those who prey on the unwary and those who feel the average collector should become self-educated about all aspects of fake pieces.

Perhaps the ultimate comment on the whole thing is this probably-not-true story. A dealer sold a notorious fake knife at a hefty price. It was paid for with a bad check.

CHAPTER VII

ACQUISITION TIPS

A year ago, a professional man with plenty of money called, stopped by, bought several of my books and asked for some advice. A non-collector, he had suddenly discovered Indian artifacts. He wanted the whole thing, an advanced collection, immediately, and how should he start?

The author suggested several reputable sources, hinted that some other books should also be read first, and cautioned a slow beginning. The man promised that he had heard every word and left with a true-believer gleam in his eyes. This story doesn't have an unhappy ending, only a so-so one. He came back weeks later with some good artifacts, nice blades, and a $200 fake. He asked advice on his purchases and what he had paid. After pointing out the good pieces and complimenting him on the reasonable prices paid, there was not much to say about the blatant fake.

The man's gain in three weeks of wheeling and dealing was the beginning of possibly a good collection, but his loss was at least $400 counting in a complete frame of no-good flint he had also managed to acquire. And the trouble is, most people refuse to take such losses, admit they were taken, and try to pass off the bad pieces to someone else. This process is endlessly repeated. Sometimes the problem is not just dealer-collector but collector-collector.

In buying, there are many things to remember, but there are four main considerations. These should be known ahead-of-time, and awareness of them can be the difference — not just between a good or a bad piece — but between a good collection and a bad collection.

Know the seller.

If there has been no personal contact, ask around. Phone calls on matters like these are welcomed by collectors, as everyone encounters the problem of fakes, and most are willing to contribute solid information. Sellers can be divided into three categories: Those who sell fakes, those who don't, and those who, unaware, have passed on a bad piece. The latter will usually make good or take back a fraudulent Indian knife. For fear of legal entanglements, the modern fake-seller is never openly accused, as in print, but word gets around just the same. Listen for that word.

Know the knife.

Dealers, after all, cannot be expected (unless they themselves collect, as some do) to know all the details of what other people collect, as in the case of what is being faked. Their interest, as it should be, is mainly in a certain profit per sale. It is thus the collector's responsibility (the word cannot be stressed too much) to know as much as possible about what the dollars go out for. Anyone who expects the dealer to educate the buyer about what is being bought should not be contemplating the purchase.

Know the value.

Yes, values are all relative, but in the free market system, firm values also exist. Here, collectors should know two things. One, what knives like a certain specimen usually sell for. Two, what the knife is worth to the collector at that moment. If too high, it may be a bad buy. If too low, it may be a bad piece.

Know the terms.

Many dealers offer some sort of money-back guarantee, such as a ten-day return privilege. But, elementary as it sounds, get the promise in writing, including item description, date and amount paid. It does no good to approach a dealer with a complaint that begins with, ''But I thought you said...''. If basic steps are taken, there is no need to invoke a guarantee because the price and piece were right in the first place.

There are many sources for good Indian knives at fair prices. These include auctions that specialize in Indian material, antique shops and shows, and other collectors. Even flea markets are all right if the buyer has enough accurate information to be solidly guided. At auctions, the value is the high bid. At shows and shops, the value is the tag or sticker price. This at times can be less if the collector asks if the price is firm (it may be lowered to make a sale) or has a tax number, at least one sign of being a dealer.

This chapter on acquisition tips can be summarized with five solid suggestions. Follow these tips and you can avoid most losses and acquire Indian knives that will enhance your collection.

1. Select an area of collecting that really interests you. Don't necessarily collect what is currently ''in'' or what someone you respect collects.

2. Take the time to learn what you really want to spend money on. The early blades have been around for thousands of years, and likely will be for a few more. Don't hurry. Relax. Think.

3. Don't make panic-purchases. The overall goal is not to spend money but to get superior specimens. After all, an agony of thought (backed by facts) should go into the purchase of art objects, whatever the kind or age.

4. Learn all you can about the field you collect in. This comes partly with experience, and is something that cannot be taught.

5. Decide for yourself which way your collection should go. Listen to the experts, but also listen to yourself. After all, it is **your** collection.

CHAPTER VIII

THE FUTURE

The future of collecting Indian artifacts in general and knives in particular isn't really difficult to ascertain unless one tries firm predictions. It is very popular to predict, but few such statements about the future ever have much validity, and the greater the distance in time, the less accurate the results. However, based on some current trends and not wild guesswork, here are some things the collector can expect.

Values will go up (even factoring in inflation, and no matter the strength of the U.S. dollar) because this has been the long-term trend since the late-1800's. A century of steady performance is behind this observation, and it is strengthened by other occurrences. Indian kinves, **wisely acquired,** are an investment. This means they have value, will hold value, and increase in value for years to come.

This is true, though the pieces should never be purchased with this consideration only in mind; after all, one might do just as well with rental units. The investment aspect takes place automatically if value determinants have been observed, plus careful collecting. In two words, it is plain common sense. After all, it is never so much what one collects, but how well one collects. And if high quality is respected, and acquired, the quality will always be recognized.

Not so much predictions as informed suggestions, here are some things the collector can expect to happen.

There may be difficulties with federal and state laws aimed (correctly) at the site-looters and pot-hunters. The average collector of course has a perfectly legal collection, and no laws, regulations or statutes were broken or infringed in putting the pieces together. In some states, regulations are so strict (or restrictive) that even the landowner of a registered site may not be able to remove artifacts, even those surface-found.

Almost certainly, there will be some spill-over for the collector with perfectly legal material. Such instances have already taken place on certain public lands in the West. One of the interesting things is whether a collector has the requirement of proving that the artifacts either came from legal areas, or, did not come from a restricted area. This is one more reason to keep totally accurate records on each piece acquired.

Conversely, and a positive counter-balance, will be the general perception that collecting surface-found artifacts from agricultural lands and digging sites about to be demolished in some way is a public service of the highest order. Such collecting will be seen for what it is. And that is the salvaging of a past thousands of years old, and a recognition of the works of a proud and ancient people whose creations delight to this day.

Throughout the book, quality has often been mentioned, but quantity also has a place in values. Very many people collect Indian artifacts, especially points and knives. The number of authentic specimens is limited, while the number of potential collectors is unlimited. This is the supply and demand aspect. Competition, bidding for scarce resources, pushes prices upward. This relates to the investment mention, why knife prices go up, or if not up why they are never likely to fall. This is the scarcity, if not rarity, factor.

There's something else happening in the land, and collectors above all should be aware of it and take appropriate action. It is so important that several collectors asked the author not to write about it to prevent the information from being widely known. This is the agriculture technique known variously as non-plowing, low-till/no-till, or conservation tillage.

Simply, the fields are not plowed and the seed is drilled in with special equipment. Farmers are taking to it because it means fewer passes across the fields (savings in time, gasoline and equipment wear) and less topsoil erosion. This is because the raw, uncovered soil is not exposed to heavy spring rains which greatly reduces gully formation and runoff, and the residue of last year's crop slows water and allows it to soak into the earth.

Many collectors already are aware of the above. However, few know that there is still another reason why farmers are going to conservation tillage. Non-plowing prevents something else, which is the hard-packed layer just below the plow blade, this formed partly by the weight of the plow and tractor. What this means is that the compacted earth becomes thicker and harder each year, preventing plant roots from penetrating; plants get less water and nutrients, and are not firmly anchored, susceptible to wind damage. Once the sub-plow plate layer is broken, and plowing stops, conservation tillage can continue.

All of this is very important to the collector. It means that the ''annual crop'' of artifacts — which has been supplied for well over one hundred years in most parts of the country — is not being ''renewed'' as more and more acreage is not turned each fall or spring. The artifacts are not brought up to be found. This means that a fairly steady source of art objects is gradually being eliminated, the supply diminished while demand ever increases.

While some collectors insist that the land must be turned every three or four years anyway, to recycle crop debris and put organic material back into the soil, they are not farmers and this may be only wishful thinking. Meanwhile some of the best fields, due to scientific advancement, no longer produce that hidden crop, the debris of prehistoric civilizations. Another result is that there is more ''hunting pressure'' and traffic on sites that formerly were considered very secondary sites in terms of hunting hours and artifacts found. Each collector must weigh what fewer artifacts and more collectors really mean, and collect accordingly.

Another trend is that Americans — who have admired and sometimes feared Indians and the Indian way for several centuries — have at last accepted almost anything truly Indian as desirable and collectible. This positive approval means that Indian knives will also shine brightly for the known future. And, there will certainly be more fake pieces as the supply of original and authentic artifacts dwindles. Still another thing that is happening, and the cause or at least inspiration for many collectors' complaints is the fact that some individuals with seemingly unlimited funds are now bidding artifacts (including knives) to previously unheard-of heights. Rightly or wrongly, it is commonly said that these bidders are pricing the average collector out of the market. The future will very likely see more rather than less of this. What this seems to mean is that if the trend continues the value of the average good collection will increase but so will the cost of acquiring top specimens — pretty much the way things have always been.

All things considered, the collecting future looks healthy, promising, exciting and challenging.

CHAPTER IX

PALEO KNIVES
(Early 12,000 BC - 10,000 BC)
(Late 10,000 BC - 8,000 BC)

In the past half-century, the age of Early Indians in the New World has been steadily pushed back. Around AD 1900 and into the 1930's, scientific interest revolved mainly around "Mound Builders" as the oldest pre-Columbian societies, peoples now known to be Woodland-era. Far-side theories were much in vogue, such as the Indians having a rootstock in one of the Lost Tribes of Israel. Even the Great Serpent Mound in Ohio's Adams County was once touted as the site of the Garden of Eden, wishful thinking building upon vague fable.

Now, Carbon-14 and other carefully calibrated dating methods steadily push back the temporal frontiers. It is no longer unusual to see responsible publications suggesting ages of 20,000, 50,000 and 100,000 years ago. Even an age of 200,000 years has some support from geological evidence.

Today's student of Amerind knives will draw small comfort from the probable fact that the very first North American blades were not chipped in flint at all. Knife-like edged cobbles or choppers or knives have been found in much of the country in very early contexts. However, "green" or fresh bone can also be chipped, and this material may have been the first knives or even points. And a bone scraper or serrated-end bone artifact from Canada has been dated at 27,000 years BP, well before any known chipped points or blades.

In the well-accepted if not understood Paleolithic or Paleo period, at least nine types of early knives are identified. Some are remarkable similar (the uniface blades) throughout the country, even North America. Apparently this tool technology was simple and effective and reliable, hence widespread. These may not be the oldest chipped-flint or obsidian knives or points in North America (Sandia Types I and II are actually pre-Paleo, ca. 18,000 BC) but they are the best-documented.

Students of early artifacts — and the longer ago such things were made it seems the greater the number of views — are divided as to whether such ancient blades had handles, or were hand-held. (The same questions arise about unhafted knives in the Archaic period.) The author, well aware of the differences between breaking new ground and going out on a limb, can only present some facts and photos. The reader, in the last analysis, will have to decide on this "hafting factor".

Here are nine Paleo knife types, and several no doubt remain to be described and placed firmly in the early or late Paleo period. It is difficult to date these artifacts, except in a broad time-span way, since so few excavations have been made and the results published.

Point-Like Knives

East or West, points seem first to have been fluted, early, and then became more elongated or dagger-like later. (**Sandia**, of course, was stemmed.) A few knife forms seem to have been patterned on the points, and simply seem to be larger or different versions of them. Standard wisdom for all time periods suggests that large examples are knives, small examples points, but it gets complicated. Small chipped artifacts can also be knives, though it is more difficult for large artifacts to be points.

Knives copying fluted points tend to be either exaggerated (extra-wide, tip unimportant, like **Ross County** Paleos), or have wide bases, sometimes fluted, and blades angled to left or right. These artifacts, quite simply, are not convincing as points and appear much more suited to be knives, with edge-use important.

In the **Lanceolate** department (lance-like, late Paleo) many examples exist that are either much larger or wider than were ever necessary as points for dropping game. Often, they are much better made (material, chipping, finish) than a throw-away point, whether hafted as a spear or **Atl-atl** dart. A few such early knives do not evidence the expected impact damage associated with thrown weapons. Instead, they have the mundane resharpening of edges, the ultra-careful edge treatment given knives in regular use. Some were so very beautifully made that even at that very early time their purpose must have been ceremonial in nature.

Uniface Blades

As the name suggests, Paleo Uniface blades are worked or chipped entirely or mainly on a single side or face. They tend to be large and fairly thick (up to ½ in.) and as much as 2 or 3 in. wide, up to 6 or 7 in. long. The underside or reverse is fairly flat and bears the slight ridges of the original "parent" block, these the percussion ripples. (Good flint shows them, much chert does not.) This side is usually concave to some extent, again relating to the strike-off process. The amount of force needed to drive off such a large spall is very great.

Though called Uniface, very often edge retouching is done on some portion(s) of the reverse edges, which tend to be straight or excurvate. The main face has percussion flake-scars, some shaping for knife use, with careful edge retouch. Due to the haphazard early large flake, Paleo Unifaces tend to be almost any elongated shape, but always sturdy and most useful. Resharpening, when done, will eventually alter the original outline of the blade.

A number of Unifaces appear to be made-on-the-spot tools, perhaps to be picked up and used again, and some show very little wear. Others are well-worn, evidencing intensive or long-term use. Uniface blades up to 8 in. are known.

Most Uniface blades are formidable instruments, designed for many cutting purposes. Some, however, are as delicate as a surgeon's knife, suited for many light cutting purposes, and may be no more than 3 in. long.

Uniface Blades with Tools

Many Paleo Uniface blades seem to have been the Swiss Army Knife of 10,000-plus years ago. In one small package the knives combined a number of features, being multi-purpose tools. The main working or cutting edge might be nearly full-length, but often involved only a portion of the original flake edge.

This main edge may be excurvate, fairly straight or incurvate, as with the general-category Uniface knives. There may be secondary knife edges, smaller, and with smaller flake-scars. The main feature of this Paleo knife type, however, are such things as shaft-scrapers. Some were chipped in, then enlarged by use, while others simply have been worn into thin edges by sheer use, gradually enlarged.

The shaft-scrapers (some call them ''spokeshaves'') are half-moon shaped indentations, up to ½ in. across, though some are indentations in elongated shapes. This would seem to correspond to the size and shape of wooden spears or lances used at the time. Graver tips, usually located near one end, are short, sharp and strong. Many are backed by the thick ridge of the original obverse for additional strength.

It is thought the purpose of the graver tips was to cut into bones, scouring them for breaking, this to obtain the marrow for food or bone for weapons or tools. Another use may have been to help cut out long splinters of bone for projectile points, most of which have now disintegrated with time.

Multiple tools were made on Uniface blades for several reasons. One was the shortage of highest-grade flint or obsidian, requiring that the best material ''go farther''. In traveling, the early groups simply could not remain always close to the best material sources.

Importantly, the nomadic lifeway meant that many knives were left behind, the reason so many Paleo Unifaces are found on short-term or seasonal campsites. Multi-purpose tools had less weight and more utility, and it is not surprising that so many were made. Likely, these were so useful they were carried with any major move.

Rectangular Blades

Fairly rare — at least compared with the huge numbers of Uniface knives — are the Paleo Rectangular knives. Usually they were made from the best available flint. They are biface, which means both flat faces were chipped equally well, though they seem to have a definite top and bottom in some cases. They range from under 1 in. to over 2 in. wide, rarely more, and may be from 2 to 6 or more in. long. Both percussion (large flake-scars) and pressure (small flake scars on edges) chipping was very well done, and it is unusual to see one of these blades that is not extremely well made.

Smaller Rectangular knives may be chipped-down versions of larger specimens, especially when fairly wide and thick. Average thickness is from ¼ to ⅜ inches, making them quite sturdy. An interesting aspect of these Paleo blades is that the working or cutting edge is a fairly small surface, located always at one of the small ends.

The edge itself may be fairly straight or raggedly incurvate or even angled slightly to one side. Often, during resharpening, the working edge was sharply beveled, or chisel-shaped. This gave a cutting edge that was both quite sharp and very strong. And, being chipped on only one surface, it represented a savings in flint. These angled edges may in fact be the earliest beveled-edge blades in the New World.

While most Rectangular blades have only one cutting edge, and with a somewhat thinned base that may well have had a handle, a few examples seem to have working edges at each end. In the latter case, they may have been hand-held only, or had a large ''cross-wise'' handle, used with both hands. Most of the Paleo knives were quite possibly hafted in some manner, except some Unifaces with combination working areas.

These would have been hand-held in a manner that brought whatever necessary working area into play. Likely, Rectangular knives were heavy-duty butchering knives, and some have battered areas that suggest somewhat violent use, as if pounded by a club or hammerstone or used as a chopper. Resharpening, the care with which made and their relative scarcity suggests a permanent, personal use. As with most Paleo artifacts, these are random surface finds, and a concentration of them is highly unusual. They are thus unlike Paleo Unifaces, which may be found in small numbers at any one campsite. Note: There are reports that these unusual blades have also been found on early Archaic sites, so use may have continued for thousands of years. Or, perhaps the Paleo people had simply been on the same sites before the Archaic people. A Wisconsin type has a stemmed base.

General-Purpose Knives

Beyond the specialized Paleo knife forms described, there is another type that can be called "general-purpose". They are fairly widely known to collectors as Paleo pieces, because they are often found on Paleo sites. They are also different from Archaic forms, and use the flints common to the Paleo period. Both good flint and average cherts were used, somewhat similar to the Uniface materials.

General-purpose Paleo knives have been so-named by the author because of their great resemblance to the average modern belt or sheath or hunting knives, all of which they may once have been. They are amazingly modern-looking, strikingly so. The faces are flat, length is from 4 to 6 or more inches, and the main long edge is always excurvate. Often the tip is dull or otherwise unimportant, though some are quite pointed.

Always, the main cutting edge was very carefully chipped from both sides, and beveling is unknown for the type, though it may be very steeply chipped from both faces. While some General-purpose knives have dulling or damage-in-use, most surviving examples have a "clean" edge. The opposite side received little attention, and the best way to describe this "backing" edge is to call it "straightish", and often not particularly well chipped. Seen from the side, these blades are quite asymmetrical.

Sometimes the baseline of this knife type seems to be angled or directed a bit to one side, obvious in some extant examples. There are only two logical reasons for this. One is that the knife was originally made in a blade-direction that matched, in-line, the direction of the base. Frequent one-edge resharpening may have shortened one edge, making the base seem out-of-line with the rest of the blade.

Or, as was likely in Paleo times since few woodworking tools exist, the handle was of bone, horn or antler. This may also be the reason the base is usually only 1 to 1⅜ in. wide. These organic materials have natural curves, and may have been used to keep handle and fingers as far as possible from the cutting work. This not only made cleanup easier, and provided a tight grip on the haft, but would have made knife use more efficient. Similar innovations were probably made with other Paleo knives, handle and blade working together. Simply said, the angled base may have allowed the employment of a curved handle.

Beyond speculation, and adding to earlier mention of Paleo affiliation, there are several other reasons for placement in this time period. All deal with the basal preparations for hafting. Some examples have a full or partial angled chipping platform, ground by abrasion into the base. This enabled the higher edge to serve as the contact point for basal thinning or fluting. This was likely done by indirect (bone punch struck with hammerstone) percussion. The chipping angle varies slightly in degrees, but is rarely as great as 45, never as shallow as 20 degrees.

This basal platform was left on a number of General-purpose knives, and may have been a spinoff from point fluting. Some examples exhibit true flutes, definitely not enlarged basal-thinning scars, of course a touchmark for the Paleo period. Usually there is only one on one lower base face, not both, since the purpose was a good solid haft area, not deep balanced pentration as with fluted-base points. Some examples lack basal platforms and/or fluting, but the base is still thinned for the handle. Such examples still retain the identical blade configuration for the type. Some writings place these blades in the Archaic, but the overall indications are certainly Paleo in origin and at least first use. A key to identifying these blades at a glance is that they are all long and slender, at least when originally made, and have the single excurvate edge.

Blades With End-Scrapers

Very closely related to the Uniface tool category are Uniface Blades with End-Scrapers, but different enough to be separately described. These tend to be 2 to 4 or 5 in. long, about 1 in. wide, and quite thick. Even the obverse or worked face presents a somewhat crude appearance, though some extremely fine and well-made examples exist. Many are long, thick and narrow, with somewhat steep and irregular edges. A sub-variety is smaller, thinner, and much more carefully made and with a very tapered blade that has straight edges. One feature of this sub-type is that the blade face is fluted on the obverse, this flute in the direction of the scraper edge.

Blade use is indicated by the long shape and slightly excurvate edges, possibly the result of resharpening, though some edges are straight. The wider end is the familiar snub-nosed or thumb-nail scraper, though one example has a straight edge that is highly polished, as if from wood-working. It is likely that some examples will have a graver tip or spur on one side of the scraper.

The opposite, usually smaller end also shows signs of use of various tasks. Often there is a fairly sharp tip here, as if for graving or penetration tasks, though it is usually much larger. Due to thickness and all-around task use, these blades may not have been hafted. Rarely are other tools associated with this Paleo knife type, and it seeems to be mainly an unsophisticated knife and scraper, the blade being the scraper handle.

Uniface Blades with Notches

Lesser-known but possibly widely distributed Paleo knives exist. One is the **Waller** a late Paleo knife-scraper from Florida. It has a Uniface structure, is 2 to 4 in. long, and has the typical irregular Uniface outline. The major feature is basal notches, these chipped in from both sides of the base. This gives the type somewhat of a stemmed appearance; the notches are fairly large and roundish. Apparently, this type is one of only a very few notched Paleo blades anywhere.

Triangular Uniface Blades

The Nuckolls Site, Tennessee, with a large number of late Paleo artifacts, has produced a triangular knife type. The two long sides of the Uniface blade are carefully chipped, and they meet to form a fairly sharp tip. The basal region is the blade's widest part, and it may be fairly straight or markedly irregular. This is a fairly large blade type that undoubtedly exists in adjacent states, and one version of it is found in Ohio.

Flute Knives

Flute knives are exactly what the name suggests, and they are extremely rare. Some have been found on Eastern sites in the U.S. They are simply the material removed from the lower face of a fluted point, usually the last chipping step in finishing the point. One side will be Uniface, while the other has the flake scars made while shaping the point. Some were used "as-is" while others had delicate edge retouching. These Paleo pieces are so scarce that most collectors have never seen an actual specimen, let alone found one.

Though Paleo knives are rather limited in quantity because they were relatively few in number to begin with and were widely scattered in early hunting times, surprising numbers exist. Collector interest remains quite high, since these are the oldest artifacts that can generally be found. And, most Paleo knives are well made and attractive, fairly large and with good visual appeal. The aura of mystery because of their distance in time adds much to their mystique.

Sometimes it is difficult to tell if any one knife form is early Paleo, late Paleo, or both, although fluting is believed to be early. It is important to remember that there is no precise cut-off date for early-late Paleo times. That is, at 8000 BC knife forms were not abruptly dropped and new ones invented. Likely, many (or at least several) centuries were involved in the slow process of knife style changes from type to type.

Side view of UNI-FACE knife from first example in photo on page 31.
Courtesy Tom Hendrix, Florence, Alabama

PALEO

Left to right: All UNI-FACE Paleo found in Lauderdale Co., Ala. 5-1/16 x 1-1/2 in. light gray in color. Made of a flake that contains the striking platform. Very fine chipping on both edges of the blade. $35. 5 x 1-3/4 in. excellent chipping on one side and distal end. $30. 4-7/8 x 1-3/4 in. made from a single core flake. Very smooth uniform flaking on the edge ranks this piece among the finest of Paleo knives. $40. 4-1/8 x 2 in., one edge has very fine chipping while the other edge on the same side has coarser chippings. $25
Courtesy Tom Hendrix, Florence, Alabama

(Reverse sides of above knive)

PALEO

Left to right: Uniface knive, 3-7/8'' x 1-1/4'', buff color, Paleo, Madison Co., Illinois. Found on Monk's Mound (Cahokia mound) on Oct. 16, 1927. It was undoubtedly carried up in a basketful of dirt when the mound was being built. This piece is finely chipped on all three edges while no secondary chipping is seen on the uni-face of the artifact. $35
Uni-face pointed knife, 3-3/16'' x 1-3/8'', buff color, Paleo, Lauderdale Co., Ala. Finely chipped on both edges. $15
Uni-face, 5-7/16'' x 1-1/2'', gray, Paleo, Lauderdale Co., Ala., chipped very finely on both edges. On the uni-face surface, one edge had a 3/4'' space of chipping, the other edge had a 2-1/4'' chipped area. $30
Uni-face knive, 4-3/16'' x 1-3/4'', gray, Paleo, Lauderdale Co., Ala., very finely chipped around the entire piece. $45
Uni-face knife, 4'' x 1-9/16'', tan, Paleo, Colbert Co., Ala., fine chipping around the periphery of the piece. $45
Courtesy A. W. Beinlich, Jr., Sheffield, Alabama

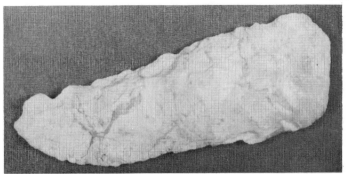

PALEO GENERAL-PURPOSE. 4-7/8 in. long, in brownish-tan mottled chert. This piece also has a flat basal chipping platform that was partially used (one side) for basal thinning. Good size here, mediocre/poor material.$20
Private collection

PALEO UNIFACE BLADE, 2-3/4'' long in a brown-black cobble flint, poss. of glacial origin. Incurvate blade edge (top left) has a sharp graver tip at lower blade corner. Fairfield County, OH and ca. 10,000 BC, from Valley Knoll site.$20
Private collection

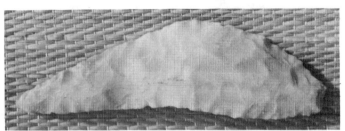

KNIFE, Paleo, 1-1/2 x 4-3/4 in., white, pink and brown Flintridge, from OH. $50
Courtesy Marguerite L. Kernaghan Collection; photo by Stewart W. Kernaghan

Left to right
LERMA ROUND BASE, 2-7/8 x 1-1/16 in. Gray Colbert Co., Transitional Paleo to Middle Archaic $7
THOROTOSASSA point or commonly called a coral knife found Trap Creek, Tampa, Florida, Hillsborough Co. Obtained from Son Anderson May 26, 1984. Similar to the Lerma Round Base. Made of Coral. White color with various shades of pink and black streaks. 3-7/8 x 1-1/4 in. Transitional Paleo to Middle Archaic. $12
LERMA ROUND BASE, 3-1/8 x 1-1/4 in. Gray, Colbert Co. Transitional Paelo to Middle Archaic $5
Courtesy A. W. Beinlich, Jr., Sheffield, Alabama

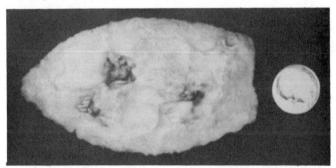

PALEO BLADE, 1-15/16 x 3-1/4 in., made of tan chert. This piece is very thin and has multiple basal flutes. It is from Graham County, KS, and came from a ''sand-blow'' area, scooped out by the wind. Such ''blow-outs'' produced thousands of Early Man points in the dustbowl Depression years of the 1930's. $125
Photo courtesy David G. Shirley, Michigan

BLADE, banded agate, 4 in. long, from Columbia River, Oregon. This is a sturdy, well-made piece. $40
Photo courtesy Jim Cressey, California

Beautiful PALEO UNI-FACE MULTI-PURPOSE TOOL. Left, graver tip. Bot. excurvate knife edge. Right, scraper end. Top, straight. Knife must have been unhafted. Black Zaleski flint, 4'', Fairfield County, OH. $30
Hothem collection

EDEN type (?), Wisconsin, 1-1/4 x 5-1/2 in. Note the parallel flaking, which (along with good length and narrow form) may mark it a Paleo piece.
Photo courtesy Bob & Gerry Rosberg Collection, Illinois   Museum quality

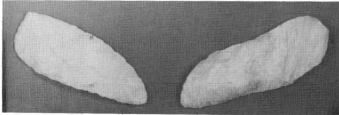

Two fine PALEO KNIVES.
Left, tan flint, GENERAL-PURPOSE, with one edge excurvate, other fairly straight, perfect condition, 3-3/4''. $35
Right, UNI-FACE BLADE, striped flint, with the reverse or flat side up. Like many unifaces, the blade shape follows the contours of the large detached flake that became the knife, 4''. $25
Hothem collection

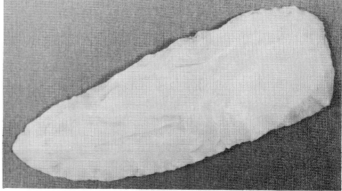

PALEO GENERAL-PURPOSE KNIFE, beautiful example, 3-7/8 in. long. It is in a tan flint with light brown at one basal corner. Design here is classic, with one excurvate edge and angled tip, with backing edge fairly straight. Note the basal chipping platform just 1/4 in. wide at obverse base. $50
Private collection

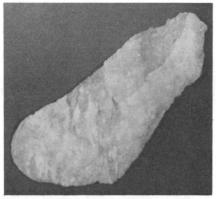

PALEO UNI-FACE KNIFE, showing obverse. Lower left section of this big blade seems to be the main working edge (rounded) while haft region is at top right. Made from a blue and white Coshocton County material, a grade found over much of the eastern Midwest via early trade, 4''. $35
Hothem collection

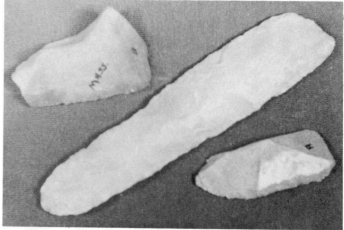

PALEO KNIVES, with center example 5-1/4 in. long.
Left, UNIFACE BLADE, Massachusetts, with minor ''B'' face created by abrasion. $20
Center, GENERAL-PURPOSE, Kentucky, tan flint, nice size. $50
Right, UNIFACE BLADE, Ohio, with minor face ''A'' worn flat by abrasion. $20
Private collection

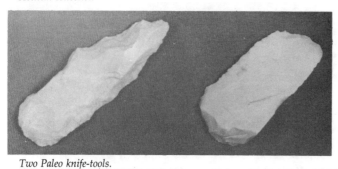

Two Paleo knife-tools.
Left, END-SCRAPER ON BLADE, pale grey, high-quality flint, thick, 3-1/4''. $25
Right, END-SCRAPER ON BLADE, cream and tan flint, upper left edge the main working knife portion. 2-5/8''. $20
Hothem collection

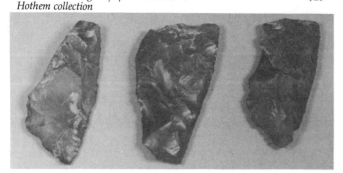

Very early blades.
Left, edge lower right and lower left, Paleo. 3-1/4'' $8
Center, probably early Archaic (from site where found) with fine edge on right chipped in from both faces. 3-1/4'' $15
Right, Paleo blade which has a 1-1/2 in. basal flute at top center. 3'' $15
Hothem collection

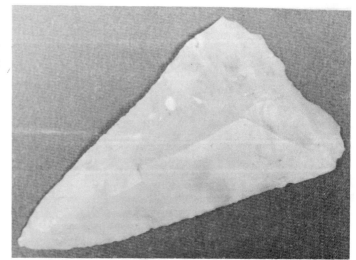

PALEO TRIANGULAR KNIFE, 3-1/2 in. long. Of uniface construction, such blades are very scarce. There is a small shaft-scraper at the base of the upper edge and main edges have several areas of retouch with very delicate chipping. Material is Flintridge chalcedony with cream inclusions. $45
Private collection

LEAF-SHAPE, 4 in. long, made of flint. A faint stemming indentation can be seen on both sides of the base. San Diege area, CA. $150
Photo courtesy Jim Cressey, California

KNIFE, 1-3/8 x 4-1/2 in., of tan flint, found in Vernon Co., WI. The end opposite stemmed hafting has a short sharpened edge, which appears to be beveled. This form suggests Paleo affiliation (see PALEO RECTANGULAR knives, elsewhere). $30
Courtesy Mert Cowley collection, WI; by Mohr Photography

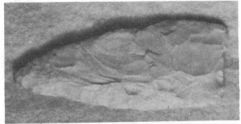

Paleo blade, yellow-brown jasper, 3-1/4 in. long. It is ground on base and lower side edges; knife is from Union County, Pennsylvania. $100-150
Photo courtesy Fogelman Collection, Pennsylvania

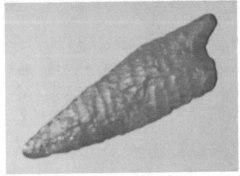

Paleo knife having characteristics of several ''name'' types. It is 3 in. long and chipped from brown flint; this is a Kansas find. $50
Photo courtesy Gerald Riepl Collection, Kansas

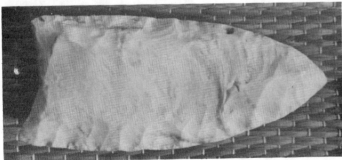

FOLSOM knife (note tip canted to one side) 1-1/4 x 3 in., of chert. Excavated from pit with animal remains at Folsom, NM, in the summer of 1964. Rare piece, and ca. 8000 BC. $300
Courtesy Marguerite L. Kernaghan collection; photo by Stewart W. Kernaghan

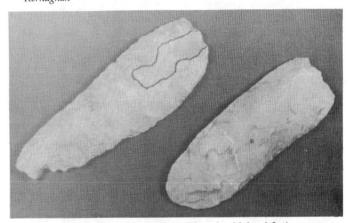

Chalcedony KNIFE, 2 x 2-5/8 in., found by a diver in an underwater cave in St. John's River, FL, about 50 miles N. of Orlando. This piece is probably very early. $30
Courtesy Marguerite L. Kernaghan collection; photo by Stewart W. Kernaghan

PALEO GENERAL-PURPOSE KNIVES, each with basal fluting on one lower base face. Left, irregular tip is early damage; on this specimen the basal flute has been outlined in black ink to show size and location. Made of red chert, it is exactly 4-1/16 in. long. $25
Right, flute visible at obverse base, light grey flint, 3-1/2 in. long. $30
Hothem collection

PALEO RECTANGULAR BLADE, concave beveled cutting edge to left, hafting area to right. Made from a glossy caramel-colored flint, it is unusually large for the type, 1-1/2 x 4-1/2 inches. From an old collection, Fairfield County, OH. $50
Hothem collection

PALEO RECTANGULAR BLADE, *angled and beveled cutting edge to left, hafted area to right. It is made of a black flint, and is 3-5/8 in. long, perfect condition, from OH.* $25
Hothem collection

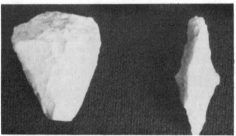

Paleo knife-like tools: *Left, knife made from flake with cutting edge on each side. Isle of Wight Site, Virginia, Cattail Creek Chalcedony.* $5
Right, double-bitted chisel-graver, same site, same material. This is a very rare Paleo Indian tool. $100
Photo courtesy R.M. Peck Collection, North Carolina

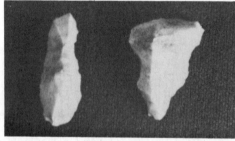

Paleo knife-like tools: *Left, chisel-graver from Isle of Wight Site, Virginia, and found in association with Clovis-like projectile points. Material, Cattail Creek Chalcedony from Williamson Site, Virginia.* $5
Right, Paleo combination tool; end-scraper, graver spur, two spokeshaves and chisel-like graver on tip close to scale. Isle of Wight Site, Cattail Creek Chalcedony. $25
Photo courtesy R.M. Peck Collection, North Carolina

Paleo Indian knife *with large spokeshave on one side of the blade. Squared base was probably hafted to a bone or wooden handle. From Swain County, North Carolina; material is a light tan chalcedony, probably from Tennessee. Discounting the spokeshave, note the great resemblance of blade outline to other Paleo knives in these pages.* 4'' $55
Photo courtesy R.M. Peck Collection, North Carolina

Paleo lancet *(cutting edge at top, the sharp tip), a rare and unusual tool. From the Williamson Site, Dinwiddie County, VA. Material is Cattail Creek Chalcedony, native to site.,* 1-1/2'' $30
Photo courtesy R.M. Peck Collection, North Carolina

Paleo Indian lancet, *cutting tip at top left, highly unusual tool from the Isle of Wight Site, Virginia, of Cattail Creek Chalcedony. Note also the cutting edge along entire top of this tool.* 2'' $30
Photo courtesy R.M. Peck Collection, North Carolina

Paleo Indian knife, *in this case a Clovis point reworked into a blade. It has extremely fine secondary flaking, done in a high grade white flint, origin unknown. Note the smoothness of the lower base edges, the result of grinding, typical for the type.* 3'' $150
Photo courtesy R.M. Peck Collection, North Carolina

DALTON blade, *late Paleo/early Archaic, evidencing the sturdy bifurcated base for which the type is known. At 4-7/16 in., this is an unusually large piece in light-colored chert. Main width at lower shouldering is 1-1/2 inches. With much useful ''life'' remaining in this knife, the Indian maker must have been unhappy when this blade was somehow lost.* $275
Photo courtesy Arnold Moore collection, Missouri

*Lanceolate knife of bluish flint, from Waynesboro (Shenandoah Valley) Virginia. Note slight stemming on one lower edge side near base. $45
Photo courtesy Swope Collection, Virginia 4-5/8''*

*Paleo knife, 5-1/2 in. long, Alibates flint, perfect condition. $95
Photo courtesy Gerald Riepl Collection, Kansas*

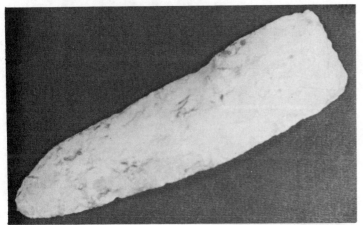

*PALEO GENERAL-PURPOSE KNIFE, 1-3/8 x 4-3/4 inches. It is made from a tan-cream flint common to the central Midwest, with lower edge the main working area. It has a basal area that is very lightly ground, and the piece offers fine length and condition. A better-than-average knife from Paleolithic times. $55
Private collecton*

*PALEO GENERAL-PURPOSE KNIFE, in pale cream flint, 1-1/16 x 4 in. long. The lower and longer working edge has been steeply rechipped (resharpened) from both faces. Upper "backing" edge has been very heavily ground and the basal area is lightly ground. Tip area on upper edge has been worked into a shaft-scraper. This piece is well-used, in contrast to many Paleo g.p. knives. $35
Private collection*

*PALEO RECTANGULAR BLADE, 1-5/8 x 2-1/2 inches, in a mottled cream and brown material that may be of glacial origin. Base at left has a flat-ground chipping platform. Working edge at right is steeply beveled away from the obverse and there is a graver spur at left blade edge. Interesting piece. $35
Private collection*

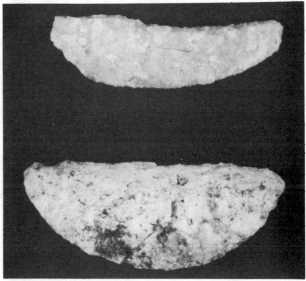

*PALEO CRESCENTS, ca. 9000-7500 BC.
Top, CRESCENT, 2-3/4 in., in spotted colored chert that is white, cream and tan. Only the long lower side has been edged. $30
Bottom, CRESCENT, 3 in., in light brown chert. Good design and condition, it has a good edge all around. $50
Photo courtesy Randall Olsen, Utah*

*AGATE BASIN KNIFE, 1 x 3-1/2 in., rounded base style. It is made of a dark grey jasper, good quality, fine flaking for the early piece. From NE. Unlisted
Photo courtesy W.R. Eckles, Nebraska*

*UNHAFTED BLADE, 1-1/4 x 5-1/4 in., in high quality blue-grey jasper native to the region, NE. Very well made, this is likely Early Man or Paleo period. Unlisted
Photo courtesy W. R. Eckles, Nebraska*

PALEO LANCEOLATE, (poss. Plainview-related), 1-1/8 x 3 inches. From Vernon Co., WI, material is a white and grey flint. The slightly incurvate base is typical of some late Paleo knife types. $100
Courtesy Mert Cowley collection, WI; by Mohr Photography

PALEO KNIFE, 1-1/8 x 3 in. long, in glossy white flint. It is fluted and has basal thinning; from Barron Co., WI. This piece is early Paleo. $140
Courtesy Mert Cowley collection, WI; by Mohr photography

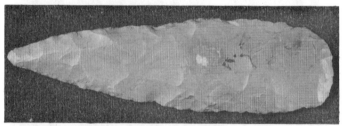

KNIFE, 1-1/8 x 4-1/2 in., from Vernon Co, WI. The material is a waxy brown flint and piece has basal thinning. Style and length suggest Paleo period placement. $80
Courtesy Mert Cowley collection, WI; by Mohr Photography

Left, UNHAFTED BLADE, NE, 1-1/4 x 4-3/8 in., in a brown jasper blade native to NE. Possible early knife. Unlisted
Middle, UNHAFTED BLADE, NE, 1-3/4 x 5-7/8 in., made in blue-grey petrified wood, also NE. Unlisted
Right, UNHAFTED BLADE, 1-1/4 x 5-1/4 in., in blue-grey jasper of high quality. This form too may be Early Man for the area, NE. Unlisted
Photo courtesy W. R. Eckles, Nebraska

PALEO RECTANGULAR BLADE, 1-1/2 x 3-3/4 in., in glossy dark grey and tan flint. From Chippewa Co., WI, this is likely a stemmed version of the rectangular knife form. Note the beveled edge on smaller edge to left, typical of the type. $55
Courtesy Mert Cowley collection, WI; by Mohr Photography

PALEO GENERAL-PURPOSE BLADE, 3-3/4 in. long, in a quality black flint. Tip is missing (lower left) and blade edges have received some wear. Such blades are usually random finds on Paleo campsites, frequently on tops or sides of small valley ridges. $35
Private collection

CODY KNIFE, 3-1/4 in., dull white chalcedony with slight greenish tint. This bade may have been reworked. Early, (ca. 7500-6500 BC) these knives are often found with Scottsbluff points at giant longhorn bison kill-sites. Scarce type, with main blade the longer edge. $75
Photo courtesy Randall Olsen, Utah

STEMMED BLADE, 7/8 x 2-7/8 in., material a reddish flint. Edges have fine chipping. Overall length to width ratio suggest Paleo placement, along with stemming. $35
Courtesy Mert Cowley collection, WI; by Mohr Photography

PALEO

ANGOSTURA KNIFE, brown flint, late Paleo Indian period. Surface find on a Sandhill site, Gaines County, TX. Found by Monte Covington in 1984; broken bone was also present, suggesting either a kill-site or butchering station. A classic piece.   5-1/4'' $500
Photo courtesy Wayne Parker Collection, Texas

Late Paleo blade, Dougherty Cty., GA, which is 5-11/16 in. long. It was found underwater in Muckafoonee Creek, and has turned black by long immersion. Perfect condition, excellent flaking, with 1-1/2 in. of lower sides and base being ground. Flaking technique is collateral and random. $500
Photo courtesy Jack M. Hall Collection, Georgia

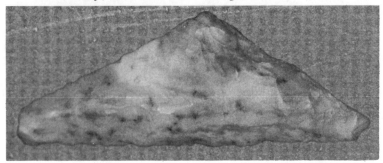

THREE-POINTED KNIFE, made of petrified wood, surface find in Palo Dura Canyon, Randell County, TX. Age unknown, but piece has characteristic features of the CODY knife, Paleo Indian period. Rare   2-3/4'' Unlisted
Photo courtesy Wayne Parker Collection, Texas

Knife, 4-1/8 in. long, of dark brown Pennsylvania jasper; time period is unknown for this very large flake knife. It is from Northhampton County, Pennsylvania. $20-50
Photo courtesy Fogelman Collection, Pennsylvania

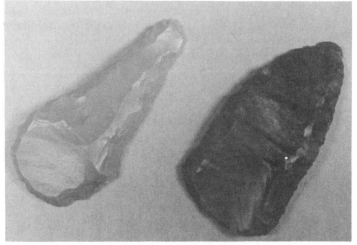

Two extremely rare artifacts, PALEO END-SCRAPERS ON TRUE BLADES. Additionally, both have been fluted on the obverse face, the scar starting at small end of blade.
Left, pale grey flint, blade edges dulled, from IN.   3'' $25
Right, black glossy flint, OH.   2-1/2'' $25
Hothem collection

STEMMED BLADE, 7/8 x 2-5/8 in., in a glossy white flint. It is from Vernon Co., WI, has transverse chipping and thinned base. Overall configuration and stemming suggest late Paleo period. $55
Courtesy Mert Cowley collection, WI; by Mohr Photography

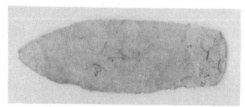

Āngostura, 3-1/4 x 1-1/8, Cream colored, Colbert Co., Ala. Late Paleo, Early Archaic. $45
Courtesy A. W. Beinlich, Jr., Sheffield, Ala.

PALEO KNIFE, 1-3/4 x 2-1/8 in., in tan flint. It is extremely thin with delicate chipping, basal thinning, very sharp edges. Configuration is early Paleo. $70
Courtesy Mert Cowley collection, WI; by Mohr Photography

4-3/4 x 2 in. Brown, Middle Archaic, Colbert Co., Ala. $175
Courtesy A. W. Beinlich, Jr., Sheffield, Alabama

*Canadian historic Indians: Morley Beaver (right) with wife and child, ca.
1906. Note the fine decorated knife sheath being worn at front.
Photo courtesy Public Archives Canada*

41

Cheyenne Indian encampment with staked-down buffalo (bison) hides, with skin tipis and meat being jerked or air/sun-dried in background. This was put up on long poles beyond reach of the camp dogs. Women in right foreground may be using a knife as a scraper to thin the hide.
Photo courtesy South Dakota State Historical Society

Indians butchering for a feast or celebration. Note several knives in use, which would be late-1800's steel-bladed, wooden-handled. The axe was often used for making major cuts like splitting carcasses.
Photo courtesy South Dakota State Historical Society

CHAPTER X

ARCHAIC KNIVES
Early (8000 BC - 5000 BC)
Middle (5000 BC - 2500 BC)
Late (2500 BC - 500 BC)

As the above dates suggest, the 7000-plus years of the Archaic period were by far the longest of any prehistoric timespan (except the completely unkown pre-Paleo) and not surprisingly, had by far the greatest number of knives and other artifacts. (In fact, CH XII, Hafted Knives, mainly concerns the Archaic.)

The name itself isn't much of a help in understanding the vast and perplexing period. The word Archaic means two things: Belonging to a much earlier time, and, something antiquated, no longer current, out-dated. The name in short does not well-serve to explain the more than 70 centuries after Paleo's big-game hunters and before Woodland's pottery and agriculture.

The Archaic is known as a hunting-and-harvest time, and in a sense it combines the earlier and later eras. Reliance was on hunting smaller game animals and harvesting wild plants, nuts and seeds. Of course, as in all periods, fish and wildfowl were also obtained.

The Paleo period has long received popular attention, as the general public is interested in "firsts". So also the late-prehistoric cultures of most U.S. areas have received much publicity due to imposing earthworks, open-to-all sites, evidence of impressive ceremonies, elaborate artifacts, or actual contact with Whites. Somehow in all this, the crucial Archaic period — in many ways the most Indian of Amerind lifeways — has been slighted, almost lost.

Though a number of very important Archaic-inclusive sites exist, only three have been deeply dug, thoroughly analyzed, well-written up and the results widely published so that the findings are easily available today. They are the St. Albans Site, West Virginia, the Indian Knoll Site, Kentucky, and the Koster Site, Illinois. Also, there are many hundred known point types from the Archaic, and probably half as many knives, though some points appear to be knives.

One aspect of all this, explored in this chapter, is that a number of unhafted Archaic knives of recognized types or at least numbers of the same close family do not have well-accepted type names. Some have only regional designations and are referred to be different names. Many others are called simply "knives" with no cultural or temporal additions that will aid the collector in identification. Everyone knows chipped knives are old. The basic question of course is this: How old?

So little has been done with Archaic unhafted knives that direct evidence — such as controlled excavation from firmly dated levels — is very difficult to find. Indirect evidence has to be relied on many times, such as surface finds from Archaic sites, manner of chipping, and type of material used. Even negative evidence, such as a knife form not found in earlier or later cultures, has had to be utilized.

The difficulty is that there are few diagnostic basal features to pinpoint a type. So, all unhafted knives of the Archaic period tend to have a well-made, good-material sameness, and this is generally true no matter the size or the configuration of the knife.

Unlike earlier or later knife types, there is no such thing as a relatively few well-documented types. The forms run into the scores and hundreds, with almost any shape imaginable. To the average collector, it must seem that Archaic craftsmen spent less time hunting and harvesting, more time chipping out confusing knife forms. Here are some of them.

Bifacial Triangular Knives

Usually 3 to 5 in. long, of a local, good-grade material, these blades probably range somewhere between late Paleo and middle Archaic. Well-chipped, nicely bifacial, all have one side that is straight or slightly excurvate, the main working edge. A few, heavily resharpened, are a bit incurvate. The blade is fairly thick, $\frac{3}{8}$ to $\frac{1}{2}$ in. in most cases.

Unusual features include a basic triangular form, much different from the Paleo Triangular Unifaces. The type never seems to have a sharp tip. The edge opposite the longest main blade is usually irregular and quite rough, shorter in length from tip to base. Basal or tip portions may appear to be battered, as if by pounding, but the main or leading edge shows only knife use and careful resharpening. Depending on the specimen, the base may be the widest or narrowest part of the blade.

This knife is likely (from sites found, which included bifurcated points) to be early in the Archaic, although a true basal flute now and then hints at Paleo association or a technique that carried over from earlier times. Also, there is usually some effort made at basal thinning, one sign that at least some of these blades were hafted.

Other diagnostic signs are very large percussion flake scars that appear on one or both faces, plus long, thin flakes detached to form the cutting edge. An unusual feature is the frequent presence of a ground-in chipping platform (sometimes natural or partly natural) on the shorter side opposite the main working edge. While thinning from a platform is a Paleo technique, the platforms were not used as in Paleo knives to thin or flute the base, but to thin one or both faces of these blades. And the platforms are never ground in with the precision of Paleo pieces, but are fairly rough, almost an afterthought.

These blades are not really so distinctive that a single specimen would excite much curiosity. It is only when one examines a number of them that the similarities really make much sense.

Asymmetrical Knives

Unhafted, bifacial knives from the known Archaic were made in large numbers, and most collections have several examples. On these, one working edge might be vastly different than the other in shape or chipping. Or, the base is not "lined up" with the two other similar edges, and may be at a different angle, a bit off to one side. Such knives range from several inches in length to 8 or more, with varied dimensions elsewhere.

Usually, as is typical for most Archaic blades, they are very well made with a combination of percussion and pressure flaking. Some, depending on type, are rather rough, certainly in many cases a preform or unfinished artifact. Photographs in the book of unhafted asymmetrical blades will indicate both the size and shape ranges, nearly endless. Of particular interest is the offset blade, with baseline in almost any configuration, incurvate, straight, excurvate, angled, irregular. In this respect, they are somewhat like the General-Purpose Paleo knives, though otherwise entirely different. There are no chipping platforms or basal fluting, for example, and most examples are much wider and with more sophisticated chipping.

The offset or angled base may have been a purposeful design to accommodate hafting or the result of continual resharpening of one blade edge. Often — as with some Archaic hafted examples, as will be seen — the two edges had different designs in terms of chipping patterns. One may have been very finely chipped, as if for precision cutting. The other may have been rough-chipped, as if for heavy-duty work. Not surprisingly, damage-in-use signs are usually more severe on the less-well-made blade edge. Or, one edge may be beveled, the other left alone or chipped (resharpened) from both faces.

Asymmetrical-edged or -based knives seem to have been made and used throughout the Archaic period. There is one puzzle here that has not been, and may never be, sufficiently explained. Many of the bases are quite wide, much more broad than other Archaic hafted examples. Yet, on many well-made examples, the base was thinned, the baseline never used as a cutting edge.

The only explanation is that the bases were thinned for hafting, for a knife handle, yet such sometimes seems impossible. In some cases, the cutting edge goes right to the base corners, precluding any idea that the base had wrap-around thongs for the handle. In other cases, blade edge resharpening stops an inch or so from the base, showing clearly where the handle thongs were located. It is known that prehistoric Indians had several kinds of glue, so perhaps knife handles were attached in some cases in this manner.

Overall, from the large and still-useful size of many asymmetrical blades from the Archaic, it would appear that they were purposefully made that way. Collectors today sometimes fault them because they do not seem to be "balanced", and because they lack the extra workmanship that went into stemming or notching, being therefore just a bit less as an example of prehistoric artwork. This should not be the case, for they are authentic representatives of their time, valid in and of themselves. Many asymmetrical blades have at least one beveled edge, though some are steeply chipped from both faces to form the edge.

Asymmetrical blades of course are not exclusive to the Archaic. Paleo times had them as utilitarian forms, Woodland times had them as ceremonial pieces. Even in the Archaic, some very large and unused blades may have been more for show than actual use. One of the sad things is that so many large Archaic knives (like Paleo Lanceolates) have received strikes from agricultural equipment, and are so damaged that key features are lost. This complicates matters.

Symmetrical Knives

"Balanced" unhafted knives are known thoughout the Archaic, but they probably exist in smaller numbers overall than asymmetrical specimens. Even symmetrical knives — with tip opposite the base center and with two similar sides — may show use of one edge more than the other. Frequently, as with hafted Archaic knives, one edge will also evidence more in-use damage than the other.

While often better grades of flint or obsidian were employed for many examples, a number were also done in lower-grade materials. Often the quality of the finished knife, as with some other kinds, depended less on workmanship and more on how well the material could be worked. Most Archaic symmetrical knives, ranging from several inches to a foot or more in length, have some indication that they were hafted. The base is not usually specially prepared, except for thinning that made handle attachment easier. Most are of a width that would have allowed for a bone or antler handle, this from 1 to 2 or more inches across.

A few examples may have basal grinding to some extent, but others simply have a slight difference in edge sharpness at the logical hafting area, and often not even that. Sometimes the sharpness difference cannot be seen, but can be felt by running a finger along the edges. It is surprising sometimes, on blades that have definite hafting changes, how little of the blade base was attached to the handle.

Unhafted-Hafted Knives

Other unhafted Archaic symmetrical knives have the beginning of hafting in the form of very shallow and small corner notches, actually tiny for blade size. These seem to occur more in the U.S. East; Western hafting in the form of stemming the blade was introduced very early with the **Sandia** points or blades. Knives with these hesitant corner notches seem to be both Archaic, and early in the period. The knives themselves may have the shape of large late Paleo artifacts, lance-like, and with fairly straight or rounded baselines. Incurvate, of course, would suggest Paleo affiliation, especially if the base edges are ground. Unhafted-hafted knives have the first appearance of not being hafted, but such signs can be found after a closer look.

One of the characteristics of these knives is doubled efficiency. Both edges were used to about the same degree, usually, so the Indian knife-user had two working edges on one piece of flint. Asymmetrical knives often had just the main edge and a minor, backing edge, as did the Paleo general-purpose knife.

It is not too much to expect that throughout the many thousand years of the Archaic that successful inventions were made in flintworking. There were three major Archaic discoveries that relate directly to flintworking and to knives.

Unhafted Beveled Blades

One is beveling, angle-chipping one or both blades edges. Like most great discoveries, it is simple. Though begun in Paleo times with the small working edge of rectangular knives, the Archaic period developed and refined beveling to a tremendous extent. The drawback to beveling was that it took a bit more very careful skill to resharpen an edge from one side only.

The benefit was an enormously strong "chisel" edge backed by the mass of the blade, giving an edge that was flush with one face for total proximity to the cutting task. And, since resharpening flakes were taken only from one face, the knife did not wear out quite as fast as when flakes are taken from both faces. For most blades, beveled edges mean both Archaic period and use as knives.

The second major Archaic innovation was serrated edges. This was chipping an edge so that it was saw-like to tooth-like. Just as with beveling, Archaic craftsmen developed serrating to a high art form, one that persisted until White or Contact times with later cultures. Even some true arrowheads were later serrated.

Serrating involved special chipping that left projecting tips in regular rows along knife edges. Usually these pointed more or less out from the blade edge, but in rare cases they were angled forward or back. In use, the projections served as small teeth, providing a ripcut. Serrations on even very small hafted Archaic knives suggest use in such tasks as skinning small game or more careful butchering of larger game.

General thought today is that small to medium sizes could have been projectile points, while medium to large were knives. Though this approach seems to have obvious validity, more subtle signs sometimes indicate other directions. It was only a few decades ago, after all, that all corner-notch artifacts were believed to be points, all side-notches knives. And that was advanced thinking for the time.

On the matter of Archaic knife beveling or serrations, there are some comparisons. Beveled edges appear with equal frequency on unhafted and hafted knives alike, as even a beginning collector has probably noticed. This particular edge design seems to have worked equally well with both major Archaic knife types. Simply put, beveling gave a stronger edge, serrating an edge that was sharper.

On the other hand, serrated edges are found mainly on Archaic hafted specimens, almost always basal notched types, or even the stemmed early **Dalton**.

Serrated-edge Archaic unhafted knives are quite rare, and when one is found a close examination may show it to be reworked from a hafted blade. Why unhafted blades do not often have serrations is another of the great mysteries to come out of Archaic times.

These observations are qualified by Archaic specimens, again usually hafted examples, that uniquely combine the edges. They are both beveled and serrated. This happy marriage puts together the ripcut precision of serrating and the basic strength of the long-lasting bevel. In some examples, serrations are worn down to the bevel, and the knife continued in use.

Too, beveling on Archaic blades was on one or both edges of unhafted examples, usually on both edges if hafted. One side may be more worn down than another, the serrations short or broken, giving the appearance that only one side was ever serrated.

Archaic Reverse Bevels

Beveled Archaic blades, viewed from base to tip and laid flat, usually have a right-hand bevel, the edge high to the right, low to the left. A small number of these blades are left-hand, with the technique just the opposite. This may in fact indicate "handedness" or may simply be a cultural difference.

Much harder to explain are beveled edges, usually on unhafted blades, that change bevel angle from tip to base. They begin at the tip as typical right-hand bevels, move to straight-edge and shift again to left-hand at the base. This is all on a single edge, and the feat is accomplished in a length of 3 to 6 inches. A few Archaic hafted blades also have this unique feature.

If one assumes these blades had no handles, they could have been used by turning the blade around and using it as if it had two tips and four edges. (In fact, the Texas late-prehistoric **Harahey** blade did just that, though of a totally different design.) However, most Archaic knives with this reverse beveling have a definite tip and base, the latter having basal thinning, the sign of preparation for a haft.

Even after a quarter-century of field collecting and studying the few available specimens, the author is unable to explain this lithic trait. It seems to be a complex solution to a simple task, or it may be the other way around.

Fracture-Chipped Knives

The third major Archaic knife innovation was fracture-chipping. This seems to have been an Archaic development or at least refinement, for one could argue that Paleo fluting was fracture-chipping on a large scale. Most collectors know very little about knives that have this, and it is true that most of them are hafted types. However, a number of hafted Archaic knives are indeed fracture-chipped in a roundabout way. Often a broken blade was fracture-chipped at the break area, the knife portion then turned into another useful tool.

Fracture-chipping involved the striking off of a splinter or sliver of flint, this always done from either a finished knife or a blade in the process of making. The marks, frozen forever in time, were made when a small bone or antler punch was placed at the point of percussion, and then struck with a short billet or club. This drove off the desired edge, leaving the surface a long, fairly shallow scar. As opposed to normal percussion and pressure flaking, which involved far larger face scars, fracture-chipping usually removed edges prepared by the first two methods.

The name itself comes from the fact that when the force of the flaking blow terminates in flint or obsidian, it leaves a hinge-like fracture mark. Once seen, this cannot be mistaken for anything else. Often, fracture-chipping was done on an edge that angled the directional energy away from the material, and the silver was thrown off without leaving the characteristic fracture mark.

Oblong Archaic Knives

Unhafted Archaic blades exist in many oblong and rounded forms of all sizes. They are assigned this period because of materials used and sites where found. These are bifacially chipped and symmetrical to some extent. Most have one end larger than the other, suggesting handle attachment to the smaller end, but some are equi-ended whether large or small.

Occasionally a side-line is deeply incurvate in one small area, suggesting use as a lance-shaft scraper (sometimes called a spokeshave) or other specialized function. These seem to be all-purpose blades, and scraping edges are not usually present, though beveled cutting edges sometimes are.

Elongated Archiac Knives

Still other elongated Archaic blades, fairly thick and sturdy, have a well-pointed tip and rounded base. There is rarely any basal grinding and some examples are probably preforms that would have been further finished before use. There are yet enough of these random finds to suggest they were used as-is, and edge-wear exists on some.

Flake Knives

While earlier and later cultures made fairly wide use of the most common Indian artifact ever made — the reworked percussion flake — the Archaic Amerinds excelled in this direction. Overlooked or frowned-upon by many collectors, the reworked chips seemed to have served well as mini-knives, hafted or hand-held, large or small.

The secondary chipping on the flake is often awesome in miniature, with up to 20 tiny pressure flakes per inch. Often the highest grades of flint or obsidian were used, because only these could take the minute chipping required for flake knives. Generally the greater the distance from the high-quality material source, the more likely that flakes would be reworked and reused. Several site studies bear this out, that something rare and excellent was treasured and kept as long as possible.

Contracting Base Knives

The classic unhafted knife form from the Archaic is symmetrical with excurvate edges. The widest blade part is about mid-section, and the base in unused specimens is slightly less wide; resharpened examples make the base relatively wider each time resharpening occurs.

Typical length is about 4 in., with size range 3 to 6 inches. The base on most examples is fairly straight and unground. An average specimen with some resharpening leaves the blade about the same width from mid-section to base. These are sturdy, well-designed knives, and totally lack the triangular appearance of the later Woodland blades. Chipping is well done and good materials are usually found.

Archaic Lunates

The **Lunate** is a knife form with rounded back and straight or curved cutting edge, very uncomplex in outline. It somewhat resembles half a circle. The form (Ulu) is still used by the Eskimos, though in modern steel. The **Lunate** seems to be a fairly late type in the North. Yet, similar forms are from the early Archaic.

These have the round back, are 3 to 8 in. wide, and the straightish edge is sharpened from end to end. At least one example has an edge that is steeply beveled, indicating resharpening from a much larger size. Beveling on the piece, fine material and chipping style strongly indicate an Archaic placement. Other than the fact that some have come from Archaic sites, little else can be said about these mysterious knives.

Triangular Archaic Knives

Symmetrical triangular unhafted knives that are bifacially well-worked can be found in the early Archaic. From 2 to 10 in. long, the shape is largely the result of long-term edge resharpening of the original knife form. The base remains a constant width while the sides narrow until they become straight or very slightly excurvate, but still appearing overall very triangular. Most Archaic triangulars have base corners **rounded.**

The baseline is also straight or very slightly excurvate, and the base area is unground. Here again the edge-bevels reach very nearly to the base corners, leading one to wonder just how the handle was really attached. Keys to this type are the triangular shape (when it reached this configuration it may have been discarded) and beveled edges.

As a first guideline to the collector of unhafted Archaic knives, if the piece is definitely not Paleo or Woodland or Mississippian — and these all have a fairly limited number of knives — then it is probably Archaic. Expect to expect some very unusual forms. Many of them have never received acknowledgement in any official journal, have never had an article written on them, and may be known only by word-of-mouth, shared knowledge, among regional collectors.

Unhafted Archaic blades is **the** field in which an aware person can yet put together a large and authentic collection of many different types.

6-1/2 in. shaped BENTON type knife. Note fine chipping on right side & left side showing considerable use, which proves the use as a knife. $175
Courtesy Tom Hendrix, Florence, Alabama

Buzzard Roost type knife, 5 in. light jasper in color. Surface find Lauderdale Co., Ala. $65
Courtesy Tom Hendrix, Florence, Alabama

6-1/4 MAPLES type knife, surface find Lauderdale Co., Ala. $150
Courtesy Tom Hendrix, Florence, Alabama

SYKES knife, 5-1/4 in., light gray, Middle Archaic finds in North Ala. Found in association with Benton Stemmed and Buzzard Roost points. $75
Courtesy Tom Hendrix, Florence, Alabama

Shaped knives 6-3/4 x 8 x 6-1/2 in. Lauderdale Co., Ala. Middle to Late Archaic find in N. Ala. $175-$225-$145
Courtesy Tom Hendrx, Florence, Alabama

Ceremonial Knife, 9-1/2 x 2-1/4 in. 5/8 in. thick. Woodland, Lauderdale Co., Ala. Fine degree of workmanship, secondary chippng very evident, gray. $125
Courtesy A. W. Beinlich, Jr., Sheffield, Alabama

Ceremonial Knife 11-1/4 x 2-1/8 in. Lauderdale Co., Al. Archaic percussion chipping, used to make this knife. A minimum amount of secondary chipping was used to finish the piece. Pointed on both ends suggesting that it was not hafted. Sometimes pieces are found broken indicating that they were ceremonially broken. $175
Courtesy A. W. Beinlich, Jr., Sheffied, Alabama

(The reason that the collections from North Alabama are lacking in color is because the Indians had easy access to Fort Payne chert that is very plentiful in this area.)

Top to bottom:
COBBS TRIANGULAR, 4-1/4 x 1-9/16 in. Gray. Early Archaic, Lauderdale Co., Ala. $25
COBBS TRIANGULAR, 4-7/8 x 1-7/8 in. Gray. Early Archaic, Lauderdale, Co., Ala. $45
COBBS TRIANGULAR, 4-3/8 x 1-1/4 in. Gray. Early Archaic, Colbert Co., Ala. $35
COBBS TRIANGULAR, 3-1/4 x 1-5/8 in. Gray. Early Archaic, Lauderdale, Co. $35
Courtesy A. W. Beinlich, Jr., Sheffield, Alabama

BEVEL, the common or regular beveled knife has its bevel on the left side when looking toward the distal end. Another bevel has its bevel on the right side and is rare in Northwest Alabama
1. BEVEL on the right side, 2-1/4 x 1-1/2 in. Gray, Colbert Co., Ala. Late Archaic-Woodland $35
2. BEVEL on the right side 2-1/4 x 1-5/16 in. Pink, Colbert Co., Ala. Late Archaic-Woodland $35
3. BEVEL on the left side, Lost Lake, 3-1/8 x 1-5/16 in. Gray with brown tip, Early Archaic, Colbert Co., Ala. $35
4. BEVELED on the right side 1-1/8 x 1-11/12 in. Gray-brown, Lauderdale Co., Ala., Late Archaic-Woodland. $35
5. BEVELED on the right side 2-1/4 x 1-5/8 in. gray, Colbert Co., Ala. Late Archaic, Woodland. $35.
**Cataco Creek points are more apt to be beveled on the right side than are other types of points.*

Courtesy A. W. Beinlich Jr., Sheffield, Alabama.

GAHAGAN knife or blade found in association with cache of eighty broken blades in Lauderdale Co., Ala. length 6 in. $35
Courtesy P. A. Everhart, Sheffield, Alabama.

This large knife (6-3/4'') was found on what appeared to be a kill or butchering site in Lauderdale Co., Ala. In association with this knife were several smaller broken knives and fragments of bones of wood bisons. Several bones showed use of the flint knives in the butchering process. $250
Courtesy P. A. Everhart, Sheffield, Alabama

6-1/2 in. Unsharpened knife found in Lauderdale Co., Ala. $125
Courtesy Tom Hendrix, Florence, Alabama.

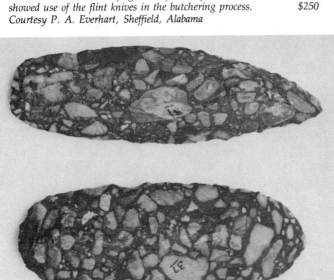

Top to Bottom:
Conglomerate knife, 5-3/16'' x 1-1/2'', Lauderdale Co., Ala., late Archaic. Pictured in ''Sun Circles and Human Hands'' by Emma Lila Funderburk and Mary Douglas Foreman. Conglomerate is a rock composed of gravel embedded in a matrix of very fine sand and is found all over the world; however, the late Archaic people of Northwest Alabama, Northeast Mississippi and adjoining Tennessee were the only people to use this rock for tools and implements. The conglomerate shown in this photograph is bonded by ferroginous cement. $90
Conglomerate knife, 4-3/4'' x 1-3/4'', Colbert Co., Ala. $90
Conglomerate knife, 3-7/8'' x 1-1/4'', Colbert Co., Ala. $90
Courtesy A. W. Beinlich, Jr., Sheffield, Alabama.

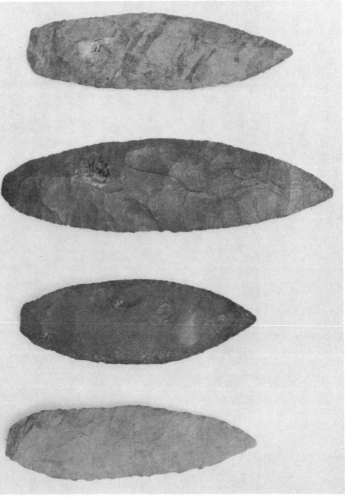

Top to bottom:
4-11/16 x 1-5/16 in. Gray and tan Colbert Co., Ala. Archaic $6-$20
5-11/16 x 1-9/16 in. Gray, Colbert Co., Ala. Archaic $6-$20
4 x 2-1/2 in. Gray, Colbert Co., Ala. Archaic $6-$20
4-9/16 x 1-1/4 in. Light tan, Colbert Co., Alabama $6-$20
Courtesy A. W. Beinlich, Jr., Sheffield, Alabama

5-1/2 x 2-1/2 in. MAPLES type knife - surface find, Lauderdale Co., Ala. possibly hand knife? $150
Courtesy Tom Hendrix, Florence, Alabama.

This unusually long (7-1/2'') and finely chipped blade was a surface find in Lawrence, Co., Tenn. $250
Courtesy Tom Hendrix, Florence, Alabama.

The following examples of shaped knives are from Lauderdale and Colbert Counties in Alabama. They range in length from 7-3/4'' to 4-1/4''. Of all the knives, these are the most difficult to classify, as they come in such a variety of shapes and sizes. These examples are from the late and middle Archaic periods in the Tennessee Valley of Alabama.

Clockwise top to bottom:
Scottsbluff, 4-1/4'', light gray, $50; Little Bear Creek, 6-1/4'', light gray, $75; Elk River, 7'', light gray, $175; Benton Stemmed, 7'', dark gray, $100; unclassified, 7-1/4'', gray with cream bands, $125; Expanded Barb Pickwick, 7-3/4'', pink, $250; Little Bear Creek, 7-1/4'', mottled gray, $125; unclassified, 7'', light gray, $90; Little Bear Creek, 6-3/4'', dark gray, $125; Little Bear Creek, 5-3/4''; dark gray, $100; Elk River, 4-1/2'', Jasper, $125.
Left, top to bottom:
Hardin, 5-3/4'', yellow, $115; Little Bear Creek, 4-3/4'', light gray, $125; Benton Stemmed, 5-1/2'', see cover photo for color combinations, $275.
Courtesy Tom Hendrix, Florence, Alabama.

Top:

EXPANDED BARB Pickwick, recently known as Spring Creek. Middle to late Archaic. Gray in color. 4-1/2 x 1-1/8 in. Lauderdale Co., Ala. $100
EXPANDED BARB Pickwick, 4-5/8 x 1-15/16 in. Dull gray in color. Colbert Co., Ala. $45

Center:

EXPANDED BARB Pickwick, 5-1/8 x 1-1/2 in. Gray in color. Lauderdale Co., Ala. $125

Bottom:

EXPANDED BARB Pickwick, 3-7/8 x 1-3/8 in. Gray & brown in color. Colbert Co., Ala. $55
EXPANDED BARB Pickwick, 4-3/4 x 1-1/2 in. Gray in color. Colbert Co., Ala. $1175
EXPANDED BARB Pickwick are middle to late Archaic in North Ala. Broad shallow flaking with a minimum of secondary chipping was used in the making of these knives.
Courtesy A. W. Beinlich, Jr., Sheffield, Alabama

Top to Bottom:

5-1/8 x 1-3/4 in. Gray, Archaic, Colbert Co., Ala. $15
6-3/8 x 1-7/8 in. Gray, Archaic, Lauderdale Co., Ala. $35
6-1/4 x 1-9/16 in. Gray, Archaic, Lauderdale Co., Ala $35
5-3/8 x 2-1/8 in. Gray, Archaic, Colbert Co., Ala. $40
Courtesy A. W. Beinlich, Jr., Sheffield, Alabama

STANFIELD KNIFE BLADE, 6 in. long, white, light brown and tan, from Dane County, Wisconsin, the KouBa site. It is early Archaic, ca. 9642 - 8920 BC, to be shown in Perino's book, Vol. I. An excellent piece. Museum quality
Photo courtesy Bob & Gerry Rosberg collection, Illinois

Early Archaic blade, Baker City., 4 in. long. A thin, well-made Georgia blade, it has a tip nick and the blade is broken and glued. Fine lines to this piece. $10
Photo courtesy Jack M. Hall collection, Georgia

Pickwick blades from the Tenn. Valley, in Northern Ala. 3 x 4-1/2 in. Three of these examples were found in association with deer antler handles.
Each: $40-$65

Courtesy Tom Hendrix, Florence, Alabama.

SLOANS DALTON, variant of about 10 different types in family, 1-7/8 x 5 in. long. It has transversal flaking, is very thin, ca. 7500 BC. This is a rare type with great age. Examples such as this have sold for several thousand dollars.
Photo courtesy Bob & Gerry Rosberg collection, Illinois

All l. to r.:
KNIFE, chert, 1 x 2 in., Agate Springs, NE.   *$9*
KNIFE, made of breccia, same source.   *$6*
Yellow jasper KNIFE, with large percussion flakes from face, NE. *$10*
Courtesy Marguerite L. Kernaghan collection; photo by Stewart W. Kernaghan

ARCHAIC KNIFE, 3-3/8 in. long, in a striped grey flint. Piece was roughly shaped by percussion and has little edge retouch. A typical generalized knife form from the Archaic area.   *$10*
Private collection

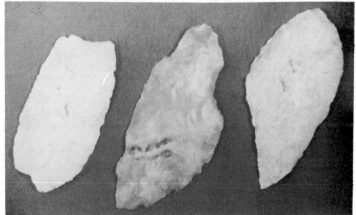

PREHISTORIC KNIVES, center example 3-3/4 in. long.
Left, PALEO OR ARCHAIC period, yellow-cream flint, pseudo-fluted base.
    $8
Center, ARCHAIC KNIFE, offset stem, tan and brown with two purple inclusions   *$15*
Right, cream and grey flint, ARCHAIC; long straightish edge is beveled.$15
Private collection

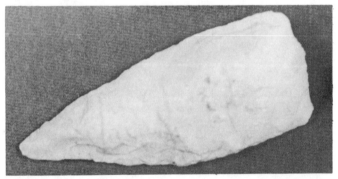

PALEO OR ARCHAIC KNIFE, 3 in. long, in white-cream chert. This is a thick (5/8 in.) artifact, the worn-down stub of a much-longer blade. The base is not as well-made as most PALEO GENERAL-PURPOSE blades, so this may well be Archaic.   *$5*
Private collection

KNIFE, early Plains Archaic (Oxbow phase), 5500 - 3000 BC. It is 1-1/4 x 5-5/8 in., in tan and red chert. Note the very long excurvate edge, at bottom. From Lewis & Clark County, MT.   *Value unlisted*
Photo courtesy John Byrd, Helena, Montana

KNIFE, late Plains Archaic (Pelican Lake phase) and 1500 - 100 BC. It is 1-1/2 x 3-1/2 in., in a translucent honey-colored agate. (Note how this particular form resembles other Archaic blades shown elsewhere.) From Lewis & Clark County, MT.   *Value unlisted*
Photo courtesy John Byrd, Helena, Montana

KNIFE, Nevada, 4 in. long, in quality white flint. While pre-historic period is unknown, basal style has been found in the Archaic.   *$45*
Photo courtesy Jim Cressey, California

EARLY BLADES, Top to Bottom:
LOAF-SHAPE, 5 in., basalt.
LOAF-SHAPE, 3 in., basalt.
TRIANGULAR, 4 in., basalt.
Age here is likely 5500 BC - 2500 BC. Unlisted
Photo courtesy Jim Cressey, California

UNKNOWN KNIFE TYPE, 5-3/4 in., made from light tan chert. From Crawford County, Arkansas. $250
Photo courtesy Pat Mahan, Texas

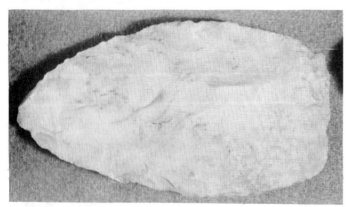

SQUARE-BACK KNIFE, 2-5/8 x 5 in. long, Vernon Co., WI. It is made of a yellow and white chert known in the area as Cold Water agate. Good size, fine condition. $55
Courtesy Mert Cowley collection, WI; by Mohr Photography

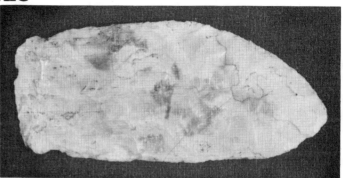

NOTCHED KNIFE, 1-7/8 x 4-1/8 in., of a pink and grey flint. This is attractive material, and blade has basal thinning and shallow side notches. Knives of a similar configuration may be from the Archaic. $40
Courtesy Mert Cowley collection, WI; by Mohr Photography

Top, Archaic blade, grey-brown chert, 2-1/4 in. long. Base, notches and lower edges are ground. From Lycoming County, Pennsylvania.$10-$15
Bottom, Archaic knife, black flint, base ground, 2-1/8 in. and ca. 3000-2000 BC. Also Lycoming County. $10-$15
Photo courtesy Fogelman collection, Pennsylvania

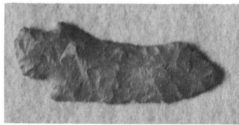

Unusual shape for an Archaic knife, with edges excurvate/incurvate. Of a local grey-brown chert, it is 3-1/8 in. long. It is from Union County, Pennsylvania. $15-$20
Photo courtesy Fogelman Collection, Pennsylvania

Top, ovate knife, Archaic, brownish chert, 3-3/$6 in. long, Lycoming County, PA. $5-$10
Bottom, leaf-shaped knife, Union County, PA, 3 in. long, of grey siltstone. It is a knife form from the Piedmont Archaic. $5-$10
Photo courtesy Fogelman collection, Pennsylvania

ARCHAIC

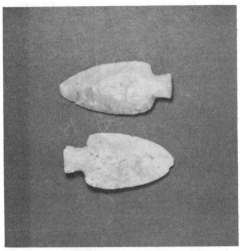

Two TABLE ROCK or "BOTTLENECK" knives, top example 1-3/8 x 3 in. long, of glossy taffy-colored flint. Bottom, 1-1/2 x 2-7/8 in., in grey and white flint. Both have the heavy stem grinding typical of the type, and are very well made with pleasing lines. They were found the same day about 100 feet apart, on one sand bar, November, 1984.

Top $50
Bottom $40

Photo courtesy Richard L. Warren collection, Missouri

Top, grey glossy flint, 1-5/16 x 3-1/16 in., poss. Archaic.
Bottom, 1-1/2 x 3-7/16 in., in blue-grey flint, steeply beveled edges, squared base. An interesting piece, the outline (triangular, shouldered) greatly resembles Ft. Ancient knives from eastern Midwest. The beveling, however, suggests Archaic affiliation. From western Johnson County, Misouri, and a fine blade. $55
Photo courtesy Richard L. Warren collection, Missouri

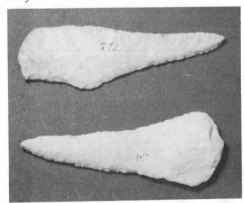

Top, Archaic, pronounced basal grinding, slightly beveled, off-white flint, length about 4 inches, unusual shape. $50
Bottom, Archaic blade with basal grinding and slightly beveled, off-white flint, blade-line gently curved. $50
Photo courtesy Richard L. Warren collection, Missouri

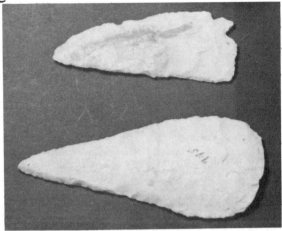

CORNER-TANG blade, top. It is 1-1/2 x 4-1/4 in. long, and light tan with a grey streak. Interestingly, the handle angle on these blades is unknown at present. They may have projected "back", "up" or at the same angle as the corner tang. $125
Bottom, unhafted beveled-edge blade, white flint. This was found in western Johnson County, Missouri. $100
Photo courtesy Richard L. Warren collection, Missouri

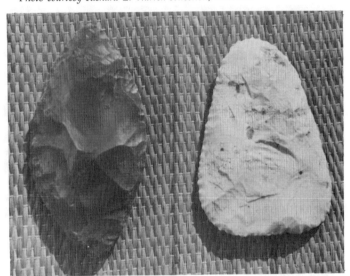

Left, LEAF-SHAPE knife, 1-3/4 x 3-1/2 in., high-grade chert or flint, surface find in Susquehanna Valley, PA. $35
Right, white chert, 2-1/4 x 3-1/4, similar provenance. $25
Courtesy Marguerite L. Kernaghan collection; photo by Stewart W. Kernaghan

All l. to r.:
Chert or flint KNIFE, 2 in., Agate Springs region, NE. $9
KNIFE, chert, same provenance. $5
KNIFE, chert, surface find, NE. $7
Courtesy Marguerite L. Kernaghan collection; photo by Stewart W. Kernaghan

All l. to r.:
ANGLE-TIPPED knife, chalcedony, surface find in Co. $10
Yellow jasper BLADE, 1-1/4 x 3-3/4 in., Cook Ranch, NE. $10
Chert KNIFE, 1-1/4 x 2-3/4 in., NE. $8
Courtesy Marguerite L. Kernaghan collection; photo by Stewart W. Kernaghan

KNIFE with base slightly angled as is so often the case with Archaic knives. Piece is 2 x 4 in. long, in high-grade blue-grey Flintridge chalcedony. Surface-find, from site that is Archaic and Woodland; main cutting edge is the more excurvate side. $35
Hothem collection

BLADE in cream flint, main cutting edge just an inch long; Archaic.$7
Hothem collection

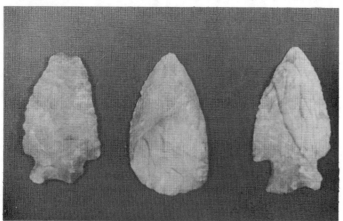

Large ARCHAIC BLADES, all l. to r.:
Tan flint, prehistoric damage at each end, early bifurcate form. $10
Leaf-shape, right edge beveled, good flint. $20
Mottled and veined flint, slight damage bot. right. $15
Hothem collection

Left, BLADE, 1-1/2 x 2 in., chert, TN. $5
Right, ELONGATED KNIFE, 1-1/2 x 3-3/4 in., mottled flint. This came from an Archaic layer, TN. The flute-like flake scar is interesting. $20
Courtesy Marguerite L. Kernaghan collection; photo by Stewart W. Kernaghan

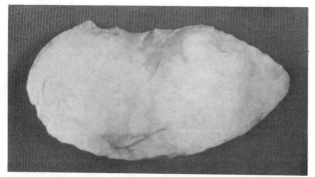

Archaic KNIFE with shaft-scraping surfaces worked into upper edge; knife is 2-1/2 in. long, in a cream-colored chert. From Archaic site. $12
Hothem collection

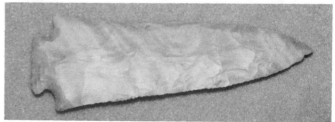

STILWELL, perfect in every respect, in fine flint, 2-1/8 x 6 in. long, early Archaic. This knife has it all, solid notching, excellent chipping and length, perfect condition. As an early collector piece, it would be difficult to match, and even some lifetime collectors have not field-found its like. $450
Photo courtesy Arnold Moore collection, Missouri

ARCHAIC knife, 1-1/2 x 3-1/2 in., Benton Co., TN. Excurvate edge was the primary working edge; glossy flint. $35
Photo courtesy Arnold Moore collection, Missouri

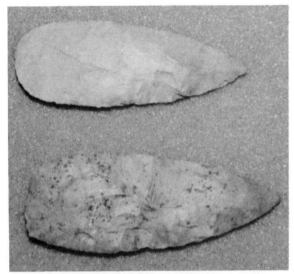

Two fine ARCHAIC knives, Benton Co., TN.
Top, 1-1/4 x 3-1/4 in., very fine basal configuration. $60
Bot., 1-1/2 x 3-5/8 in., good flint in two shades. $60
Photo courtesy Arnold Moore collection, Missouri

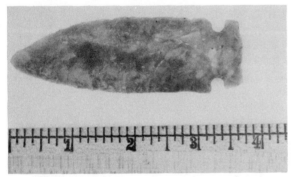

Knife of Tennessee flint, semi-translucent, from Tennessee, with well-executed base, balanced notching. $80
Photo courtesy Swope collection, Virginia

Archaic blades, Kansas, 2-1/2 in. long.
Left, bifurcated-base type, white to off-white flint. $15
Right, glossy grey-white flint, stemmed and shouldered. $15
Photo courtesy Gerald Riepl collection, Kansas

ARCHAIC KNIFE, in reddish-pink and white flint, 2-3/8 in. long. This blade has been well-used and the stem area (right) has grinding on lower (bottom) edge as knife is positioned in phto. $10
Private collection

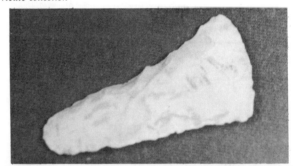

Flint knife, probably ARCHAIC BLADE, 2-1/4 in. long. Material is a milky whtie opaque flint, and the tip was purposely left rounded. $8
Private collection

ARCHAIC LUNATE, eastern Midwest, 1-3/4 x 3-3/4 in. It is made of Flint-ridge in pale grey with cream inclusions and is translucent. The lower side is the knife edge, and it is very steeply beveled away from the obverse. This is a rare piece. $95
Private collection

Archaic knife, 2-1/4 x 4-3/4, in grey-black flint. This piece, unhafted, has the very rare REVERSED-BEVEL edges in which the bevel angle changes from one side to the other on both edges. Most blades of the type are very well made of top material and are quite large. $250
Private collection

ARCHAIC KNIFE, early beveled blade, unhafted. Midwestern, of blue Coshocton flint with white fossils, it is 1-3/8 x 3-5/8 in. Beveled edges on both side stop about 1 in. from base, where edges ended and handle began. Basal edges are very lightly ground; unusual knife. $55
Private collection

Archaic knifes, each about 2-1/4 in. long.
Left, CORNER-NOTCH, agricultural strike scar top left, fossil inclusion, dark blue flint. $20
Right, BIFURCATE, black flint, thick for size showing resharpening, right shoulder removed by fracture-chipping. $30
Private collection

ARCHAIC KNIFE, 2 x 3-3/4 inches, in a solid grey-black flint. The rather irregular baseline and width are typical of the period. $40
Private collection

UNKNOWN KNIFE TYPE, 4 in. long, light brown Edwards Plateau flint. From Llano County, TX, Lake Buchanan. $200
Photo courtesy Pat Mahan, Texas

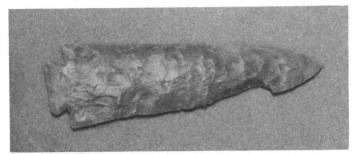

STILWELL, 2 x 6-3/4 in., Clay County, AR, in a quality dark flint. Though it is dangerous to "read" too much into a photograph, it appears that the incurvate section high on lower blade edge was done in later prehistoric times, when a pickup or Indian find was reworked. Note darker interior compared with patina on blade surface. Perino (OAS, #4/p. 94) puts these time-wise in the early Archaic, the age averaging 6000 BC. Farming equipment broke this specimen in two pieces. $150
Photo courtesy Arnold Moore collection, Missouri

BENTON blade, 1-1/2 x 7-1/4 in., quality dark flint, from Clay Co., AR. It is beautifully chipped and tiny missing tip, for a knife, does not detract greatly from appearance or value. Main center of distribution for this type was the Tennessee River Valley (Bell, OAS, #2/p.6) and the period was middle-late Archaic, ca. 3600 - 1200 BC. This piece was broken into four sections, and all were found on the same day. $250
Photo courtesy Arnold Moore collection, Missouri

Left, chert blade 3-1/2 in. long, from Leonard Farm, Clarion, IA, 1963.
Right, 1-3/4 x 4 in., all data same as above. Archaic. Each, $25
Curtesy Marguerite L. Kernaghan collection; photo by Stewart W. Kernaghan

TSA-LA-GI KNIVES, from southeastern Kansas, mainly Cherokee County. The largest complete blade is 6-1/2 in. long and made of pinkish chert with white fossil inclusions. Most of the blades are beveled back to the hafting notches. Each... $50-$500
Courtesy Col. Floyd B. Lyerla collection, Kansas

McCORKLE stemmed bifurcate blades, in wide range of styles and materials, early Archaic. The dark Ohio flints are characteristic of early blades. Type was named at the St. Albans site, WVA, and examples were found above KIRK CORNER-NOTCHED (hence, not as old) types and below (older than) ST. ALBANS SIDE-NOTCHED types.
Lengths here are about 2 in. to 4-1/2 in. (top rt.), a beautiful example, as is its lower rt. companion. Many McCorkles have serrated edges, and all have the wide, twinlobed bases, almost always ground. Each, $25-$125
Photo courtesy J. B. Geyer Collections, Michigan; photograph by Mark Petrosoff

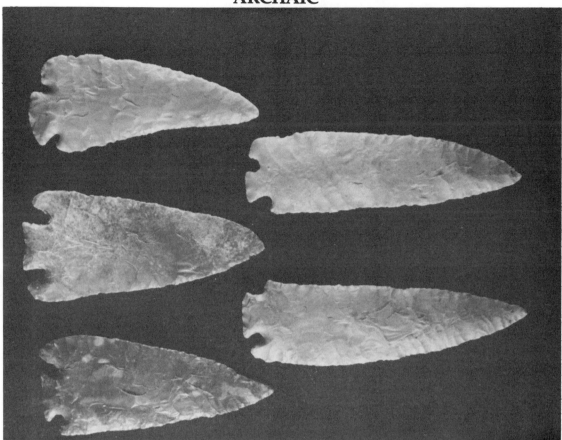

BASE-TANG knives, Texas, 4-1/2 to 5 inches. They are made of a local grey and tan chert, and are very well chipped. As this photo illustrates, and as Mr. Rogers noted in another publication, probably 90% of Texas knives have a definite curve to one blade edge. Values, each... $250-$300*
Photo courtesy D. Rogers collection, Houston, Texas

Exclusive, ultra-fine Texas blades: Diagonal corner-tang knives, Bell and Coryell Counties. Materials, tan and grey cherts from local sources. The size range here is 4-1/2 to 9 inches. For the smaller specimens, values are, each... $400-$800*
The largest tang blade is ''...very expensive''.
Photo courtesy D. Rogers collection, Houston, Texas

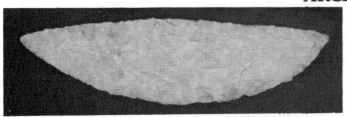

ARCHAIC KNIFE, unknown type, 4-3/4 in. long, material a yellow-brownish chert. This is a very thin and finely chipped piece, in perfect condition. Design shows the wide variety of Archaic knife forms, wherever found in the country. $90
Photo courtesy Randall Olsen, Utah

Archaic blade of yellow jasper, Northumberland County, Pennsylvania, from along the Susquehanna River. $40
Photo courtesy Swope Collection, Virginia

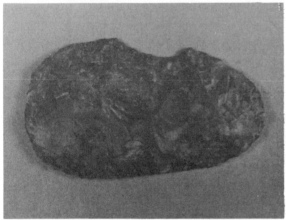

Archaic blade with concave shaft-scraper on upper edge, chipped in very nicely. From an Archaic site, and made of blue mottled Coshocton County flint. $20
Hothem collection

TRIANGULAR KNIFE, light Edwards Plateau chert, surface find, 3''. This piece is probably from the Archaic period. $35
Photo courtesy Wayne Parker collection, Texas

A good range of solid ARCHAIC KNIVES, all l. to r.:
CORNER NOTCH, ''Ohio Blue'' flint. $12
STEMMED, canted blade, mottled flint. $14
HEAVY-DUTY in black flint. $15
BIFURCATE, black flint, serrated. $12
Hothem collection

DOUBLE-POINTED KNIFE, Edwards Plateau chert, surface find from Robertson site, age period unknown. 4'' $50
Photo courtesy Wayne Parker collection, Texas

TRIANGULAR KNIFE, reddish quartz material, probably Archaic period. A surface find from Fisher County, TX. 5-1/2'' $75
Photo courtesy Wayne Parker collection, Texas

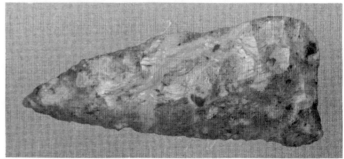

TRIANGULAR KNIFE, surface find, material moss agate. From Blanco Canyon, period unknown. 3-1/2'' $50
Photo courtesy Wayne Parker collection, Texas

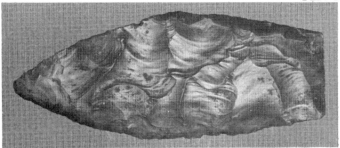

TRIANGULAR KNIFE, dark Edwards Plateau chert. A burial knife, it is Archaic and from Crosby County, Texas, the Llano - Estacado region.$150
Photo courtesy Wayne Parker collection, Texas   5-1/2''

Very early blade, size 1-1/2 x 3-3/4 inches. Material is either quartzite or schist, and estimated age is 6000 - 4000 BC. It is from the high sierra mountains, California. $35
Photo by Ray Pace Associates; courtesy Cliff Morris collection

TRIANGULAR KNIFE, 5-5/8'', light-colored Edwards Plateau chert, from ring midden site, Sutton County, TX. Triangular knives with rounded basal corners are usually Archaic, and found over much of the Central U.S. $50
Photo courtesy Wayne Parker collection, Texas

TRIANGULAR KNIFE, grey Edwards Plateau Chert, from a flat-top mesa in Blanco Canyon, Crosby County, TX. Archaic period.   5'' $125
Photo courtesy Wayne Parker collection, Texas

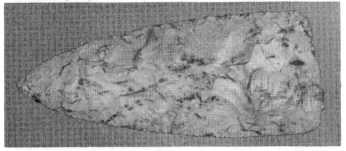

TRIANGULAR KNIFE, light-colored unknown flint. From a large cave rock-shelter in Arkansas. This is a well-shaped piece, and is Archaic.$100
Photo courtesy Wayne Parker collection, Texas   5''

SEKAN STILETTOS, possible knives. Name: ''Sekan'' from location in SouthEast KANsas, ''Stiletto'' because of shape and possible prehistoric use. (FBL) Longest specimen is about 6-1/2''. They are common to ''Bevel Trait'' sites, and are associated with the late Plains Village and Buffalo Hunter Cultures. So far the sites where SEKANS are found are located along small streams only. Each... $50-500
Photo courtesy Col. Floyd B. Lyerla Collection, Kansas

CHAPTER XI

Woodland (1000 BC — AD 800)
Mississippian (AD 800 — AD 1650)

It is difficult to combine the late-prehistoric eras, early Woodland to the end of Mississippian, this being over fifteen centuries that need to be condensed and sorted out in some way. The lifestyle changed greatly, from the last of late Archaic to Contact times, a period of agriculture, increased ceremonialism, and later, confusion and altered Amerind values.

The shift was also from full utilization of the natural world to taking control of portions of the environment. Scattered seasonal villages were out, permanent settlements in, a process that had begun in the middle Archaic. Man no longer went to the streams for a drink, but brought water in pottery vessels, these built up with ropes of damp clay before being fired. Small wild seeds were no longer enough, and fields of domesticated corn, beans and squash were tended.

Along with these improvements came a revolutionary change in weaponry and warfare. Somewhere around AD 500, the date different in various U.S. regions, the long-standing **Atl-atl** and dart were replaced by the bow and arrow. The slow-speed spear had been gone since Paleo times, the medium-impact lance was old-fashioned, the high-speed arrow the new technology.

Unhafted knives, however, returned to a very basic form, triangular, suitable both for stabbing stroke or cutting. Utilitarian blades were fairly large, 2 - 6 in. long, medium-wide at the base, and the types rarely show beveling or serrations. Plain and simple, these cutting tools perhaps indicate greater dependence on farming, less on the hunt. The knives may reflect an emphasis on ceremonialism, less on real and rigorous every day use. Some examples, however, do show extreme wear and/or in-use damage. Whatever the reasons, there is nothing even approaching the huge range of blade types and sizes from the Archaic.

Adena Knives (1000 BC - AD 700)

The well-known Adena people (named after an Adena-associated mound opened on Thomas Worthington's estate near Chillicothe, Ohio) spanned the late Archaic into middle Woodland times. Their high conical burial mounds, for example, may have been inspired by the high glacial knolls used by the Glacial Kame peoples for burials. Adena artifacts, spread over much of the Eastern U.S., are sturdy and utilitarian. It would seem that the bow could have been used in the last of the period, but few small Adena true arrowheads are known.

Cache Blades

The Adena are famous for both their graceful, lovely leaf blades, and for **caches** or underground deposits of blades. Adena knives may consist of hundreds, even thousands, of quarry blanks, roughly chipped, deposited near Adena village areas. Sometimes the deposits are isolated, and as is usually the case, are discovered by accident. The material may be fairly rough, various cherts, but the best obtainable material was also used.

For Adena, the caches of large blade-blanks seem to represent a practical hiding away of valuable weapon or tool materials, to be dug up and used at a later time. Although some deposits would appear to have ceremonial meaning, most may be semi-finished artifacts, temporarily sidetracked along an early trade route.

Adena true cache blades were made in two varieties, these from a few inches to over half a foot in length. The first is the basic Adena leaf-shaped blade with excurvate sides and base. The second is probably made from the first, but at times may be a distinct variety. This is the hafted Adena with the central protruding basal stem.

Often such knives forms are found in mounds, sometimes placed by themselves in small groupings, at other times associated with burials. Both blade forms have two characteristics. They are extremely well made, being flat from percussion flaking, and the edges are beautifully retouched by pressure refinishing. The very highest obtainable flint grades were usually used. Whatever ceremonial purpose these knives had, it seems to have been quite meaningful to those who made them and placed them in secure places. The Adena also had stemmed utilitarian knives in several styles.

Hopewell (300 BC — AD 600)

Within the Adena timeframe, another mound-building people called the Hopewell (after a site owned by M.C. Hopewell, also near Chillicothe, Ohio) developed. Speculation continues as to whether they were a separate Indian group, a related offspring, or even the ceremonial aspect of the Adena lifeway. However that is eventually decided, the Hopewell also were pottery and agriculture people, with larger towns rather than the scattered hamlets typical of Adena.

Though Hopewell had notched points and blades, there are also three very well known knife types. Even more than Adena, Hopewell traders sought out the very highest material grades and great distances were traveled or traded over to acquire special flints and obsidian. These blades in general are very well made for whatever cutting tasks, and illustrate some of the best chipping of the Woodland period.

Triangular

The main large Hopewell knife is attractive in simplicity, being triangular, from 2 to 5 or more inches long, and without any indication of stemming or notches. The base with fairly sharp corners is rarely ground but always thinned, and side are fairly straight. Though there are exceptions, most examples are thin with sharp edges, and usually do not show heavy use. Some examples were placed in burials intact, but in 90% of the cases, burial inclusions in charnal houses were either broken or burned.

Bladelets

The second Hopewell knife example almost needs no introduction, for these are the famous tiny, core-struck mini-knives. From ¾ to 1½ in. long, most are about ¼ in. wide and very thin. The majority have long flake scars on the obverse face, the marks of blades that were struck off earlier from the "parent" block.

If Hopewell triangular knives were made of high-grade flints, the core-struck bladelets were made of the best of the best, because superb fracturing qualities were needed. Otherwise, maximum length and minimum thinness could not have been achieved almost every time. An interesting aspect of these percussioned-off flake knives is that they were indeed hafted.

On many examples, one end (usually this is the squared or rounded end, not sharp-tipped) will have both edges ground or dulled. This can be felt, if not seen, and the dulling exists for about ⅜ in., rarely more. The lower working edges and the very important tip may have minute secondary chipping, but not always. There is no confusing these tiny blades with any other culture.

Because the Hopewell seemed to center on burial rites and ritual dismemberment of bodies, the "Cult of the Dead", one theory suggests that the bladelets were used for this purpose. While an easy explanation, the fact is that these tiny artifacts are wdely found on any Hopewell village site, these often far from any major ceremonial earthworks or mounds. The bladelets appear to be suited for any intricate cutting task, especially for small game which no doubt supplemented the field-grown crops.

Ceremonial

Hafted ceremonial Hopewell blades, large and dramatic, were key adjuncts for burials in important central sites. Often they were made with great care, and then ritually broken or burned, shattered as if to represent the departed life they honored. Some ceremonial knife forms have blade configurations or notching never seen on everyday utilitarian forms, and designs were reserved for the ceremonial pieces.

Mississippian (AD 800 — AD 1650)

These seem to have been various warlike bow-and-arrow people, who in the late prehistoric period occupied lands held by faded cultures. Their projectile points were triangular, sometimes notched. Their knives had a squared hafting area at the base, and while they often lacked the clean lines of the classic Hopewell shape, they no doubt were effective.

A feature of Mississippian points (Erie, Ft. Ancient, and others) was serrations on both edges. No doubt some "points" served as knives, especially longer examples. The pure triangular knife form, however, did not seem to be serrated. Whether saw-edged or smooth, the typical point was about 1¼ in. long, knives from 2 to 5 inches.

The Mississippian period also had ceremonial aspects, and saw the rise of the giant temple mounds and associated earthworks. Very large blades were created, these straight or curved, often duo-tipped as were some smaller utilitarian knives. (As if to get double use from artifacts, some drills were also pointed at each end.) Some of the ceremonial blades were up to two feet long, but a deterioration in flint-working seems finally to have arrived.

WOODLAND-MISSISSIPPIAN

Copena Classic & triangular knives, Colbert & Lauderdale Co., Ala. Late Archaic to Woodland period in North Alabama.   Group: $125

Top row:
* Copena Triangular, 2-1/2'' x 15/16'' Lauderdale Co., Ala.*
* Copena Triangular, 2-3/4'' x 1-1/8 Lauderdale Co., Ala.*
* Copena Triangular, 2-5/8'' x 7/8'' Lauderdale Co., Ala.*

Top to bottom:
* Copena Classic, 3'' x 1-3/16'' Colbert Co., Ala.*
* Copena Classic, 3-7/8'' x 1-1/8'' Colbert Co., Ala.*
* Copena Classic, 3-1/4'' x 1'' Colbert Co., Ala.*
* Copena Triangular, 2-1/16 x 1'' Colbert Co., Ala.*
* Courtesy A. W. Beinlich, Jr., Sheffield, Alabama*

Top to bottom:
* Mississippian Knife, 5-5/16 x 1-3/8 in. Tan late Woodland Colbert Co., Ala.* $25
* Mississippian Knife 5-1/16 x 1-1/2 in. Gray and Tan late Woodland, Colbert Co., Ala.* $20
* Courtesy A. W. Beinlich, Jr., Sheffield, Alabama*

Bottom row:
* 4-7/8'' x 1'' Gray, Colbert Co., Ala. Woodland* $7-$30
* 4-9/16'' x 1-3/8'' Gray, Colbert Co., Ala. Woodland* $6-$30
* 4-9/16'' x 1-1/4'' Gray, Lauderdale Co., Ala. Woodland* $6-$30
* Courtesy A. W. Beinlich, Jr., Sheffield, Alabama*

LEAF-SHAPE, serrated edges, made of Felsite, 4 in. long. It is ca. 1000 BC - AD 1500. $150
Photo courtesy Jim Cressey, California

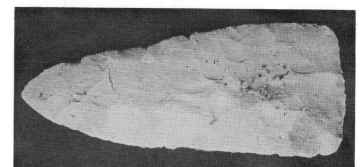

Large triangular blade, Worth County, GA, 4-1/2'' long. It is in average condition, in a brown chert patinated white. In the Eastern U.S., many similar blades are from the Woodland period. $15
Photo courtesy Jack M. Hall collection, Georgia

Archaic to early Woodland knives. Lauderdale Co., Ala. Knife on right shows degree of grinding along base and sides, length, 3-1/2'' x 3-3/4''.$15-$20
Courtesy P. A. Everhart, Sheffield, Alabama

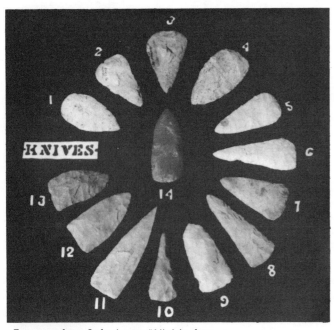

Frame numbers: Scale, (center #14) 4 in. long.
#1-NORTH, Illinois
#2-TRI-BLADE, Wisconsin
#3-NORTH, Illinois
#4-NORTH, Illinois
#5-TRI-BLADE, Wisconsin
#6-TRI-BLADE, Tennessee
#7-TRI-BLADE, Illinois
#8-TRI-BLADE, Illinois
#9-BOAT-SHAPE, Missouri
#10-TRI-BLADE, OH River Val
#11-TRI-LADE, Georgia
#12-TRI-BLADE, Illinois
#13-TRI-BLADE, Illinois
#14-BOAT-SHAPE, Wisconsin
Photo courtesy Bob & Gerry Rosberg collection, Illinois

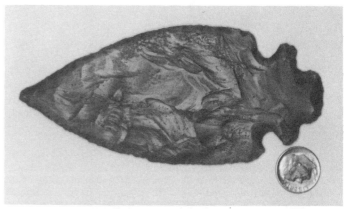

Fine knife, DOUBLE-NOTCH OR NOTCH/STEM TYPE, from the late prehistoric Turkey-tail culture. It is 2-1/8'' x 4-5/8'' long, of Indiana hornstone, from the Kent and Ottawa County line region. This is a very specialized knife form, and does not seem to be widespread. Excellent size, chipping, design. $425
Photo courtesy David G. Shirley collection, Michigan

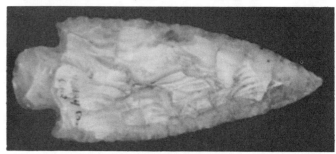

STEMMED WOODLAND BLADE, 1-3/4'' x 4-1/2'', from Henry County, OH. It is made of translucent tan Flintridge chalcedony, a gem material, which adds to value. This piece carries G.I.R.S. authentication no. 0-8. Note the well-balanced shoulders, fine base, good length. $275
Photo courtesy David G. Shirley, Michigan

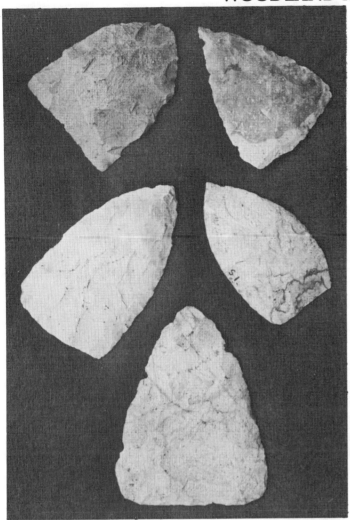

TRIANGULAR-BLADES, each 4 in. long, from Mojave Desert region. The material is agate and yellow jasper. Time period is ca. 1000 BC-AD 1500. Each... $45
Photo courtesy Jim Cressey, California

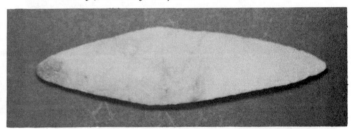

Four-blade knife, having slightly beveled edges, two per side. It is 1-3/8 x 4-7/8 inches, in light pink flint with dark pink inclusions. Slightly thicker on the short end, this is a beautiful and very well made piece, as evidenced by clean lines in photo. Found by Mr. Warren in 1960 in Missouri, this is normally a Texas type. Many are found in a Panhandle Pueblo context, AD 900-1300. $375
Photo courtesy Richard L. Warren collection, Missouri

Five triangular Georgia blades, Seminole County, in white, brown and pink cherts. Lower center blade is 2-3/8''. Upper right is an O'LENO blade, AD 200-1250, while center right is an ICHETUCKNEE, post AD 1250. Each... $3-$10
Photo courtesy Jack M. Hall collection, Georgia

Archaic or Woodland stemmed blade, with one white ''lightning line'' toward tip, which itself received some prehistoric damage not harming outline.$12
Hothem collection

SIDE-HAFTED KNIFE, 3/4'' x 3-1/4'', Plains period, AD 1500-1700. Material is pink porcelainite and item was found in Cascade County, MT. These blades were side-hafted into a slot at the end of a bone or wood handle, with the tip protruding just beyond the handle end. Here, the excurvate edge remained within the handle and the working edge is straight.
Value unlisted.

Photo courtesy John Byrd, Helena, Montana

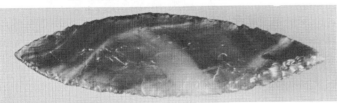

BIPOINTED KNIFE, 1 x 4 in. long. It is from the Prairie phase, AD 1000-1500. Knife is made of translucent banded agate and is from Teton County, MT. This is a very beautiful blade in a gem material. Value unlisted.
Photo courtesy John Byrd, Helena, Montana

WOODLAND knife, 2 x 3-1/2 in., done in a striped or layered flint. Size, differing shoulders and strong hafting all blade indications; this is a robust artifact from the late prehistoric. $45
Photo courtesy Arnold Moore collection, Missouri

WOODLAND-MISSISSIPPIAN

Large and fine triangular blade, probably Woodland. It is of brown jasper and from Union County, Pennsylvania. An interesting feature of this knife is that it balances perfectly on the dorsal ridge without leaning either way. 5'' $100
Photo courtesy Swope collection, Virginia

Large ADENA blade over 6 in. long, made of a light chalcedony flint. It has very straight sides for a distance, unusual in an Adena. $150
Photo courtesy Swope collection, Virginia

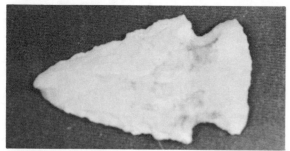

HOPEWELL BLADE, Woodland, 2-1/4'' long, in white flint. It has the typical excurvate Hopewell base, wide and thin, unground. Knife edges show some signs of use. $25
Private collection

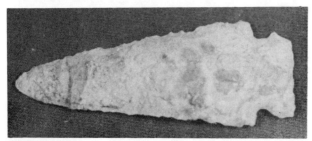

ARCHAIC KNIFE, 3 in. long, side-notch, eastern Midwest. This piece has good form, length and workstyle, but the material is very low-grade. Of a grey and brown chert with rough inclusions, low grade hurts value.$9
Private collection

NODENA blade, 1-1/8'' x 4-1/2'', a beautiful specimen. From Pemiscot Co., MO, these are very late in prehistoric ca. AD 1500. They are sometimes found as CACHE offerings with burials. $195
Photo courtesy Arnold Moore collection, Missouri

Late prehistoric knife, probably HOPEWELL BLADE, 1-1/2'' x 3-3/4''. It is made of translucent Flintridge in gem quality pale grey flint and is extremely thin. Two small spots at lower left are not inclusions, but grease and dirt form a tractor toolbox. $40
Private collection

FT. ANCIENT KNIFE, 1-3/4'', in grey-white stripped flint. Slight squaring of base suggests cultural ties; a delicate and thin blade. $15
Private collection

Late prehistoric knife, probably FT. ANCIENT BLADE, judging from the very faint signs of hafting at 1/2'' of base sides. Piece is 1-1/4'' x 3-1/2'', in gem quality Flintridge with cream and quartz inclusions. Fairly thick, this knife was originally much larger before long-term resharpening.$25
Private collection

HOPEWELL BLADE, Wayne County, MI. It may be a trade piece, and is made of Knife River flint from SD, or at least of material brought in from that source. At 2-1/8'' x 7-1/2'', it is very large, possibly ceremonial. Comparable pieces hve been found in Indiana and in Wisconsin. While notching is atypical (not scoop-like) the Hopewellians produced a wide variety of basal designs in their ceremonial pieces. $1400
Photo courtesy J. B. Geyer collection, Michigan; photograph by Mark Petrosoff

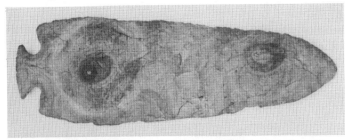

HOPEWELL BLADE, (2-1/4'' x 7'') made of nodular Bay Port chert. The two dark areas are caused by two nodules forming close together and are rather balanced in the piece. Basal notching resembles the NORTON Hopewell style from Michigan, Northon Mounds, Grand Rapids. Rounded tip and small base are reminiscent of the huge ROSS obsidian blades from Ohio, and this may be a related piece. From Michigan, ex-coll. Warner. $1000
Photo courtesy J. B. Geyer collection, Michigan; photograph by Mark Petrosoff

ADENA KNIFE, early to middle period, 2 x 8-3/4''. Of brown and light grey translucent flint, it is fairly thick, well-stemmed. Old markings: ''Finley at Derby, Ohio/Found in 1906''. (Derby is in Pickaway County.) A Mr. Hess picked it up. Almost always, such large Adena pieces were mound inclusions, and this may have been an excavated find, or one plowed up. Ex-coll. Dave Warner; blades of this size are extremely rare, which adds to value. $1000
Photo courtesy J. B. Geyer collection, Michigan; photograph by Mark Petrosoff

HOPEWELL BLADE, 8-1/16 in. long, of Flintridge material. It has the common Ohio Hopewell traits, including large base, corner notches, monoface-beveling and broad flakes (JBG). This is an extremely large specimen made in gem flint. It was found about 50 years ago northeast of Greenville, MI, by Kent Scott. The piece may have been traded North into Michigan, perhaps for finished copper artifacts, which were exported in prehistoric times. At any rate, it is a rare and beautiful piece, with only slight damage to one shoulder tip. $1000
Photo courtesy J. B. Geyer collection, Michigan; photograph by Mark Petrosoff

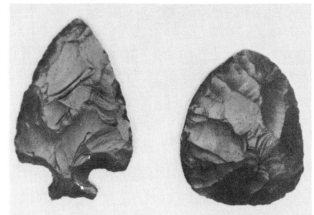

MIDDLE WOODLAND BLADES, left, notched Hopewell (4-1/4''), Indiana hornstone, Barry Co., MI. $125
Right, NORTH blade, one of an eleven-piece CACHE, all made of Indiana hornstone. Ex-coll. Wills, Marion, IN. 4'' $90
Indiana hornstone (Harrison County flint) plus Illinois flints and Ohio Flintridge were traded into southern Michigan during Hopewell times.
Photo courtesy J. B. Geyer collection, Michigan; photograph by Mark Petrosoff

SNYDER, Woodland, knife 3-3/4'' long, excellent chipping and such smooth edges they appear to have been ground. From Calhoun Co., IL, such examples were probably ceremonial in original use. Hopewell Indians, noted for their ritual creations, made this fine example. $175
Photo courtesy Arnold Moore collection, Missouri

Large BEAVERTAIL knife from Oklahoma, brown flint, just over 5 in. long. $80

Photo courtesy Swope collection, Virginia

HARAHEY KNIFE, Edwards Plateau Chert, from Early Plains Apache site, Blanco Canyon, TX. It is Neo-Indian, AD 1300 - AD 1700. $75 Photo courtesy Wayne Parker collection, Texas   *4-1/4''*

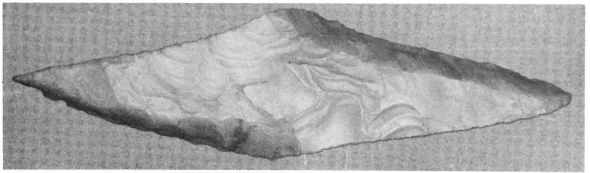

HARAHEY KNIFE, Alibates Flint, Classic form. It is Panhandle Plains Aspect, from site of that period, Hutchinson County, TX. Neo-Indian, AD 900 - AD 1300.   4-1/2'' $175 Photo courtesy Wayne Parker collection, Texas

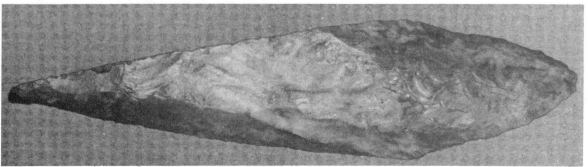

HARAHEY KNIFE, Alibates flint, Classic form. Surface find in Crosby Co., TX. Neo-Indian period.   4-1/2'' $175 Photo courtesy Wayne Parker collection, Texas

HARAHEY KNIFE, dark Edwards Plateau Chert, from Early Plains Apache site in Blanco Canyon, Crosby Co., TX.   3-1/2'' $100 Photo courtesy Wayne Parker collection, Texas

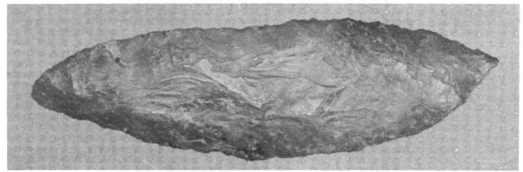

DOUBLE-POINTED KNIFE, Edwards Plateau chert, probably a blank for
a beveled knife. It shows some beveling or resharpening which had already
begun. Blanco Canyon, Crosby Co., TX. It is Early Plains Apache.$100
Photo courtesy Wayne Parker collection, Texas   3-1/2''

HARAHEY KNIFE, dark Edwards Plateau chert, surface find on Robertson site, Crosby Co., TX. This fine piece is Neo-Indian. $100
Photo courtesy Wayne Parker collection, Texas   4-1/4''

HARAHEY KNIFE, Potters Chert, surface find, Robertson site. Crosby Co.,
TX. Note that the beveled edge is unusually long and delicate. $125
Photo courtesy Wayne Parker collection, Texas   5''

HARAHEY KNIFE, dark Edwards Plateau chert, Early Plains Apache,
AD 1300 - AD 1700. From Blanco Canyon, Crosby County, TX$100
Photo courtesy Wayne Parker collection, Texas   3''

WOODLAND-MISSISSIPPIAN

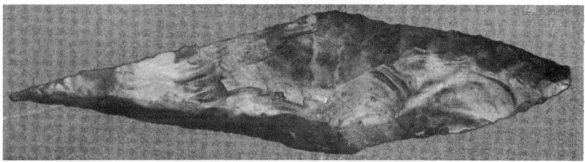

HARAHEY KNIFE, Alibates flint, Panhandle Plains Aspect site, Hutchinson County, TX. Neo-Indian period, AD 900 - AD 1300. $175
Photo courtesy Wayne Parker collection, Texas 4-1/2''

DOUBLE-POINTED KNIFE, possibly a blank for a HARAHEY knife.
Alibates flint, Panhandle Plains Aspect site, from Hutchinson Co., TX,
AD 900 - AD 1300. 4-1/2'' $100
Photo courtesy Wayne Parker collection, Texas

DOUBLE-POINTED KNIFE, grey Edwards Plateau chert, from early Plains
Apache site, Blanco Canyon. It is AD 1300 - AD 1700, Neo-Indian, Crosby
County, TX. 3-1/2'' $100
Photo courtesy Wayne Parker collection, Texas

HARAHEY KNIFE, four-way beveled, of Tecovas jasper. From early Plains
Apache site, Blanco Canyon, AD 1300 - AD 1700, Neo-Indian, Crosby
Co., TX. 4'' $150
Photo courtesy Wayne Parker collection, Texas

HARAHEY KNIFE (or four-way bevel), Alabates flint, Panhandle Plains Aspect site. From Hutchinson Co., TX, period AD 900 - AD 1300. Note the extreme length and narrowness of this piece.   4-3/4'' $175
Photo courtesy Wayne Parker collection, Texas

HARAHEY KNIFE, Alibates flint, classic form. Panhandle Plains Aspect site, from Hutchinson County, TX. Neo-Indian.   6'' $250
Photo courtesy Wayne Parker collection, Texas

HARAHEY KNIFE, Edwards Plateau chert; surface find, Crosby Co., TX.
4-1/4'' $100
Photo courtesy Wayne Parker collection, Texas

HARAHEY KNIFE, Edwards Plateau chert. Notice flute on base of obverse. This is a refashioned Clovis projectile point made into a four-way bevel. From an Early Plains Apache site. This is a very rare piece, having the cultural touchmarks of two completely different early people. $250
Photo courtesy Wayne Parker collection, Texas   3-1/2''

Young Indian male, Northwest Territories, Canada. The very large general-purpose or fighting knife attached to the cartridge belt has a leather sheath that is decorated with rows of brass tacks.
Photo courtesy Public Archives Canada

74

An Indian named Big Star, shown cutting a type of Indian tobacco. Note large knife to his left.
Photo courtesy South Dakota State Historical Society

Indians cutting up a steer, ca. 1895. The man at left seems to be sharpening a small blade on a whetstone.
John Anderson photo, courtesy South Dakota State Historical Society.

CHAPTER XII

HAFTED KNIVES

Rather than continue this chronological overview with the next logical step, historic times (post AD 1650 or so) and the influx of White-made knives, we go back to the beginning. This is done to keep all prehistoric knives in one section, unhafted and hafted alike, all chipped artifacts. ''Hafted'' as used here means special and obvious treatment to the blade base, this in the form of either notches or a stem.

Notches usually exist in pairs, the same size, depth and location on or near the blade base. The most common notching is in the lower side or the corners, the least common in the base bottom.

Stemmed blades have a projecting central basal column, for the handle, and sometimes (as with later Adena types) much of the lower blade corners and sides were chipped off. This seems to be a waste of good flint, but gave the blade an immensely strong central base. At times, the two hafting methods seem to combine, as in many of the early Archaic bifurcated or split-base types.

Some technically unhafted knife forms from all prehistoric periods do indeed have hafting areas at the base. These may be squared areas, a contracted region, basal grinding or basal thinning — all indications of hafting. A very few seem to have even the actual handle chipped in flint, somewhat similar to some of the Danish prehistoric daggers.

Knife Characteristics

In trying to understand early chipped knives, it would be wise to reconsider what a knife (as opposed to a point or scraper, for example) really is. A knife is used for one major purpose, cutting, and one secondary purpose, penetration, which is why many have sharp tips. A point — whether spear, **Atl-atl** or arrowhead, was for piercing. A scraper usually had a short edge of whatever kind and a very short length so that great pressure could be placed on the edge.

Further, prehistoric Amerind knives in some cases seem to have been general purpose — probably most of the symmetrical notched and stemmed types — or very highly specialized. The last might be the rectangular Paleo with the small beveled edge. Bases were ultra-important because if the handle (for knives that had them) could not be well and solidly attached, the knife itself ranged from inefficient to nearly useless.

In most cases, the basal area seems to have been appropriate in size and shape to suit the blade. If the knife is large, the base tends to be robust, as with a number of Archaic hafted knives. If small, the base correspondingly is somewhat delicate, as with Hopewell bladelets. All this stands to reason and is about what one would expect.

There are exceptions to the size extremes. Some chipped blades have quite short lengths and edges, with comparatively large bases. Most of these specimens are simply the result of wear and resharpening, which hardly ever included changes to the basal region. And, some large blades (one example is the small-base Dovetail) may have a very small base for size. Generally, though there are exceptions, if an artifact of whatever period and style looks like a cutting instrument, it should be so-considered and without a lot of effort to make it into a point.

For an unknown reason, probably representing dramatic thoughts about life long ago, projectile points for the collector seem to have more attraction than knives. Perhaps — since more men than women collect Indian artifacts — points are considered more masculine. This perception is now changing, and who can say which blades were actually used by which sex, and for what. Sometimes the psychological aspect of collecting Amerind art can be revealing.

Sign of Wear

Obvious as it may seem, a close examination of artifacts may indicate knife use. The tip is important, and if it is worn down by use, this suggests a blade that was for a time heavily used in one area. This may relate to the sides or edges, which may or may not be similarly dulled. Note that this is not damage or breakage, but the wearing away by contact with other materials.

Knives may have wear at the tip, anywhere on the sides, even near the base. Sometimes one edge or both edges where entirely resharpened (rechipped), sometimes only small areas of either.

Extremely dulled blades are good to collect for two reasons. One is that the piece is in fact larger than it would have been after the last resharpening, at least width-wise. It also has authentic evidence of knife use. And, such examples are unusual in themselves. Probably 95% of these chipped blades are sharp enough to use today for many purposes. Very likely, the blades were cleaned and rechipped after repeated use, kept sharp and ready for the next time they were needed.

Experimental use of blades for modern cutting tasks has some documentation, including the successful use of obsidian bladelets in open-heart surgery. In another case a bear was skinned and butchered using an obsidian blade. It was noted that extra care had to be used because it was sharper than a steel knife.

The degree of everyday wear and dulling on prehistoric knives has several task or time aspects. One suggests that a deer could be skinned and cut up without sharpening the knife used. Findings indicate that deer were one of the most utilized prehistoric meat sources, so many knives were no doubt employed in this fashion throughout North America.

In-use Damage

Beyond use-signs on knives — worn-down serrations, dulled edges or tip — there may also be typical damage marks. While most such signs detract to a large extent from collector value, they also add authenticity to the piece and something of a glimmer as to how the knives were used. Except for the basal aspect, such damage will be seen on hafted and unhafted blades alike.

Often, close inspection of fragmentary blades will prove that the massive damage is ancient, that however it happened, the knives were actually destroyed in use. This means an undisturbed patina even in the break area, an interior color that is indentical to that of the exterior.

Tip damage is different from the occasional "impact fluting" seen on the tip and upper face, though more will be said on this later. Tips may be snapped away from either face, leaving one side slightly lower than the other. Or, the break may be more jagged, suggesting that a twisting motion was the cause of original breakage.

Many times opposite areas of a symmetrical blade will have heavy wear that created "break-chipping", or flake removal when the knife was used. Such signs are fairly unusual, because the Indians seemed to know the stress limits of their blades and did not abuse their basic properties. Even more often seen is shoulder damage, especially when this part of the blade was fairly wide and thin, this pertaining mainly to hafted knives. One or both shoulders may appear to be battered or broken off, probably unintentionally, major damage in the course of heavy use.

Hafted blades of many periods, especially the Archaic, seem to suffer from something of a design deficiency. Some blade types had side or corner notches that went too deep, and only a fairly small amount of flint or obsidian remained between handle and blade. Eastern U.S. beveled blades often had this problem, especially larger examples. The connection between the opposing forces (handle power, blade resistance while cutting) was not sturdy enough. This can be seen on some examples that somehow survived, probably because their users treated the knives with special care.

This is also why surface-hunting collectors often find whole or nearly whole blades without bases, or find bases only without the blades. Hafted blades with wide, thick and strong bases generally survived even rough treatment, including heavily battered blade edges.

Salvaged Knives

Prehistoric Indians sometimes misplaced or abandoned completely useful knives for reasons we will never know. This is why superb authentic examples exist in museums and collections. More common, though, was the practice of getting every last bit of work out of a blade. Examples are knives with very short, thick blades on normal-size bases, these on types that are normally much longer or wider. Rechipping to retain usefulness is in a way a form of salvage itself.

Another form of salvage is much different and somewhat rare. This was when later Amerind found and used the chipped artifacts of much earlier peoples. There are two hallmarks of such salvage. One is when the patina of the piece is definitely disturbed, showing work at a later time, perhaps separated by thousands of years. One example is the tip of a beveled Archaic blade reworked into a triangular arrowhead.

Sometimes later people found an early blade and "played" with it. One example is a notched-base Archaic **St. Charles** of unknown tan flint. It was found just above the waterline of an ice-age lake, 60 feet from a tiny Ft. Ancient campsite. Saw-like notches had been chipped from one part of the edge, a shoulder was removed from another side, and the tip was rechipped. It forms no known tool type. It may have been an amusing toy to those who found it or perhaps someone tried to take it apart to see what it was made of.

The final salvage of early blades (even sometimes projectile points) was when later people picked up the artifact and kept it, unchanged. This creates much confusion for today's students, as when Archaic blades are found in Woodland mounds. If purposely placed there, and assuming the artifacts were not just scooped up with midden debris when the mound was put up, this suggests a prehistoric respect or interest in the objects of earlier Indians. The fact is that the artifacts indeed came from the late sites, but they were second-hand items.

The Shaft Factor

In considering whether any one artifact is a point (spear, lance or arrow) or a knife, the shaft factor must be taken into account. Consider: Most Paleo points have a basal width that averages about an inch; the average piece has some divergence either way, but not much. This suggests that Paleo spears (knives in some cases) had handles with diameters of an inch or so to provide deep penetration of the target animal. Diameter could have been an inch or even greater when a much thinner bone foreshaft was used, known to have happened on at least one Paleo kill-site in Mexico.

HAFTED KNIVES

There is evidence if no sure proof that the **Atl-atl** or lance thrower may have been in use as early as 6000 BC, in the early Archaic. This comes from finds in various Southwestern caves including Utah's Hogup Cave and Nevada's Lovelock Cave. Given the probable early appearance of the lance-thrower, points have a certain relationship or ratio to the lance shaft.

If the thrower did indeed appear that early in much of the country, this would explain the smaller points of the period. Most evidence indicates the lance ranged in length from 4 to 7 feet, and perhaps averaged 5 feet and about ⅜ in. in diameter. So point notches would generally be ⅜ in. or so apart, unless narrower foreshafts were used. In this case the notches could be as close as ¼ inch. For true arrowheads with the ¼ in. diameter arrowshafts, points again must have notching that corresponds to this measurement. Of course, with the omni-present triangular arrowheads, unhafted, such considerations are not nearly so important. In all cases notching can be wider than the shaft, but rarely smaller. For stemmed blades, the handle can be wider than the stem, rarely less wide.

Hafted knives had much wider handles than any of the points, perhaps ranging from 1-⅛ to nearly 2 inches. So, the stem can be much thicker (**Adena**), or notches much wider apart (**Meadowood**). Some types have such large notches (**Ashtabula**) that an actual stem is formed. Related to the shaft factor is the sheer size of many blades. Not even considering the dozens of knife-use indications, one or more of which may be present, the concept of throwing too much point should be considered. Just enough size and weight and velocity were used, for overkill in design would have been underkill in use. All this relates to knives, in that something likely not a point was likely a knife, especially if other knife traits are present.

Knife Traits — A Checklist

Large shoulders. If hafted, extra-wide shoulders suggest that the edge was more important than the tip, and would have made a poor point design. Points needed to pierce and angled, or expanding lower sides would have increased resistance, lessening penetration. Indian chippers knew what they were doing, and did not design against the purpose. So, very wide shoulders and flared shoulders indicate a knife.

Mismatched shoulders. As with mismatched notches, such examples do not usually indicate a point made in a hurry, but were use-designed basics. If, for example, the main knife working edge is on the side with the lower notch, this provides a longer uninterrupted working edge. Two-level notching will usually provide a firmer handle attachment because a greater length of binding can be used. There is little to be gained if points are secured in this way.

Shoulder removal. Long before this book was written, during the course of collecting, the author was struck by a strange sort of "damage" that occurred on some artifacts. The tip portions of some projecting shoulders were missing. Since these areas are relatively fragile, and many of the artifacts were field-found, it was thought that this was damage due to disc strikes.

Yet, over time, a pattern began to emerge. The damage was almost always in the same place, and one or both lower sides might have the missing shoulder tips. And this chipped-out section always left behind a short, flat flake scar which terminated somewhere in or near the notch area. Further, this shoulder removal occurred largely in one family of artifacts, the many members of the early Archaic bifurcated-base group.

Any one of this family of very early artifacts might have the shoulder tip removed, one or both sides. However, other very similar examples might have the shoulder regions intact. It was perplexing because it became obvious that this was not accidental damage at all, but intentional work and highly specialized fracture-chipping.

Two more curious things were noted. Often the artifacts, of whatever size, had serrations or saw-tooth edging, though not always. And, the unique chipping rarely seemed to be done on very large and full (little used) specimens, only those of whatever size that showed much use. Actually, indirectly, the missing shoulders are probably the best sign of heavy, long-term use on any one of these artifacts.

There are two keys to the solution of this puzzle of the "disappeared" shoulders on these knives, for this they almost certainly are. One is the general observation that prehistoric Amerinds, in their utilitarian flaked knives, always had a good reason for this or that shape or size or modification. They were practical and there was always a line of reasoning regarding how a tool not only worked, but how to make it work well. After all, if the Indians' tools for living were not right, neither were their lives.

The second key is that these early Archaic bifurcated-base knives — with their split twin basal lobes — are invariable smaller in length or width or both than the average of the largest known examples of the type. This in turn means several things. Missing shoulder tips are not a wierd cultural trait, but something done on shorter, well-used knives and done for a solid reason.

An examination of large specimens of the family (**Kanawha, St. Albans, Lake Erie, LeCroy, MacCorkle** and others) indicates that when shoulders were left untouched, the blades still had good length and width and were fully useful. Or, "new" blades had intact shoulders. As the blades were worn down and rechipped, reducing the width and sometimes the length, the basal area remained the same size. Finally, the basal width in effect became too large for the remaining blade size to be effectively used, because the lower blade corners were then in the way of the work.

HAFTED KNIVES

At this time, the Indian user had a choice. The knife could simply be discarded and a new one made (and this often happened), or, one or both shoulders could be knocked off. This was both a form of salvage (conserving time and material) and the creation of a new and smaller blade, once again totally useful on a smaller scale. Many collectors, if they examine their acquisitions closely, will find just such a progression on their blades.

There is a second form of shoulder chipping that may be related to the type already discussed. Instead of the shoulder being chipped down into the body of the blade, it is chipped along the outside edge. That is, the indirect percussion blow began at the corner of the shoulder tip and fractured-off the lower shoulder outside edge. Sometimes the hinge fracture can be seen farther up the blade edge and at other times the fracture terminates in a direction away from the material and it does not show the hinge. This is a highly unusual and rare form of shoulder removal and few specimens exist.

Tip flattening. On a number of hafted artifact types, especially from the Archaic, there is a unique form of damage-chipping or flake scars, whatever the reason turns out to be. This is at the tip, and resembles the fluting at the base of a Paleo **Clovis.** That is, the flake scar looks like an indirect percussion scar, generally on one face and extending as much as an inch, with varying width, toward the artifact face center. The concentric circle segments within the flute-like channel radiate back from the tip, proving place of impact.

Standard collector lore has it that these are accidental impact-flutes, the sign of a rare and violent contact against a solid object. It would have to had struck at just the right speed and angle, a one-in-a-million shot. No doubt, some of them are indeed that. For others, the fluting of the tip was likely not accidental. While few examples exist, they suggest that the flake was deliberately and carefully done.

This step, in fact, may not even have been a cultural trait of whatever period, only an expedient discovered by single individuals. In the case of knives, this tip-fluting or thinning was done on relatively thick, sometimes worn-down blades. The purpose seems to have been to thin the top and upper portion of the blade for better cutting, or even for different cutting tasks. While these observations are valid, and the examples exist, more research is needed before regarding the presence of a tip flute as a true knife trait.

Sometimes knife tips were fracture-chipped (see, earlier) on one or both side edges, and the long, thin scars remain. This was evidently to remove ragged tip edges or make a much more pointed tip, likely for a tool form similar to a graver. The region sometimes received heavy wear, and the scars must be seen closely and in good light, just like the faint flake-scars on some fractured-base blades.

Knife faces. Probably unrelated to the Paleo Uniface blades known throughout North America, hafted later knives may have one flatish face, the opposite humped or ridged. Practical for knives, poor for points, such designs may be crude in execution but nonetheless effective. Often, but not always, the obverse or upper face may have the bulk of the chipping, while on other examples the chipping is done equally well on both faces.

Tip Indications

Obvious as it might seem, many knives are still termed points even when the blade tip is entirely inappropriate for a projectile form. The tip may be dull or squared and angled to the extent that it forms a third, smaller edge. Many examples have tips that could simply be called unimportant, while the edges retain full utility for knife use.

Tip angled. Many stemmed or notched knives have a tip (compared with a line drawn from base center up the face middle) that is decidedly angled or off-center. This may be to the left or right and gives the blade two edges of slightly unequal length. This off-centeredness may be mild or extreme, but always gives the knife an asymmetrical look.

Blade angled. Rather than only the tip, some blades are angled or off center for the entire length, beginning at or near the hafting region. As with the tip, this angled blade may be great or small, even in some cases creating a main or primary edge plus a backing or secondary edge. Signs of use may exist on all parts of the edge or on selected portions of such edges.

Blade up/down. Depending on which face of the blade is examined the blade may be angled up or down. Laying the hafted knife on a flat surface, the base can touch first, followed by the tip. Or, placed flat, the tip of the other face would not touch the surface at all. While many collectors consider these deformed or poorly made points, most will have other knife characteristics as well.

Blade extra-long. Whatever the hafted artifact type an extra-long blade is a major sign that the edges were the desired working region, not the tip. Most flint-knappers in most periods were frugal with flint or obsidian and did not over-design a utility piece. Length does not provide a better-penetrating tip, though specialized tipping would have added a plus.

The greater mass, if used as a point, would not greatly have aided penetration and made the artifact more prone to breakage during rigorous use. Many extra-long pieces whether of a recognized point type or not, will have other indications of knife use. In these cases the makers simply wanted more edge-length, or, longer knives.

79

HAFTED KNIVES

Blade extra-thick. Whatever the blade size or type, there is one reason for a poor point design and two in favor of knives. For the first, perhaps the ancient hunter did not fully comprehend the details of point design and efficiency. Assuming the shaft end was streamlined to enter the wound-hole with little resistance, deep damage was needed for a killing strike. Here, we are dealing with two feet into a mammoth, a foot or more into a bear, at least 8 inches into a deer.

Other factors held constant (and considered equal) a "fat" point penetrates less well than a thin point because the impact force is spread over a larger point cross-section, providing more resistance. A nearly identical principal is still used today in armor-piercing ammunition. Called a kinetic energy round, the main projectile is amazingly simple, a pointed small-diameter tungsten bar which is kicked out at over 4000 feet per second. The Russians in WW-II used a solid steel projectile called an "arrowhead shot" to tear apart German armored vehicles. The prehistoric Indians would have loved it.

For knife use, extra-thick examples gave much more strength for tough cutting tasks, the edge backed by mass. This was security whether the knife was used traditionally on the edges or was employed in various twisting or prying movements. The final reason — and this can be noted on many examples by comparing base size and/or overall size with others of the type — is that the knife was simply worn down by use and rechipping. While length and width decreased, base and thickness remained about the same. So in the final version, the well-worn knife is comparatively thick.

Knife Edges

Various knife characteristics have been described, and all are of importance. Even more vital, because it shows the intent of makers and users, is the matter of edges, exactly how they were shaped, rechipped, and so forth. It might be noted that collectors tend to admire the overall piece and so may miss some of the edge detailing. Here are a dozen and more observations about knife edges, these all dealing with hafted blades of whatever prehistoric time.

The two edges may have different chipping patterns, and there are many possibilities. One edge may be roughly percussion-flaked, the other done the same but with pressure retouch that evens and smooths the edge. Still another with very delicate chipping may have a very smooth edge. Some of these "super" edges seem to have been very lightly ground or dulled, for whatever reasons. The different chipping, when found, suggests different intentions for the blade edges.

Some knives show a very unpoint-like difference in edge wear, hence, use. An edge — it can be either or both or all or part — can show the same, or different signs of wear. Edge-wear in itself indicates full- or part-time use as a knife, and it is often present in some form.

While much of this discussion about knife edges also obviously could be placed in the category of blade shapes, the focus yet remains on the edge itself. A perfect example is the **Pentagonal,** a familiar and widespread Archaic hafted type. Known primarily as the **Afton,** the word simply means "five sided". This includes the base (1), two lower sides (2&3), and the two tip or upper sides, (4&5).

The various **Pentagonal** forms range from 1 in. to over 5 in. in length, and are corner-notched. The cutting edges descending from the tip are almost always much shorter than the lower side edges, and any of the four can be straight or incurvate. The type never seems to be beveled or serrated, and the important cutting edges appear to be the upper and smaller opposing pair.

As a point type, **Pentagonals** are failures, often being too long, generally too wide, and the rapid expansion of the semi-shouldered upper edges grossly reduces any penetration. There is rarely much basal thinning for this type. Evidently the precision of the upper cutting edges outweighed any awkwardness in hafting. Many examples are very worn down by rechipping of the upper edges, and are almost blunt.

If one blade side is excurvate and the opposite side incurvate, this is again a blade no matter how slight or subtle these differences may be. On hafted examples, this may be by design, or one side (incurvate) may be more reduced because of frequent resharpening. There may also be differences in chipping patterns, one edge devoted to a certain purpose, the other to another.

If both edges are greatly excurvate, this again is an obvious sign of knife, not point, use. Very excurvate edges make penetration more difficult, but are an excellent design for knife use. On some knife types — notably some of the deep-notch Archaic forms — blade edges are so excurvate as to give an oval or spade-shaped outline. Rechipped or resharpened forms so common in collections have a more familiar triangular shape.

Some blades are a combination of the two characteristics just mentioned, and have say, an incurvate upper portion and an excurvate lower pair of edges. On other forms, the edge configuration may be reversed, and straight edges may be included. Much depends on where, and how much, a blade was resharpened. An example of the excurvate-incurvate edge is the **Copena** of the Tennessee River Valley, an artifact referred to by Bell (Oklahoma Anthropological Society Special Bulletin No. 2, p. 20-21) as "recurved". An example of incurvate-excurvate is the well known **Turkey-tail** of the Ohio River Valley, with incurvate upper edge that may produce a very pointed tip.

HAFTED KNIVES

Irregular edges — and these can be almost any design imaginable — are a strong indicator of knife use. This means that whether the edgeline is excurvate, incurvate or straight, the basic contour is at some place disturbed by an indentation, or very rarely, by a protrusion in the edgeline. Of no benefit and even detrimental to point purposes, such purpose-made irregularities can only be explained in terms of edge utility, knife use.

Retouched edges, whether completely rechipped or only in a small area, can be found on hafted and unhafted blades alike. Usually this rechipped area has a series of much smaller flake scars, as if a smaller more delicate edge was required, but chip scars may also be about the same size as the original edge. The last is especially obvious when a blade edge was damaged and the break area in the edgeline "repaired".

Irregular edges as seen from the face have been described, but irregular edges seen from the side also exist. Some have been in collections for years, without this curious feature being recognized. This may be a random movement or edge-shift in small areas from upper to lower face or vice-versa. Irregular edges of this type are probable signs of knife use, and may be caused by such mundane matters as flaws in the material, repairs, or individual experimentation.

Another broad class of hafted knives, purpose-made in that fashion, has an edgeline that shifts from one face to the other. The **Pandale** of Texas has this very unusual "twisting" edgeline, and so do a number of other specimens, mainly from the Archaic. Another, unnamed type is extremely well made, long and slender, with a short, wide stem that is moderately ground. One 3 in. example in Indiana hornstone is also serrated.

Hafted knives or points of a fairly small size may have various indications of non-point use — or non-knife use, for that matter. These include rechipped tips made into straight or hooked gravers and the presence of shaft-scrapers on the sides. Shaft-scrapers, often seen on flakes of medium size, are smallish semicircular indentations with super-smooth edges.

Despite the multitude of chipped knife edges, there are also knife edges formed by abrasion. These are so rare that most collections do not have an example, and there seems to be no one single type. Abrasion is the process of grinding the artifact against a loose-grained stone, the edge being formed by wearing away the crystalline material on one or two faces. No large examples are known, and most are medium to small in size. Typical edges may be formed by the flat surface, or one carefully rounded, which produces a straight and very sharp edge. Sometimes the faces of other flakes are ground absolutely flat, but the chipped edge remains.

A few examples of the flat-ground surfaces are found on the sides and backs of small Paleo Uniface blades. The purpose seems to have been to create a very strong and straight working edge, but one that is strangely dull by most knife standards. Sometimes this abrasion is on one edge of a chip, sometimes done on both edge faces.

A fragmentary knife specimen (fire-cracked) in the author's collection has one face flat, the opposite side rounded, no chipping visible and the whole in a white flint polished to a fine gloss. The age and reason-for-being of these unique knives is not known. While that particular specimen was found on an Archaic site, late Paleo and Woodland artifacts have also been found nearby.

More than thirty knife characteristics or at least indications of primary or secondary knife use have been discussed at some length in this chapter. There may be more, and the collector is urged to explore the subject by closely examining possible blades for additional signs. This again relates to the multitude of hafted artifacts, not the unhafted varieties that are obviously blades.

Depending on how reasonably certain one wants to be regarding hafted chipped pieces as knives, almost any number of characteristics can be used as a minimum gauge. The number can be as low as one in a case like edge beveling, indicating frequent resharpening. Heavy edge-wear and large, sturdy bases probably rate a "one" as well. From here, a combination of minor knife traits will need to be studied, and perhaps several or many will be convincing to the student of prehistoric Amerind art. It is time for such rethinking and closer study.

And, in at least two areas, this is indeed being done. One is magnified study of edge-wear. This reveals, in some cases, what an ancient knife was really used for, all speculation and theory aside, before it was resharpened and the signs removed. Some of this experimental work was done at the Koster Site in Illinois, using knives for such purposes as opening clams. Modern use-signs were then compared with the minute marks on ancient blades. Comparisons of diagnostic scrapes and chips then revealed true ancient use.

The collector can do some of this interesting work. The usual magnifying or reading glass only enlarges about three times (3-x), little more than with the unaided eye. These (at $5 to $9) are easily available and good for studying tiny, "nibble" chipping on edges. Ten-power (10-x) monoculars are available from two sources, photo supply catalogs and jewelers' shops. The price range for the 10-x is about $9 - $15.

HAFTED KNIVES

Photo lenses tend to be of greater diameter to study larger areas, while jewelers' loups are of smaller diameter but similar in power and resolution. The 10-x is fairly easy to use and will show, greatly enlarged, medium-sized wear patterns, but not very tiny marks.

For this, one needs to go to the twenty-power jewelers' loup or magnifying lens, this available at about $35. At 20-x, very tiny edge-wear marks can begin to be seen. More research needs to be done in the large-point, small-knife field, where penetration marks may resemble those of occasional thrusting marks made by knives. For those who are really into this aspect of prehistoric hafted blades, the use of a binocular microscope is suggested, though these of course are very expensive.

Even more scientific, the second "upcoming" area of blade analysis may be the study of blood on knives, some of the artifacts thousands of years old. Unbelieveable as it appears, and washed seemingly clean by time and the weather, microscopic traces of blood down to the cell level still remain in tiny crevices. In addition, sensitive testing has also revealed hemoglobin and protein-derived amino acids.

Work done at the British Columbia Provincial Museum, Victoria, Canada is nothing short of incredible. Early chipped artifacts (AD 1000 - 4000 BC) included blood samples from seven different animals, from snowshoe hare to sea lions.

One artifact firmly dated at ca.830 BC showed traces of caribou and grizzly bear blood. Perhaps not surprisingly, human blood has been found on some artifacts, but this does not necessarily mean they were used as weapons. Cutting hands or fingers during manufacture or use was probably not uncommon.

A great deal, it seems, is yet to be learned about prehistoric knives.

This particular piece shows how the knife was actually hafted to a bone handle. This piece has a 3-1/2'' blade inserted into plaster of Paris in the bone which was used for the purpose of this photo only. The Indian obviously didn't have plaster of Paris but used either pitch, animal glue, asphaltum or some other available material. The final length of the knife is 6-7/8''$75 Courtesy A. W. Beinlich, Jr., Sheffield, Alabama

LATE ARCHAIC LEDBETTER KNIVES, all Georgia.
Left, Calhoun Cty., 2-3/4'', pink-grey flint, one barb missing. (Author's note: This may be an example of purposeful shoudler-tip removal, described elsewhere in book.) $5
Left center, Seminole Cty., brown and red. $20
Right center, Clay Cty., light chert. $10
Right, Early Cty., thick, in an unattractive chert. $5
Photo courtesy Jack M. Hall collection, Georgia

HAFTED KNIVES

This unsharpened Lost Lake blade is a good example of a beautifully made shaped knife (note the deep notches for hafting). Length 4-1/2''. Lauderdale Co., Ala. $350
Courtesy Tom Hendrix, Florence, Alabama

Early blade, THONOTOSASSA SUB-TYPE 2, from Mitchell Cty., GA. Of pink and white chert, it was made by heavy percussion flaking. It is in good condition, exactly 5-7/16 in. long, but THONOTOSASSA blades are generally fairly crude. It is ca. 6000-5000 BC. $35
Photo courtesy Jack M. Hall collection, Georgia

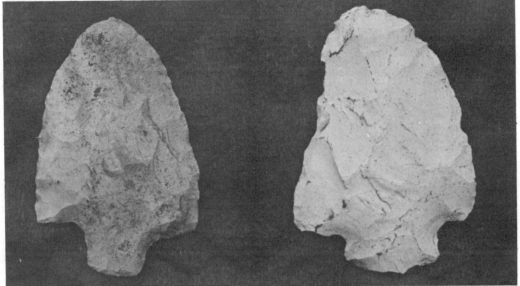

Left, stemmed blade, Dougherty Cty., GA, cream chert, percussion flaked. $15
Right, Dougherty Cty., 3-3/4'' long, crude percussion flaking , material white with rust staining. $10
Photo courtesy Jack M. Hall collection, Georgia

Late Archaic LEDBETTER Knives.
Left, blue-brown flint, Calhoun Cty., GA. $10
Center, Seminole Cty., GA, 3-1/8'', chert patinated white. $10
Right, Calhoun Cty., GA, blade with unusual angled tang; orange and cream banded chert. $10
Photo courtesy Jack M. Hall collection, Georgia

HAFTED KNIVES

Late Archaic LEDBETTER Knives, Georgia.
Left, Calhoun Cty., pink chert. $5
Center, Seminole Cty., 2-3/4", grey flint, nice size, good piece. $15
Right, Calhoun Cty., blue-brown flint. $10
Photo courtesy Jack M. Hall collection, Georgia

ARCHAIC SIDE-NOTCH, 2-1/8" x 4-1/4". It is made from golden-brown
Hixton Quartzite, has basal thinning, and reverse has a small circle of the
original blank with patina. From Vernon Co., WI. $45
Courtesy Mert Cowley collection, WI; by Mohr photography

ST. CHARLES (DOVE-TAIL) KNIFE, 1-3/8" x 4-5/8". Made of Coshocton
County flint, this is also an Ohio piece, excoll. Payne, Drake, Tilton and
Baldwin. The fine balance on this piece indicates that both sides were primary
working edges. $250
Photo courtesy David G. Shirley, Michigan

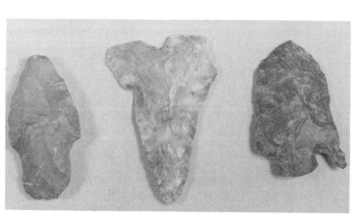

PREHISTORIC KNIVES, center example 2-1/4" long.
Left, ADENA, Woodland, black flint, tip damage. $6
Center, WOODLAND OR MISSISSIPPIAN, blue-grey mottled flint, piece
badly damaged in early times. $3
Right, ARCHAIC BASE-NOTCH, stem bottom fracture-chipped, rare.$12
Private collection

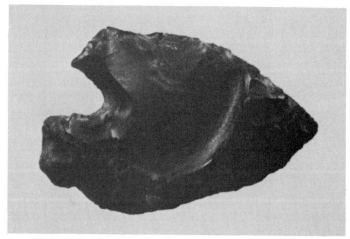

HAFTED KNIFE, middle Plains Archaic, 3000 - 1500 BC. It is 1-1/8"
x 1-5/8", of black chalcedony, from Broadwater County, MT. The basal
design on this artifact is interesting. Value unlisted.
Photo courtesy John Byrd, Helena, Montana

HAFTED KNIVES

Archaic SIDE-NOTCH, unusually "ragged" baseline, in a mottled high-quality flint. Knife tip is not damaged, but was purposefully chipped in the rounded fashion.   2-3/4'' $25
Hothem collection

LATE PALEO KNIFE OR POINT, stem very heavily ground, pale grey glossy flint. This piece has very good lines.   3'' $75
Hothem collection

EARLY ARCHAIC KNIFE, some serrations left on edges. This is another example of intentional removal of shoulders, in this case the lower shoulder, next to ruler. Only a long flake scar remains.   2'' $20
Hothem collection

TAPER-TIP BLADES, Archaic, side-notch and with bases missing. When complete, these examples would have been just over 1-3/4'' long. As yet, this type has not been named.   Each, $5
Private collection

Archaic PENTAGONAL knives, showing a good range of size and styles.
Left, heavily resharpened piece with unbalanced upper blade edges. $7
Center, unsharpened example in nearly full original size. $20
Right, resharpened specimen, which was once much longer. $15
Hothem collection

ARCHAIC CORNER-NOTCH KNIFE in an unknown flint that is reddish tan with swirls of chocolate-brown. It is 2-1/4'' long and both shoulder tips are missing. Knife edges have moderate wear. $18
Private collection

Archaic knife with blade angled downward or to left, with asymmetrical base. Edges were not serrated but intentionally made irregular. $9
Hothem collection   2''

EARLY ARCHAIC KNIFE, 1-3/4'' long. Of interest is the quality material, jewel Flintridge in several shades and the missing tip. This piece seems to have been purposefully thinned at the tip, and termination hinge scar can be seen about halfway down the face. $25
Private collection

HAFTED KNIVES

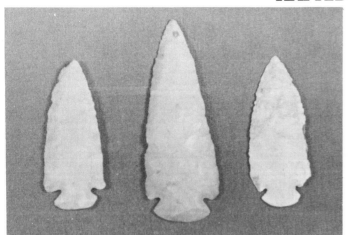

ST. CHARLES BLADES or DOVETAILS, center example 3-3/4" long, all Archaic.
Left, DOVETAIL, Flintridge jewel chalcedony. $50
Center, DOVETAIL, pale grey material, resharpened edges. $95
Right, DOVETAIL, unknown cream and purple flint. $50
Private collection

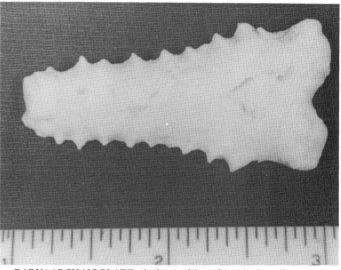

EARLY ARCHAIC BLADE, tip damaged in prehistoric times, heavy serrations, milkwhite chalcedony, well-ground basal bifurcations. The important thing about this knife is that both shoulders have been fracture-chipped off, leaving a tiny "stairstep" ledge or hinge-break. On lower edge, this can be seen directly above the 2-9/16 in. mark on ruler. $20
Hothem collection

UNNAMED ARCHAIC BLADES, left example 1-1/2" long. The name NARROW-NOTCH is suggested as notching is only 1/16" wide and only 1/8" deep. Another interesting feature is that the shoulders have been fracture-chipped off, not in toward the notch but up along the blade lower edge. Eastern Midwest. These have value mainly as study pieces and for a type description.
Private collection

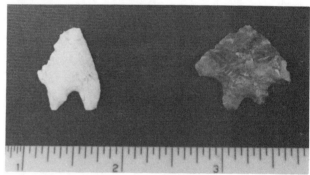

EARLY ARCHAIC BLADES, very small sizes.
Left, white flint, one shoulder has been completely rechipped off, leaving a smooth contour. $5
Right, dark flint, neither shoulder has been fracture-chipped off, something often done when the blade became this shortened. $5
Hothem collection

PEDERNALES KNIFE, 4-3/4", Edwards Plateau flint. From Travis County, TX. $400
Photo courtesy Pat Mahan, Texas

All knives, l. to r.:
STEMMED, 2-1/2", Normanskill flint, Laxarra Farm, Stockport, NY.$15
STEMMED, same material and provenance. $15
SHORT-STEMMED, same material and provenance. $10
Courtesy Marguerite L. Kernaghan collection; photo by Stewart W. Kernaghan

BASE TANG KNIFE, 6-1/4", Edwards Plateau flint. Personal find 3-26-82, Williamson County, TX, South San Gabriel River. $5000-plus
Photo courtesy Pat Mahan, Texas

HAFTED KNIVES

Top, STILWELL, 1-1/2'' x 3-1/4'', Clay Co., AR, incurvate edges from frequent resharpening. $125
Bottom, STILWELL, 1-3/8'' x 4-3/8'', Clay Co., AR, Matching notches, fine size, full blade — excellent. $225
Photo courtesy Arnold Moore collection, Missouri

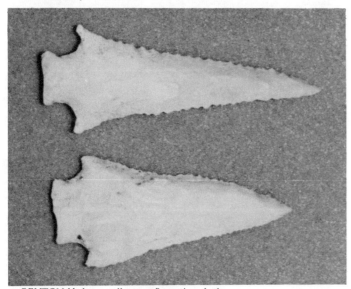

BENTON blades, excellent configurations both.
Top, 1-1/2'' x 4-1/4'', beveled and serrated edges, AR, a piece sharpened down to the shoulders. $150
Bottom, 1-1/2'' x 3-1/2'', beveled in an irregular manner, but yet a very good piece for fairly late in Archaic times. $150
Photo courtest Arnold Moore collection, Missouri

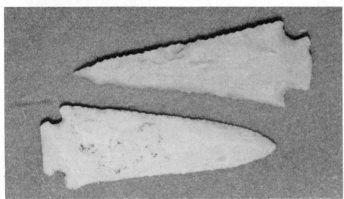

EARLY BLADES, each 1-7/8'' x 4-7/8'' long.
Top, BENTON, serrated edges, Clay Co., AR, beveled. $200
Bot., STILWELL, same provenance, excellent edging, firm shoulders, good size. $300
Photo courtesy Arnold Moore collection, Missouri

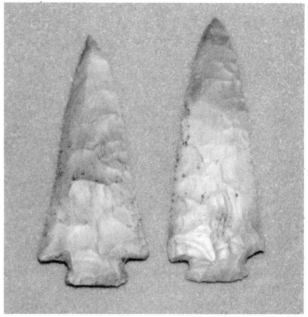

Two fine STILWELL blades, both from Clay Co., AR.
Left, 2 x 4-3/4'', beveled edges due to resharpening. $200
Right, 1-3/4'' x 5'', fine glossy flint in several shades, very good length, fine design and condition. $250
Photo courtesy Arnold Moore collection, Missouri

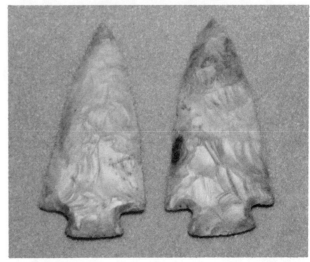

Left, STILWELL, 2-1/2'' x 4-1/2'', Clay Co., AR, so deeply corner-notched as to form a broad stem. $200
Right, STILWELL, 2-1/2'' x 4-1/2'', same provenance, it too in a very high grade of flint. $200
Photo courtesy Arnold Moore collection, Missouri

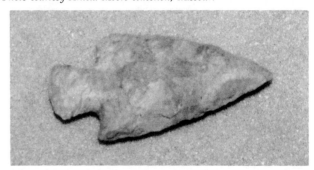

ARCHAIC knife, Benton Co., TN, a well-stemmed piece. It is 1-5/8'' x 2-7/8''. $30
Photo courtesy Arnold Moore collection, Missouri

HAFTED KNIVES

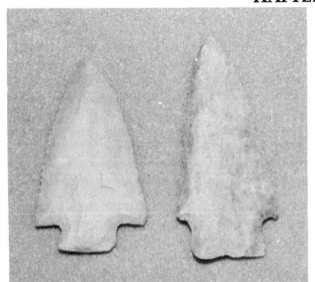

Two BENTON blades, both from Clay Co., AR.
Left, 1-5/8'' x 2-7/8'', strong shouldering, fine serrations. $75
Right, 1-1/2'' x 3-1/4'', edge-beveling, wide stem. $50
Photo courtesy Arnold Moore collection, Missouri

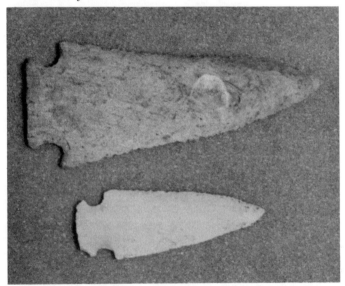

Two STILWELLS, Clay Co., AR.
Top, 1-7/8'' x 4-5/8'', strongly notched. $200
Bottom, 1 x 3 in., fine white flint, matching notches. $125
Photo courtesy Arnold Moore collection, Missouri

CORNER-TANG knife, 2-3/4'' x 5-1/8'', obsidian, from the state of Washington. This blade is unusually wide at mid-section. $275
Courtesy Marguerite L. Kernaghan collection; photo by Stewart W. Kernaghan

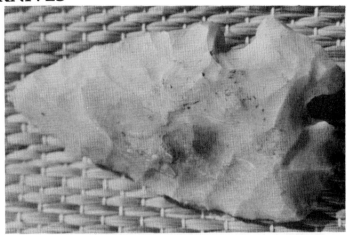

CORNER-TANK knife, 1-1/4'' x 2-1/4'', of a high grade of light-colored chert. It is from Glenwood, AR. $90
Courtesy Marguerite L. Kernaghan collection; photo by Stewart W. Kernaghan

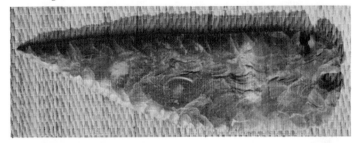

CORNER-TANG knife, 2-1/4'' x 7-1/2'', chert, from Clovis, NM. The back edge of this specimen is unusually straight. $475
Courtesy Marguerite L. Kernaghan collection; photo by Stewart W. Kernaghan

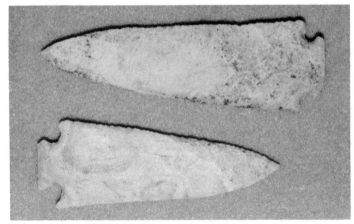

STILWELL knives, early Archaic, perfect condition.
Top, 2 x 6 in., Clay Co., AR, speckled chert. $195
Bot, 2 x 5 in., same provenance, mottled chert. $150
Both are fine early blades.
Photo courtesy Arnold Moore collection, Missouri

ARCHAIC KNIFE, Midwest, E-NOTCH BEVEL, 2-3/4'' long. This piece is very beautifully serrated and beveled, done in a cream-grey flint with black lines. $65
Private collection

88

HAFTED KNIVES

DOVETAIL, Archaic, 2 in. long, with creamy patination over brown and grey glossy flint. Patina disturbance indicates this piece was picked up and rechipped by later Indians, and such signs exist on both faces. Heavily ground base bottom and in notches, unusually short for a "Dove". $35
Private collection

ARCHAIC KNIFE, grey flint, quartz vein inclusion, 1-3/4" long. The left base corner has been damaged, and left blade edge has serrations more worn than right side. $15
Private collection

ARCHAIC KNIVES.
Top, CORNER-NOTCH, serrated edges, 3 in. long, done in a fine glossy grey flint that may be Indiana hornstone. $45
Bottom, CORNER-NOTCH that looks side-notched because shoulders have been removed by frequent resharpening. It is a glossy cream flint. This blade has been heavily used and was probably thrown away when it reached this short size. $10
Private collection

MIDWESTERN BLADES, center example just over 2 in. long. All Archaic.
SIDE-NOTCH, left, strong base and large notches. $12
SIDE-NOTCH, center, typical early knife in very typical form. $10
AFTON, right, in the usual pentagonal form, unthinned base faces. $9
Private collection

MIDWESTERN BLADES, center example just under 2 in. long. All Archaic.
Left, BASE-NOTCH, one shoulder worn off by resharpening, large notches. $5
Center, EXPANDED-STEM, black chert, varied edging. $8
Right, BASE-NOTCH, pale quality flint, very excurvate knife edges. $7
Private collection

EARLY ARCHAIC KNIVES, serrated edges, example on right 1-3/8 in. long.
Left, BIFURCATE, tan flint. $15
Center, BIFURCATE, brown and grey flint, good shouldering $20
Right, BIFURCATE, irregular edging indicates considerable use; tan flint. $20
Courtesy private collection

EARLY ADENA BLADE, also called a CRESAP, 3-1/8" long. Material is a black and grey mottled flint. This is a nicely balanced piece with short, sturdy stem. $25
Private collection

89

HAFTED KNIVES

EARLY BLADE, 3-7/8'' long, in blue-black flint with thin white inclusions. This knife is a mystery piece, with steeply resharpened edges, and an extremely short and wide basal stem, with base edge ground. Unnamed type, best guesses place this late Paleo - early Archaic. $40.
Private collection

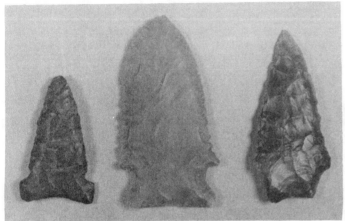

ARCHAIC KNIVES, center 2-1/2'' long.
Left, EARLY ARCHAIC, side-notch, black flint, edges resharpened right into the notches. $8
Right, ARCHAIC, originally corner-notch, edges resharpened to become a side-notch, grey flint. $30
Right, EARLY ARCHAIC, glosy brown flint, worn-down serrations. $10
Private collection

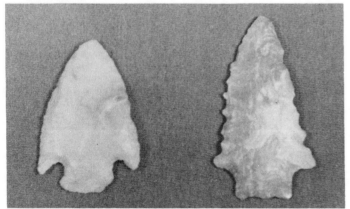

PREHISTORIC KNIVES
Left, HOPEWELL, 2 in. long, in Flintridge jewel flint. $25
Right, ARCHAIC STEMMED BLADE, mottled brown and cream material. $20

Private collection

SCOTTSBLUFF TYPE-I KNIFE, 4-5/8'', Tan-brown Edwards Plateau flint, McCulloch County, TX. $250
Photo courtesy Pat Mahan, Texas

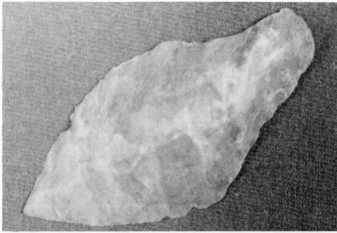

PREHISTORIC BLADE, 2-3/8 in. long, in a striped tan and grey flint. This piece has an unusual offset stem and the reverse is flat, obverse humped. Uniface design suggests Paleo placement. $20
Private collection

MONTELL KNIFE, 3-1/4'', Edwards Plateau flint in mottled tans and cream. From Williamson County, TX. $200
Photo courtesy Pat Mahan, Texas

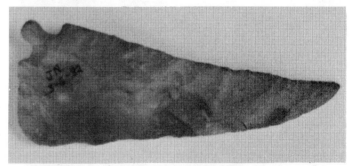

CORNER TANG KNIFE, 4-1/4'', Edwards Plateau flint in two shades of tan. From Wiliamson County, TX. $250
Photo courtesy Pat Mahan, Texas

MARSHALL KNIFE, 3-3/4'', Edwards Plateau flint, light and dark tan color. From Williamson County, TX, one shoulder tip off. $250
Photo courtesy Pat Mahan, Texas

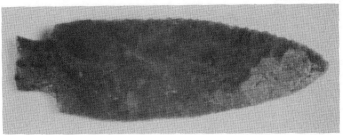

DARL KNIFE, 4-5/8", serrated edges. Of Edwards Plateau flint, from Williamson County, TX, the South San Gabriel River area. $250
Photo courtesy Pat Mahan, Texas

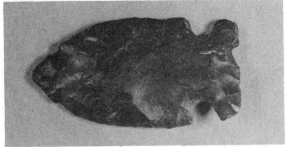

EARLY ARCHAIC KNIFE, 2-1/4" long, in shiny black Zaleski flint. Blade edges are beveled and flush with opposite faces. Most of the type are not this large, so this specimen has not been resharpened very often. $20
Private collection

TANG KNIVES, all from Eckles colleciton, Nebraska, all l. to r.:
CORNER-TANG, 1-1/2" x 2-1/2", red jasp.
CORNER-TANG, 1-1/4" x 3-5/8", high quality jasper in light and dark blue.
BACK-TANG, 1-3/8" x 3-1/2", in blue-grey chert.
CORNER-TANG, 1-1/4" x 3", grey jasper, high quality material and very well made.
Photo courtesy W. R. Eckles, Nebraska

BOTTLENECK KNIFE (also known as TABLE ROCK) in glossy white flint. Blade is 1-3/8" x 1-1/2", and basal area is very well ground from shoulder tip to shoulder tip. Blade edge is so rounded that it is almost one continuous edge, very unusual for the type. $20
Private collection

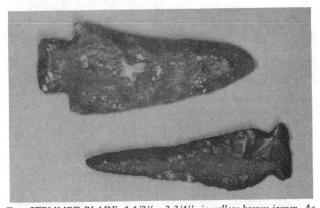

Top, STEMMED BLADE, 1-1/2" x 3-3/4", in yellow-brown jasper. As with some knives, one edge is incurvate, the other excurvate. Stem is wide and sturdy. Unlisted
Bottom, NOTCHED BLADE, 1 x 3-1/2", in a brown jasper. This knife has indications of extreme wear on both sides near the tip. Unlisted
Photo courtesy W. R. Eckles, Nebraska

Stemmed knife, ARCHIAC, with base somewhat resembling the TABLE ROCK type. From Benton Co., TN, it is 1-1/2" x 3-5/8". $40
Photo courtesy Arnold Moore collection, Missouri

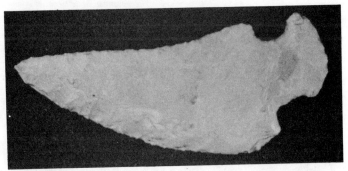

BASE TANG KNIFE, 1-1/4" x 3-1/8" of cream-colored chert. Both incurvate and excurvate edges have been finely pressure-retouched, showing both edges were used. Unusual form. From Richland Co., WI. $50
Courtesy Mert Cowley collection, WI; by Mohr Photography

EARLY ARCHAIC BIFURCATE, 2-1/4" long, in pale blue flint. Note the worn-down serrations on both edges. This piece also has the right (lower) shoulder fracture-chipped off, very commonly done in the Archaic bifurcate family. $25
Private collection

HAFTED KNIVES

Wide BASE-TANG knives, all made of Edwards Plateau tan flints. The two deep-notch blades are from the Rio Grande area and are called BELL blades. The three other examples are from Bell, San Saba and Medina Counties, Texas. Sizes, 3-1/2'' to 6''. Values for larger blades, each, would be

$350-$500

The specimen at left center is superb.
Photo courtesy D. Rogers collection, Houston, Texas

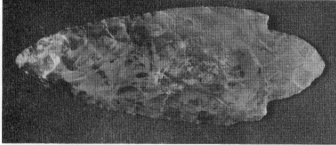

WAUBESA KNIFE, 1-7/8 x 5 in., in a grey flint. The dark stained or deposit material may be from grave association, the remains of organic material. This is a very large and fine piece in all respects. $125
Courtesy Mort Cowley collection, WI; by Mohr Photography

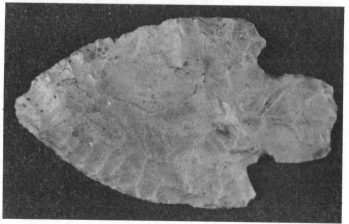

STEMMED BLADE, 1-3/8 x 2-1/8 in., in brown flint. The well-worked edges are thin and sharp; this artifact has an unusually shaped stem, almost with notches near the shoulders. $20
Courtesy Mert Cowley collection, WI; by Mohr Photography

HAFTED KNIVES

NOTCHED BLADE, 1-3/8 x 2-3/8 in., made of chert with heavy patina. This piece has very thin edges; from Vernon Co., WI. $20
Courtesy Mert Cowley collection, WI; by Mohr Photography

NOTCHED BLADE, 1-3/4 x 2-7/8 in., in pink and tan flint. This piece is thin with sharp edges. Configuration is probably Hopewell, certainly Woodland. $25
Courtesy Mert Cowley collection, WI; by Mohr Photography

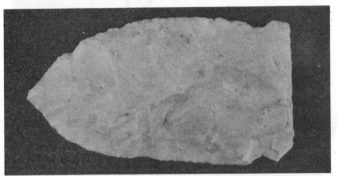

SIDE-NOTCHED BLADE, 1-1/4 x 2-1/8 in., light-colored flint. The very straight base bottom is an indication of straight-line grinding. Casual, shallow notches, very thin piece with very sharp edges. This may be Archaic. $35

Courtesy Mert Cowley collection, WI; by Mohr Photography

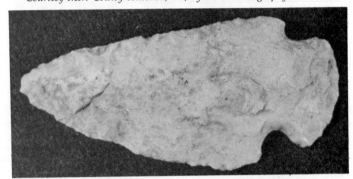

BASE-TANG KNIFE, 1-1/4 x 3 in., Vernon Co., WI. It is made from a glossy cream flint; note the different notching sizes and depths. $25
Courtesy Mert Cowley collection, WI; by Mohr Photography

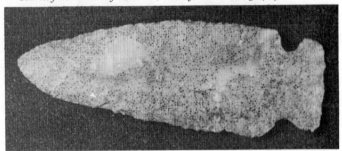

SIDE-NOTCH KNIFE, a familiar Archaic form, 1-1/8 x 3 inches. It is made of oolitic chert with pale inclusions. Material is fairly rare, making this an attractive blade. Barron Co., WI. $40
Courtesy Mert Cowley collection, WI; by Mohr Photography

NOTCHED BLADE, 1-3/4 x 3-7/8 in., from Vernon Co., WI. Material is a tan, white and grey flint, and piece is sturdy, with thin edges and some retouch. It is similar to many other Archaic side-notch blades. $50
Courtesy Mert Cowley collection, WI; by Mohr Photography

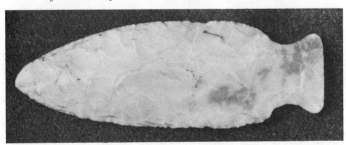

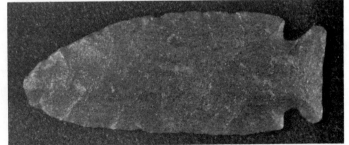

OSCEOLA KNIFE, 1-1/8 x 3 in., of purple-grey Hixton Quartzite. It is translucent, has basal thinning, and extremely fine workmanship. From Vernon Co., WI. $50
Courtesy Mert Cowley collection, WI; by Mohr Photography

TABLE ROCK KNIFE, 1 x 2-7/8 in., in a glossy tan flint. Workmanship is delicate, stem is ground, and edges are extremely thin and sharp. From Dunn Co., WI. $30
Courtesy Mert Cowley collection, WI; by Mohr Photography

KNIFE, Kansas, base lightly ground, in light tan flint. Piece is 1-1/2 x 3-3/4 in., and end has been bevel-chipped into a short scrapping edge or a third knife edge. Note that right base shoulder (lower) has been fracture-chipped off, with termination hinge readily visible. $30
Private collection

Angled blades, all from Illinois. Left, Flintridge white chalcedony, 1-3/4 x 3-3/4 inches. $65
Center, 2 x 4 in., brown chert with strong bevel on blade. $75
Right, 1-1/2 x 2-3/4 in., black Coshocton County flint. $50
Photo by Ray Pace Associates; courtesy Cliff Morris Collection

HAFTED BLADES, l. example 1-3/4 in. long; both are made of meta-rhyolite. The source is near Gettysburg, PA, 80 miles distant, evidence of early trade. (All SEP finds, Potomac Valley.) These side-notched knives took heavy use and some damage, and period is late Archaic. They have minimal value but are fine scientific specimens and excellent for study.
Courtesy Stephen E. Porcelli collection, Virginia; photo by Scott Silsby.

Very large blade, gem quality, 3-1/4 x 6-1/2 inches. Made of grey flint, the large size means it possibly was used to manufacture dugout canoes. Unusual specimen. $95.
Photo by Ray Pace Associates; courtesy Cliff Morris Collection

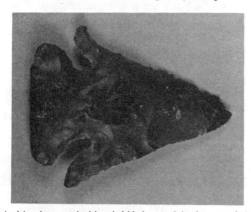

Very fine Archiac deep-notched beveled blade over 2 in. long, made in glossy black Zaleski flint. This was a reservoir find, on an Archaic site. $35
Hothem collection

L., JASPER BLADE, 6-1/2 inches. Center, OBSIDIAN BLADE, 8-1/2 inches. R., OBSIDIAN BLADE, 6 in. long. These were found in Malheur Cty., Oregon in a dry lake bed near The Narrows. Hafted types are unusual, since most blades found in dry lake beds are leaf-shaped, and up to 14 in. long. These are fine specimens from an unknown time period. Values, each would be $200-500.
Photo courtesy Ernest Cowles collection, Washington.

HAFTED KNIVES

MID—BACK TANG KNIFE, *dark Edwards Plateau chert. This is the rarest type of Tang knife, and was a surface find in Dickens County, TX.$200 Photo courtesy Wayne Parker Collection, Texas   2-1/2''*

DIAGONAL-TANG KNIFE, *grey Edwards Plateau chert, Archaic period. Surface find, Lynn Co., TX, and a Sand-hill site.   3-1/2'' $135 Photo courtesy Wayne Parker Collection, Texas*

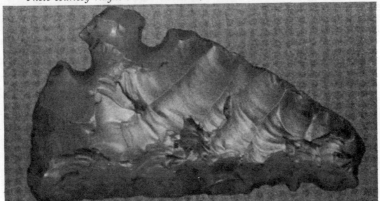

BACK-TANG KNIFE, *grey Edwards Plateau chert, Archaic period. Found by Jack Wells near May, Texas, in Brown County, 1940. $145 Photo courtesy Wayne Parker Collection, Texas   2-1/2''*

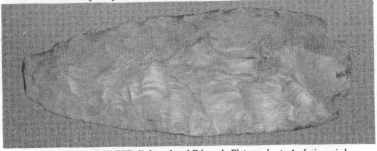

BASE-TANG KNIFE, *light-colored Edwards Plateau chert, Archaic period. This was a surface find by Amos Ellison in a peanut field near Comanche, TX, in 1940.   5'' $125 Photo courtesy Wayne Parker Collection, Texas*

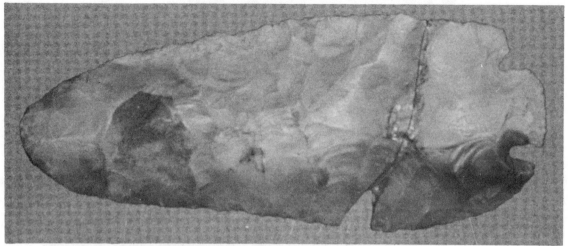

BASE-TANG KNIFE, Edwards Plateau chert, Archaic period. From Burnt
Rock Midden near Waco, TX; found by Amos Ellison in 1930. $125
Photo courtesy Wayne Parker Collection, Texas   5''

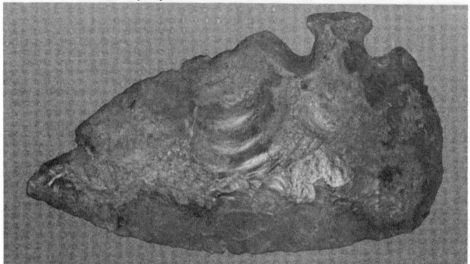

BACK-TANG KNIFE, Edwards Plateau chert, Archaic period. It is a surface find at a Sand-hill site in Lynn Co., TX.   3-1/2'' $165
Photo courtesy Wayne Parker Collection, Texas

DIAGONAL-TANG KNIFE, grey Edwards Plateau chert, Archaic period.
From a Sand-hill site, and a surface find in Lynn Co., TX. $145
Photo courtesy Wayne Parker Collection, Texas   3-3/4''

DIAGONAL-TANG KNIFE, Edwards Plateau chert, Archaic period. A surface find by Frank Runkles in 1943, near Dublin, TX along Armstrong Creek.   3'' $135
Photo courtesy Wayne Parker Collection, Texas

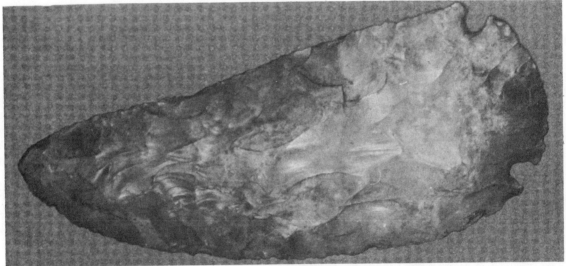

BASE-TANG KNIFE, Edwards Plateau chert, Archaic period. Surface find by a Mr. Spurgeon near Uvalde, Texas.   4-3/4'' $165
Photo courtesy Wayne Parker Collection, Texas

DIAGONAL-TANG KNIFE, Edwards Plateau chert, Archaic period. Surface find by L.D. Jones near Dublin, TX, in Erath Co. The tip of this blade has been restored. There is little value because of the restoration. $25
Photo courtesy Wayne Parker Collection, Texas   4''

DIAGONAL-TANG KNIFE, *Edwards Plateau chert, Archaic period. A surface find from Crosby County, TX.* 3-1/4'' $100
Photo courtesy Wayne Parker Collection, Texas

BASE-TANG KNIFE, *reddish quartz material. A surface find from Palo Dura Canyon, Armstrong Co., TX.* 3'' $70
Photo courtesy Wayne Parker Collection, Texas

DIAGONAL-TANG KNIFE, *3-1/2'', Potters Chert material, Archaic period. Found by Frank Runkles near Brownwood, Tx., Brown Co.* $150
Photo courtesy Wayne Parker Collection, Texas

Cheyenne warrior in full war costume, including sheath knife secured to cartridge belt. Morrow photo, courtesy South Dakota State Historical Society.

CHAPTER XIII

CEREMONIAL BLADES

Three very large classes of ceremonial knives were used in prehistoric North America. They seem to have been made in all time periods, though super-large examples are more common in the Woodland and Mississippian cultures, later times.

The first class consists of knives of almost any kind and period that seem to be more than everyday blades. While some are extra-large, most are of fairly normal size but exceptional in other aspects. The material may be unusual for the area (called "exotic", or from elsewhere) or the piece may be exceptionally well made and show no signs of use whatsoever. Simply because the material was exotic does not necessarily make a ceremonial piece, but extra-good outside material was used with some frequency.

Some blade examples, even from Paleo times, have the edges purposefully dulled by abrasion, an ultimate proof that the blades were never meant for actual use. Almost without exception, ceremonial knives of this type have extremely fine chipping, and are ultimate showpieces of excellence. Nothing more could be done to make them more attractive.

The second class is burial blades, these known from Archaic through Mississippian times. Such examples may be large and perfect in every respect, as if waiting the hand of the user in a next world. Sometimes very mundane blades were included, possible personal weapons of the deceased. The author was involved in exploring a Hopewell ceremonial site that included two knives at one place. One was a broken triangular blade, another a notched knife. Found in a field somewhere, one would not have known they were in fact ceremonial inclusions.

Burial blades can be highly specialized. An example is in William S. Webb's **Indian Knoll**, the University of Tennessee Press, Knoxville. It reports on the discovery and excavation of an Archaic village/burial site in Kentucky, and is highly recommended reading. Besides unhafted, corner and side-notched and stemmed blades and drills (the style range is instructive) one knife type stands out.

It is a stemmed blade that contracts toward the base, is fairly long (up to 4 in.) with wide shoulders. Some are almost barbed, with excurvate sides. Webb suggested that while the type found was less than 1% of the total burial inclusions, the association with bone suggested (p. 255) the knife might have caused the death of the individual. Rather than a pure offering, it may have been an executioner's knife. He further reported that the type had been found in similar burial association in Alabama.

This particular knife form has two considerations. One is that such blades for the region, found on the surface, may indicate the presence of Archaic burials. Another is that ceremonial blades may in some cases have been used for something a bit more than public ceremonies or private ritual offerings.

The third largest class of ceremonial blades consists of the odd-shaped or extra-large blades/points/spearheads/swords of later prehistoric times. These include obsidian Hopewell examples of many forms, wide-based, angled-edge or just very large. Some examples, as were excavated at Mound City Group (now a National Monument) in Ohio were either broken or destroyed by cremation fires.

The Mississippian Temple Mound people of the Southeast and Midwest chipped very unusual blades, swords and maces, and some were found in the famous Duck River **Cache.** Some of the Temple Mound ceremonial blades were duo-tipped and extremely long. Used in ceremonies, they must have been very impressive. Even more impressive is the fact that people were able to chip such specimens at all, given the flaws inherent in much flint.

The third Indian group to use large ceremonial blades was centered in northern California and these knives were made in obsidian of several colors. Popular both in late prehistoric and in early historic times, the duo-tipped blades probably served several purposes. Historic evidence suggests they were a store of wealth, valuable objects for trade, and honored in dances and other ceremonial activities. As an indication of importance in the latter, leather thongs were wrapped around them which were secured to a belt so they could not be dropped and broken.

For the extra-fine knives of whatever size and for the extra-large knives of all periods, it seems that the Indians used them as symbols and admired objects. Perhaps this was their way of honoring a tool type that made their lives possible and their lifeway richer.

CEREMONIAL BLADES

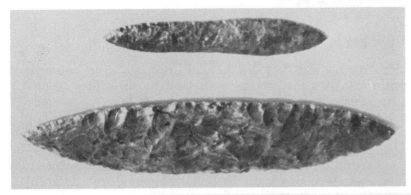

Two ceremonial blades from the Trinity River, California.
Smaller, Chimariko knife, 1-1/2 x 8-1/2 in., dark red obsidian.$500
Larger, Chimariko ceremonial knife, 14-3/4 x 3-1/2 in., red obsidian.
$1300

Courtesy Eugene Heflin Collection, Oregon

Fine large unhafted ceremonial knives from Gunther Island, Humboldt Bay, CA. Center blade is 15-1/2 in. long. The longest blade in photo is 16-1/2 in., 2 in. at one end, 2-1/2 in. at the other. Museum quality Photo by Eugene Heflin, courtesy Gene Favell, Favell Museum, Klameth Falls, Oregon.

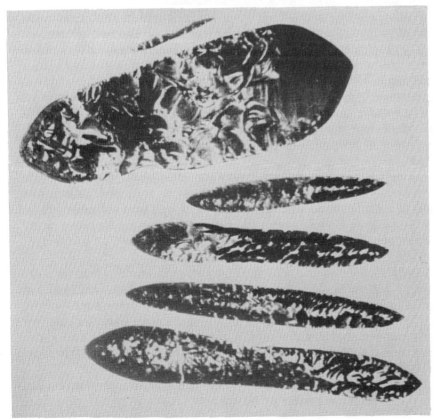

Enlarged view of the ceremonial obsidian knives from Gunther Island, Humboldt Bay, CA. The largest blade on the top is 4-1/2 x 15-1/4 inches. Authentic ceremonial blades this size are extremely rare. Museum quality. Photo by Eugene Heflin; courtesy Gene Favell, Favell Museum, Klamath Falls, Oregon.

CHAPTER XIV

KNIVES OF OTHER MATERIALS

Perhaps the earliest metal-working in North America was done by the Old Copper Culture Indians, beginning about 5000 BC and lasting for many centuries. They used native copper so extensively they created the name we know them by today. Living in the forests of the Western Great Lakes region — especially Michigan and Wisconsin — they obtained copper in raw nugget form or from veins near the surface. The copper was pounded into shape with stone hammers, and the metal may have been heated to make it easier to work.

The Old Copper people made at least three different knife types. One resembled a spearhead, as it may well have been at times, with excurvate symmetrical edges and a basal haft. Half a dozen different hafting designs were used, mainly varieties of stems and/or multiple notches, plus a hollow wrap-around or socket type.

Another knife had a long blade, straight, curved or with one excurvate edge and a straight backing edge. Hafting was stemmed, socket or "rat-tail", long and tapering. The last knife variety was very similar to the Eskimo "woman's knife", the **Ulu**. It had a wide, curved blade which ended in projecting posts for attachment of a handle. A few scarce forms were one-piece, with copper handles. Otherwise, the handles would have been of wood, bone or antler.

In the American Southeast, Mississippian peoples made a rare and ornate knife form, first carved in wood and then covered with thin sheets of copper. Occasional knives of copper turn up in other prehistoric cultures, such as the Woodland-era Hopewell, but they are very rare. Much use of copper was also made in historic times. Some Northwest Coast groups made large ceremonial and fighting daggers from copper, with long, tapering hilts and thong-wrapped handles. Some had effigy-figure handles, with head at hilt tip.

So important were copper daggers to the Alaskan Ahtna that the knives were kept in special beaded sheaths. And they were worn both night and day to be kept safe, and so that a personal weapon was always within reach. To the Kutchin Indians of northern Alaska and Yukon Territory, knives of native copper obtained from the Pacific Coast were treasured items. The blades were signs of status, prestige and wealth.

Canada's historic Tanana Indians used a peculiar form of fighting knife made from native copper. One-piece, the hilt area terminated in a long, twisting spiral. The Yellowknife was one of four sub-groups of the Chippewa. They were also known as the Copper People , and received the first name from the copper knives they made. Part of their range was along Canada's Coppermine and Yellowknife rivers. The present town of the same name is on Yellowknife Bay.

Copper — in addition to flint and obsidian — was one of the "big three" of Indian knife materials made from natural deposits. Such "from the earth" substances were rivaled by use of "on the earth" organic materials, all parts of things once living. This included animal (bone, horn, antler, ivory) and vegetable (mainly wood). Seasoned wood that has been fire-hardened can be extremely durable, and points and blades made of it are still used in the Amazon region of South America.

All indications are that organic handles were very widely used on all knives, everywhere, but most have disintegrated with time. Only under very special and protected circumstances have a few examples survived to the present. Such conditions include permafrost in the North, dry caves and rock shelters in the Southwest, and submergence under water in some other places. Otherwise, bacteria and oxygen cooperated to gradually destroy the artifact.

But not always. In 1931 a skeleton known as "Minnesota Man" was found in strata deposited by a glacial lake. (When it was discovered that the bones were that of a female, the find was renamed "Minnesota Minnie".) With the skeleton was a portion of a knife made from elk antler. The age was estimated to be ca. 8000 BC, and the knife was some 8 or 9 in. long. While very old chipped blades are known, many authorities believe bone or antler may have been the first knives. After all, the raw material came right with the food animal, and did not have to be obtained from other, distant sources.

In the Nodena mound, Arkansas, an earthwork that once covered two acres, some 813 burials were eventually excavated. Only two of them seemed to show death by other than natural causes. One skeleton had a projectile point in the skull, while another had a bone dagger or thin knife lodged in the breast-bone.

Intrusive Mound people of the Eastern U.S., late prehistoric, had a small-edge knife. This was a beaver tooth set at right angles near the tip of a long antler shaft. Such combinations were not unknown to later Indians, and it was a way to put great force onto a small cutting surface. Such blades were probably used to shape wood. The original idea may have come from watching beavers at work.

Key Marco prehistoric Indians, Florida, did elaborate and skillful wood-carvings, such things as realistic deer heads and stylized cat-like figures. It is likely that their main wood-carving knives were different sizes of shark teeth, some with serrated edges.

Beginning 400 or so years ago, there are records of organic material knives. Before metal trade knives arrived, Mountain Indians of Canada's Mackenzie Mountains had a difficult time cutting up moose, caribou or Bighorn sheep. Their early knives were beaver incisors or bird-beaks fastened to wooden handles.

The Ingalick of the North, among others, had a rough-work knife or chisel for cutting wood, made from two curved beaver incisor teeth set in a wooden handle. For finer work, a one-tooth tool was used. These may have been the original crooked knife, the multi-purpose knife of Northern regions.

Snow knives were a unique sword-like tool, probably developed by the Eskimos. It was made of wood, bone or walrus-tusk, and had a fairly wide but thin blade. It was used to shape blocks of packed snow to construct temporary shelters or wind-breaks, dugouts and snow-houses or igloos. Indians of the Yukon, the Inglaik, also used this building knife. Patwin Indians of California used mussel-shell knives to cut meat and fish into strips, so that the foods could be sun-dried and preserved for long periods.

The historic Nisenan of California used wood to make a grass knife; evidently this was a machete-like tool to harvest grass stems for thatching, etc. Wintu males of California had a special fighting dagger made from deer bone. Some 10 in. long, it was carried thrust in the top-knot of the warrior's hair.

Eastern Pomo "bear doctor" shamans sometimes carried a ceremonial dagger suspended from a belt or around the neck. The curved blade was of polished elk antler and the handle was wrapped with fur. About 7 in. long, one example has a looped attachment thong.

All available information suggests the widespread and long-term use of organic materials for Indian knives.

EFFIGY BONE DAGGER, 7'', Mixtec. ca. 950-1200 AD. Note the human form with arms, face and headdress; similar daggers were also shaped in stone. Southern Mexico. Value... Museum quality
Photo courtesy Bernard Lueck, California; from the collection of Kevin Mineo, San Diego, California.

EFFIGY BONE DAGGER, 5'', Mixtec, ca. 950-1200 AD. This blade may have served as a very large pendant; hole in effigy forehead could also have been used as a tying area for thongs, preventing knife loss. Value... Museum quality
Photo courtesy Bernard Lueck, California; from the collection of Kevin Mineo, San Diego, California

BONE DAGGER, 12-1/2'', Mixtec, found in northcentral Mexico. It is ca. 900-1200 AD. Made in human effigy form, it is also made of a human femur bone. Value... Museum quality
Photo courtesy Bernard Lueck Collection, California

ESKIMO KNIFE, slate blade with hide-wrapped handle. Ca. 1870-90. Value... Museum quality
Photo courtesy Bernard Lueck Collection, California

SNOW KNIFE, Eskimo, made of walrus tusk, 16''. It is used for cutting snow blocks for windbreaks and igloo construction. This is a beautiful piece, ca. 1820-70. Value... Museum quality
Photo courtesy Bernard Lueck Collection, California

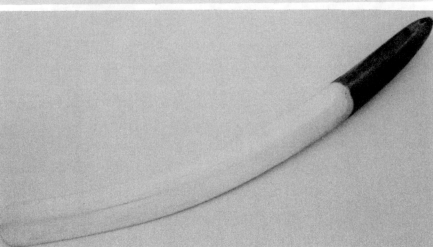

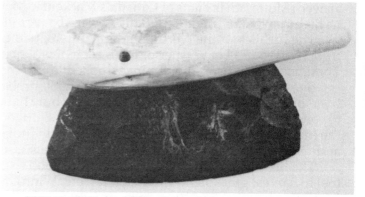

ESKIMO ULU, slate blade and ivory handle. These were all-purpose household knives. Ca. 1870-90.   5-1/2''
Value...   Museum quality
Photo courtesy Bernard Lueck Collection, California

COPPER KNIFE, Chimu culture, Peru, South America. Tumi semi-lunar blade; carved wooden figure demonstrates the use of these knives. The chieftain holds a knife in one hand, human head in the other. Ca. 1200 AD. Value...
8-1/2''   Museum quality
Photo courtesy Bernard Lueck Collection, California

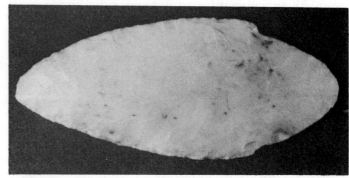

WAUBESA KNIFE, 1-3/8 x 3-1/4 in., from Rock Co., WI. It is in white flint, has beautiful flaking and overall lines, with surface patina. It is Woodland period.
Courtesy Mert Cowley collection. WI; by Mohr Photography

CEREMONIAL KNIFE, cleaver type, copper, from Chimu culture, Peru, South America. While the Incas are the most famous Amerind group for the area, there were a number of earlier people. Ca. 1200 AD.   14''
Value...   Museum quality
Photo courtesy Bernard Lueck Collection, California

Rhyolite knife about 3 in. long, from Lycoming County, Pennsylvania. It is from the Transitional Period, ca. 1500-800 BC. The base, notches and one edge are ground. $10-$15
Photo courtesy Fogelman Collection, Pennsylvania

Large triangular blade, 2-1/2 x 6-3/4 in., and 1/8 in. thick. Of light-colored rhyolite, it has exceptionally fine chipping and no damage. The blade was found in Moore County, NC, in 1965, near the town of Carthage. $200
Photo courtesy William C. Lea Collection, North Carolina

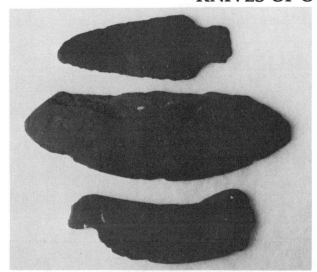

Large SAVANNAH RIVER blade, 2-1/2 x 7-3/4 in., and 1/4 in. thick. It is made of rhyolite and has very fine secondary pressure flaking. Material is almost black; the light areas are patination, now in a pleasing color contrast. The blade was found in 1979 in Moore County, North Carolina.$250
Photo courtesy William C. Lea Collection, North Carolina

Knives made of slate, with center blade 2-1/2 x 7-1/2 inches. All have extensive wear and are estimated at 6000 BP or 4000 BC. From Salmon River area, Idaho.

Range, $15-$30
Photo by Ray Pace Associates; courtesy Cliff Morris Collection

QUARTZITE BLADES, l. and r. specimens 3-1/8 in. long. Materials, l. to r.: Brown and white, pink and white, tan and grey. All, found by Mr. Porcelli, are from the Potomac Valley. These are quite thin despite the difficulty of chipping quartzite because flaking cannot be well-controlled. Values, less than $5 each.
Courtesy Stephen E. Porcelli Collection, Virginia; photo by Scott Silsby

Triangular and beveled-edge blade, 1-1/2 x 4 in., and 1/8 in. thick. It is made of rhyolite and evidences excellent chipping. Note that edge is beveled back to where it was hafted; this piece has a thin "lightning line" of darker material. Found near Eastwood, Moore County, NC, around 1963. $75
Photo courtesy William C. Lea Collection, North Carolina.

Woman skinning a rabbit, Resolution Northwest Territories, Canada. She is shown using a two-handled drawknife, perhaps a fleshing tool.
Photo courtesy Public Archives, Canada

CHAPTER XV

BLADE CACHES

One of the most unusual aspects of prehistoric Amerind life is the scarce but still-found **cache.** Pronounced "cash", the word actually means the place (hole, hiding place) where goods were deposited, but it generally also refers to the items themselves. Cache artifacts of many kinds, but especially knives, have been found ever since the first plows turned virgin soil in the New World.

Caches may range in number from several artifacts to thousands. They may be buried a few inches or many feet below the surface of the ground, such sites often in or near prehistoric dwellings, villages or mounds. Caches have been found in rock shelters, along streams, on knolls, and in areas that today seem featureless and unimportant. It should be noted that most caches are unrelated to burial activity or grave goods, and do not seem to be ceremonial in nature.

The artifacts range from obvious quarry blanks and preforms to totally finished artifacts, some even showing the wear-signs of use. Subsurface deposits of artifacts have ranged from late Paleo into near-Contact times for prehistoric artifacts. Some chipped blades — notably **Adena** cache unstemmed and the notched **Turkey-tail** are frequently found in numbers. In fact, the alert surface hunter has learned to be especially inquisitive if one of these two types is picked up.

While it is speculation to attempt to understand why caches occurred at all, why valuable economic and survival goods were buried in the gound, perhaps something can come of such speculation. An old belief that this was done to "age" the material and make it better to chip has little validity, when the crypto-crystalline structure itself is dozens of millions of years old.

The best current theory is based on the ancient coin hoards found in England and elsewhere, these dating from Roman to WW-II times. This is the safe-keeping theory. It is the protection of property by concealment. This is the simplest and most probable reason, based on the fact that what can't be seen can't be taken. Perhaps a cache was a type of prehistoric bank lock-box, the key or combination being simply the location, the secret locked unseen in a prehistoric mind.

In other cases, caches may have been a routine practice, probably along major early trade routes and trails. It is thought-provoking that many underground artifact deposits are no more weight than could easily be carried for many miles. Some could have been regular storage places, used again and again. In such cases, the site was probably known to a small number of people. In all probability, at the time the cache was put down, the place was marked by a major feature such as a tree, to aid in finding the cache again.

Two other theories may be worth examination. The catch-all possibility is that of emergency, valuable goods being temporarily buried to avoid loss. The threat could have been anything, from forest-fires to enemy action, the result the same. The ceremonial possibility is that sometimes there is powdered hemitite, red ochre, sprinkled over the artifacts. It is thought that this practice simulated life-blood, but how this relates to caches in non-burial situations is unknown.

Theories aside, the greater mystery is why the caches were never recovered, why treasures were never retrieved. This is the stuff of fiction. If the facts were known, some of these ancient stories would no doubt boggle even a stimulated imagination. A matter of side-interest is why so many caches seem to be knives or blades, though point deposits are also known.

Here is a brief survey of prehistoric North American caches. There may be some sort of overall pattern having to do with knives and their uses. A great deal of additional study, however, is needed before any firm conclusions should be made.

_____

In Michigan, a cache of Adena material — including seven blocked-end tube pipes — was recently uncovered from a knoll site during construction. At least 23 stemmed blades, whole or fragmentary, were found. They were made of Flintridge, red quartz and Harrison County flints, and lengths were from 4 to 7 inches. Another nearby cache of 27 quartzite blades was found, these pieces being up to 6 in. long. While these may have also been Adena, they more closely resembled late Paleo types. (Munger, L. & Baldwin, J., *The Redskin*, Vol. XIII No. 3, 1978, p. 86-91.)

The Bee Creek cache was found in November, 1983, and was located in a rock shelter near Bee Creek, Taney County, Missouri. (See photos elsewhere.) The cache was only 4 in. deep, and the blades had been put down in four rows, placed on edge, each row about a foot long. There were 207 blades in all, triangular in outline. They ranged from 1 to 3⅝ in. long, and only about a dozen had any damage at all. Base-lines ranged from straight to excurvate. Material was a quality dark flint that worked extremely well. A red ochre deposit covered the center of the cache and most of the blades. The knives are probably late in prehistory, possibly Woodland. (Roberts, R., "Bee Creek Cache", *Central States Archaeological Journal*, Vol. 31 No. 3, July, 1984, p. 115.)

Ca. 1940's, a cache of 116 blades was found near St. Augustine, Florida. There were many other artifacts associated with the find, but the knives are mainly of interest here. Some 18 of the blades were over 5 in. long, being shouldered, and straight-edge or excurvate edges. The smallest knife was just 1½ in. long. As with many caches (a number of them unreported in the literature) some mystery surrounds the circumstances of the find. (Kinsey, P., "The St. Augustine Sub-type...", *Artifacts*, Vol. 9 No. 3, 1979.)

About 100 years ago, a cache of at least 13 large blades was found at Mullica Hill, New Jersey. Ovate, with squared or rounded bases, most were slightly over 6 in. long, many with heavy wear signs. Of yellow-brown flint, the blades in general were very well made. They were originally collected by Lammot du Pont, the pioneering powder-maker. (Custer, J., "Prehistoric Indian Technology", *Indian-Artifact Magazine*, Vol. 3. No. 5, Oct/Nov 1984, p. 26, 27 & 43.)

On May 14, 1977, an unusual double cache of large blades was found in southern Indiana. Nine blades were in one cache, 21 in the other; they were found about 18 in. apart and the same distance below the earth's surface. Plowing fragmented three specimens, and the remainder were located by probing, then digging. The largest blade was 9⅞ in. long, and all were made of a grey-blue to beige flint, likely Indiana hornstone. All were well made; in the author's (LH) opinion, these resembled **Turkey-tail** performs, but of a nearly unprecedented size. (Lawson, J., "The Williams Cache", *Central States Archaeological Journal*, Vol. 25 No. 2, April 1978, p. 78-80.)

A cache of nine **Turkey-tail** blades (including one unnotched, the largest) was sold at the Dr. Baker auction. Item no. 250, the exceptional cache was found in Jefferson County, Indiana. (Baldwin, J., *The Redskin*, Vol. XIII No. 3, 1978, p. 114.)

In June, 1982, a large number of Adena unstemmed leaf-shape blades was discovered during plowing, in a wide range of sizes and all of multi-colored high-grade Flintridge material. The find took place in Ohio's Portage County. A small cache of seven blades had earlier been found nearby, and after the major find, another seven were found on the site of the major discovery. This consisted of 342 blades, making it one of the largest for the state. Many of the blades were exceedingly beautiful in size, workstyle and color. (Converse, R., "The Luken Cache", *Ohio Archaeologist*, Vol. 34 No. 3, Summer 1984, P. 20 & 27.)

Eight large blades were found cached at the Eva site in Benton County, Tennessee, sometime prior to July, 1983. The site has been covered by the waters of Kentucky Lake; the level drops during winter months in anticipation of spring rains. Then, like in many other reservoirs, artifacts can be found on wave-washed sites. The largest blade was a basal-notched elongated type, **Cypress Creek I,** measuring 8¼ inches. The other blades were stemmed, basal-notched triangular (two types), and, unhafted. In short, five entirely different blade types made up the eight artifacts, some from much earlier times. (Gahagan, B., "Eva Cache", *Central States Archaeological Journal*, Vol. 30 No. 3, July 1983, p. 110-113.)

In 1975, a cache of Hopewell notched blades and rounded-base unhafted knives was found in Mason County, Illinois. The material was a white, grey and tan-colored chert or flint. This deposit also had a sprinkling of red ochre, and the cache was accidently discovered while using excavating machinery. (----, *The Redskin*, Vol. XI No. 2, 1976, p. 44-45.)

Eugene Heflin and another gentleman found a cache of broken obsidian blades in the 1960's. The artifacts were deposited on a spur of the north slopes of the Main Glass Butte in the High Lava Plains of eastern Oregon. All blades were broken about mid-section; some were fine finished specimens, while others were rather crude preforms. None were hafted and some were duo-tipped (see photos elsewhere). All were made of double-flow or mahogany obsidian, and Mr. Heflin and friend were able to find and piece together some fine complete knives. Some pieces were found down-slope, where they may have been thrown or naturally displaced. (Personal communication, 23 Jan 85.)

Two large knives were excavated in the spring of 1966 in Lehigh County, Pennsylvania. Each **Perkiomen** was over 5 in. long, only ¼ in. thick, and was made from a brownish flint. The blades were found one above the other and were accompanied by fragments of a steatite or soapstone container. (Lorah, W., "A Perkiomen Broad Point Cache...", *Ohio Archaeologist*, Vol. 19 No. 4, October 1969, p. 112.)

In the late 1800's, a cache of **Turkey-tail** blades was found in Butler County, Kentucky. Made of Harrison County (Indiana) flint as is often the case, one exceptionally well-made knife was 7½ in. long, and three other specimens were even longer. A total of 25 blades was recovered. (Baldwin, J., "Copeland High Artforms", *Prehistoric Art — Archaeology '82*, Vol. XVII No. 1, 1982, p. 8.)

A cache was recovered from Tazewell County, Illinois, on October 15, 1973. A complete and several damaged blades were found, thrown up by the plow. Later searching revealed a cache, with the topmost blades damaged by plow-strikes. Some of the blades were nearly 6 in. long. Though the soil was clay, the blades were in a pocket of sand. A total of 15 whole or fragmentary blades was found, related to the **Copena** type from the early Woodland period. (Wayland, M., "Tazewell County Cache Find", *Central States Archaeological Journal*, Vol. 22 No. 1, January, 1975.)

CACHES

In Connecticut at the Smith Brook site, 499 triangular blades were excavated, these averaging 2³⁄₁₆ in. long. They were well-made of a grey-brown flint, and overall similarity suggests production by one individual. (Fowler, W., *The Redskin*, Vol. XII No. 1, 1977, p. 25.)

A cache of **Ashtabula** blades was found in Lorain County, Ohio, in 1918. Most were close to 6 in. long, and were made of a mottled flint. Whether **Ashtabulas** of the Eastern U.S. are large-notched or narrow-stemmed is a matter of opinion. (------, *The Redskin*, Prehistoric Art, Vol. XIV No. 3, 1979, p. 22 & 38.)

Four **Benton Broad Stem** blades were found in burial association in Tennessee recently, these ranging in length from 5 to 7 inches. All were of a dark flint, three varieties, and in perfect condition. (Huffines, D., "Cache Or Not", *Central States Archaeological Journal*, Vol. 31 No. 2, April 1984, p. 81.)

Sometime in the late 1970's, a cache of 39 blades was found at Lake Texarkana, Texas. The material was novaculite, in a quality grade of grey-white. There is evidence the large-notch or semi-stemmed blades were heat-treated to improve chipping. The artifacts were fairly rough, mainly chipped by percussion, suggesting the knives were semi-finished. Blade length was from 5 to 7⅛ in., and widths from 2 to 3½ inches. In time, they may be late prehistoric. (Perino, G., "A Cache Of Unusual Knives", *Artifacts*, Vol. 10 No. 1, 1980, p. 4-6.)

After recovery of three large blades on the surface in March, 1982, further searching revealed another, and finally, 19 additional blades were found under the plow zone. This took place in Putnam County, Ohio; further investigation indicated other collectors had earlier acquired artifacts from the same site, for an eventual total of 51 blades. The knives were 5 to 6 in. long, about half as wide. All were percussion-flaked to shape, and the flint was Indiana hornstone (also called Harrison County flint), a favorite cache material. (Nusbaum, P. & Harnishfeger, L., "The Carpenter and Wischmeyer Cache...", *Ohio Archaeologist*, Vol. 32 No. 3, Summer 1982, p. 25.)

In April of 1978, a cache of large blades was recovered from a plowed field, probably in the St. Louis, Missouri, area. All were unhafted, with excurvate edges and with straight or slightly excurvate bases. Of a light flint with dark specks, the longest blade was 8⁵⁄₁₆ inches. A total of ten blades were recovered. (Turin, J., "Wadlow Cache Blades", *Central States Archaeological Journal*, Vol. 27 No. 1, January 1980, p. 30-31.)

A cache of **Thebes** (early Archaic) blades was found in April, 1969, in St. Charles County, Missouri. There were seven in all, which came from a cultivated field, and four were damaged by agricultural equipment. The longest specimen was just under 6 in. long, though a damaged piece (judging from base size) may have originally been longer. (Photo caption, *Central States Archaeological Journal*, Vol. 25 No. 3, July 1978, p. 129.)

In August of 1981, a cache of preform blades was found in St. Charles, Missouri. The group of 84 blades was found during landscaping, and at a depth of four feet. Length ranged from 3¼ to 4¾ inches, quite uniform for a cache. Material was a light Missouri chert, a high-quality pinkish-white color. Workstyle ranged from very good to rather rough. The blades are Woodland in origin. (Kinker, J., "Recent Cache Find", *Central States Archaeological Journal*, Vol. 29 No. 2, April 1982, p. 89.)

On the edge of Lake Eufaula, Oklahoma, a cache of long duo-tipped blades was found in 1967. Eroded by wave-action, a section of bank caved in, exposing part of the cache. Made of Kay County flint, the knives were resharpened by bevel-chipping. They ranged in length from 6¼ to 10½ inches, and one prehistorically damaged specimen was 5 in. long. Width was from ⅝ to 1⅛ inches. The cache is believed to be late-prehistoric, because of the blade form and the presence of triangular points. (Millsap, M. and Dickson, D., *Indian Relic Trader*, Vol. IV No. 3, 1984, p. 12.)

In 1974, a blade cache was found in Washington County, Arkansas. One artifact was exposed after sliding part way down a riverbank, another was partly visible, and seven others (total, nine) were thereafter discovered. Unhafted, the longest was over 4 in., the others slightly shorter. The blades were well-formed, and with edge pressure retouch. They resemble certain Archaic knives. The find was donated to the University of Arkansas Museum, Fayetteville. (Hutton, M., "My Cache Find...", *Central States Archaeological Journal*, Vol. 25 No. 4, October 1978, p. 191.)

A cache of Adena leaf-shaped blades was found in Johnson County, Kentucky, in May, 1967. There were 63 artifacts in all, found in a cultivated field, hurriedly excavated with the aid of a hay-fork. Material was combined cream-and-grey flint with browns, origin unknown. The topmost artifacts were fragmented by the plow. The longest knife was about 4 inches, and all were very well made. (Brown, L., "A Kentucky Cache", *Ohio Archaeologist*, Vol. 18 No. 1, January 1968, p. 35.)

A cache excavated on April 4, 1976 on a reservoir ridge in Bartow County, Georgia, consisted of 58 items. This brought the total number of artifacts (including earlier finds) from the same site to 75. All were unhafted preforms, triangular and with rounded bases. Material was a dark flint or chert not common to the region, and length was from 1½ to 4 inches. The cache pit, 18 in. deep and about 2 feet across, had

CACHES

been exposed by construction equipment. (Rudolph, W., "The Allatoona Reservoir Cache", *Central States Archaeological Journal*, Vol. 26 No. 1, January 1979, p. 28-29.)

Near Marion, Indiana, in May of 1981, a cache of 13 blades was recovered by collectors while surface-hunting. Two of the rounded-base unhafted blades had been damaged, but the remainder were intact. Material seems to be a pale chert. (Moon, D., "Moons Discover Treasure Trove...", *Prehistoric Art — Archaeology '82*, Vol. XVII No. 3, 1982, p. 90-91.)

On a knoll close to the joining of two streams, a cache of blades was discovered in Madison County, Kentucky. The find took place in the summer of 1982, and was made by workmen excavating for a barn addition. A total of 28 triangular unnotched blades was recovered by the landowner, and it thought the workmen picked up additional artifacts. The blades were largely made from a dark flint not of local origin. Accompanying the blades was a 6 by 9 in. sheet of mica, nodules of what may be natural lead, and a large and fine rectangular one-hole gorget. (Wagers, C., "The Congleton Cache", *Central States Archaeological Journal*, Vol. 31 No. 4, October 1984, p. 166-167.)

EXPANDED BARB PICKWICK. Found as a Cache in Colbert Co., Ala., these blades show unusually fine workmanship. After observing the pieces one can only conclude that they were made from the same nodule. This type usually is Middle to Late Achaic finds in the Tenn. Valley. 5-3/4 x 5-1/2 in. in length. The four are valued at $1400
Courtesy of Tom Hendrix, Florence, Alabama

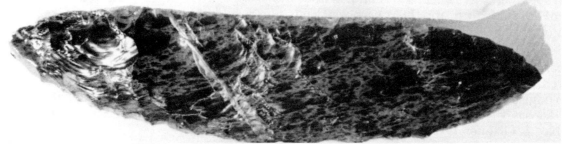

Blade found with a CACHE of other broken specimens, Glass Buttes, Oregon, 1960. It is made of mahogany obsidian and is 7-3/4 in. in length. As with a companion piece illustrated elsewhere, it was ceremonially destroyed in early times and is now glued back together. $300
Courtesy Eugene Heflin Collection, Oregon.

CACHE BLADE, large (4-1/4 x 7-3/8 in.) of Indiana hornstone or Harrison County (IN) flint. Bi-pointed, it was plowed from a mound in Harrison County, In. There were several other large blades, and one was notched in TURKEY-TAIL fashion. All were covered with a red substance, probably ochre. Workstyle is superb, with broad facial flaking and fine edge retouch. A superb piece. $900
Photo courtesy J.B. Geyer Collection, Michigan; photograph by Mark Petrosoff

CACHE BLADE, 5-1/4 in. long; found with other oval blades in a CACHE, this was the only piece with pointed tip. Material is a high grade waxy-appearing brown jasper, with sources 40-60 miles distant near confluence of Shenandoah and Potomac Rivers. This was found in Virginia below Mt. Vernon. $75
Photo courtesy Stephen E. Porcelli Collection, Virginia; photographer, Scott K. Silsby, Arlington, VA

Unhafted blades, all from Georgia, l. to r. and top down.
Dooly Cty., GA, percussion-chipped. $5
Baker Cty., GA, 4-3/4 in., tip nick. $25
One blade of CACHE of four, base heavily ground, well made. $50
Dougherty Cty., GA, excavated specimen, pink-brown flint, serrated, extremely well made piece; note serrations mainly on the single edge. $125
Photo courtesy Jack M. Hall Collection, Georgia

Blade found with a CACHE of broken specimens in the Glass Buttes area of Oregon, 1960. Chipped from mahogany obsidian, it is 8 in. long; the two pieces have been glued back together after ceremonial breakage. $300
Courtesy Eugene Heflin Collection, Oregon

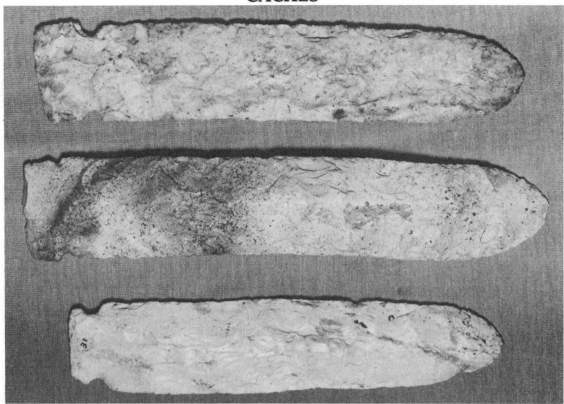

LARGE KNIVES, *from Forest City, MO. Longest example at center is 10 inches. These pieces were found as a CACHE.* $300-500
Photo courtesy Ben W. Thompson, Missouri

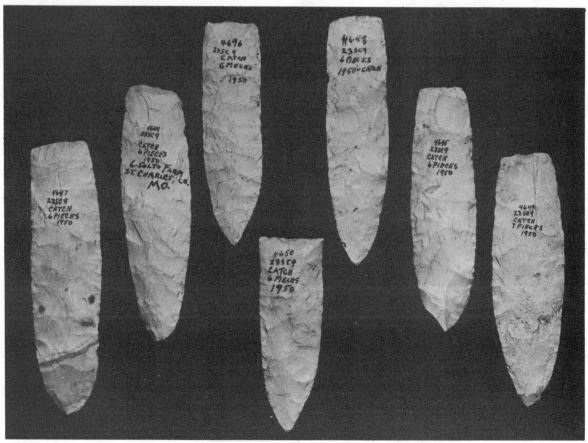

BLADE CACHE, *all found in Missouri, 1950. Material is a light-colored chert.* $100-250
Photo courtesy Ben W. Thompson, Missouri

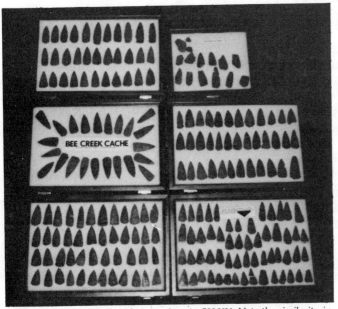

The Bee Creek Cache, described elsewhere in CH XV. Note the similarity in size, shape and material, a common feature of many CACHES. The flint is exotic, possibly from Oklahoma.
Photo courtesy R.G. Roberts Collection, Missouri

ADENA CACHE BLADES, from the Lukins Cache, found in Portage County, OH, several years ago. Of scarce bluish Flintridge gem material, the CACHE was plowed from a bog that had once been a lake. There were 356 blades in all, 17 large and 339 smaller. Red ochre was on about half the artifacts. Wood fragments were also found, indicating the knives had been in a wooden container. A rim section hinted the container was about 14 in. in diameter. In the photo, large center blade is 3 x 6-3/4 in. long. $2200
Photo courtesy J.B. Geyer Collection, Michigan; photograph by Mark Petrosoff

Closeup of one frame of the Bee Creek Cache, showing the very symmetrical outlines of most of the blades. See CH XV for full details of this find.
Photo courtesy R.G. Roberts Collection, Missouri

CHAPTER XVI
HISTORIC INDIAN KNIVES

This chapter is not so much hard facts as a general outline of historic knives, what "historic" means, what the knives were. Historic simply means the arrival of Whites and writing. Then observations could be made and put down in a permanent way, in a widely understood language. Before historic times, in prehistory, there were no written records for North America, so one can only deal directly with the artifacts themselves. This is why prehistoric Indians have no tribal names today, but are gathered into eras of thousands of years. We simply do not know what names they used, except just before the arrival of Whites when Indians themselves told the newcomers.

However, Whites brought more than pen and journal. They brought a totally new material, iron and steel, and these hard substances revolutionized Amerind lifeways. Along with beads, axes, silver ornaments, wool blankets, copper kettles, firearms and much more, the Europeans brought knives. These were an immediate success, and large quantities were involved in all trading periods.

Historic Indian knives — generally but not always made by Whites for trade with the Indians — belong to the period late-1500's to late-1800's. There were three centuries of exchange and knive production, stockpiling, transportation, trade and use. While Indians obtained knives by casual interaction with Whites, as gifts or as war booty, the vast number of blades exchanged hands in the fur trade period. So, historic Amerind knives are sometimes also known as "trade-era" knives, because the largest number of them were obtained in that way.

As with prehistoric eras, there was no abrupt start-stop of knife design or use, for Indian craftsmen continued to chip their knives even well into the 19th century. Availability was the key, and whenever possible, metal containers replaced pottery, guns the bow-and-arrow, steel the flint or obsidian.

In the latter case, the natural substances were hard but brittle, and prone to shatter. Steel knives (like axes) were stronger, more efficient, and easier to sharpen. These technological improvements were recognized and accepted. Flint and obsidian blades eventually were reserved for ceremonial occasions, while metal blades were used for everyday tasks and some ceremonies. The beautiful skill of fine flint-knapping as practiced in early times eventually became a lost art.

As suggested, direct trade was the earliest, least common method and involved relatively few people or trade goods. As with all first international commerce, both sides were tentative and exploratory. In time, great trading houses or "factories" like Hudson's Bay Company developed a full line of goods. These were tailored to, and readily accepted by, the native inhabitants of northern North America. Many businesses were individuals or partnerships and small traders were everywhere on the frontier and beyond.

Most of the early knives were made in Europe, mainly France, while England, and Germany produced a share. Americans with their own political and military problems served mainly as middlemen at first, and after 1776 also became proficient in manufacturing. Eventually Americans turned out some fine knives and these were also traded to the Indians.

Some Indians picked up the relatively simple process of pounding heated iron or steel and learned to make their own knives. Almost any source of raw material was used, salvaged gun barrels, wheel rims, kettles and so forth. A favorite was a worn-out file, since it had high-grade steel and was already almost a knife-shape. In the AD-1800's a few trained Indian blacksmiths came onto the scene and they were valued workers in their tribal communities.

As can be seen from the great variety of prehistoric blades, historic knives also came in all shapes and sizes. For the collector, three main divisions should serve as at least an introduction to the field.

Camp knives

A bewildering range of blades are in this category, from huge butchering knives to small blades used for mundane tasks like cutting sewing thread or paring fingernails or slicing roots. Most have a single edge, excurvate, and a sturdy handle of bone or wood. The main thrust is that all these are "at home" knives, often without a sheath, usually very heavily used. All could also be classed as general purpose knives.

These include knives for cutting up game large and small, skinning, hide-scraping, thong-making, peeling limbs, everything. A characteristic is that the knives were not altered and rarely, if ever, decorated in any way. They were used until no longer serviceable as knives, and rather than be discarded, were often made into another tool such as an awl. Sharpening was done with either a file or a fine-grained whetstone. The best stones (such as Arkansas' Ouchita oilstones) gave a razor edge.

A difficulty here (as with some knives in some sheaths, second category) is that Whites of whatever historic period also tended to use the same knives in about the same ways. So, unless there is a good provenance or secure historic ownership/attribution recorded for the piece, actual use by whom and when can become questionable. Fortunately, some of these blades were maker-marked so date and distribution are at least helpful in establishing even a general provenance.

HISTORIC INDIAN KNIVES

Sheath Knives

These are generally top-of-the-line specimens, competed for by advanced collectors and museums alike. And generally, this competition is not just for the knives themselves, but for the knife-with-sheath, the combination. Two main classes of sheath knives exist, eastern Woodlands and western Plains. Floral sheath designs were popular with the first, geometric designs with the second.

Not surprisingly, the knives are often actual or converted camp knives, sometimes the robust type, sometimes with small blades. Other times, the knife is a sturdy blade with crosspiece to separate handle and blade. A few examples were even made from cut-down swords. It is the sheath that sets this category apart, being a showpiece of Indian handiwork. After all, the knife was usually White-made, so the appeal here is because of Indian use and in the way artistic additions were done by the Indians. A few knives have handles that were further decorated, often with pewter or lead inlays or with brass tacks.

Usually the sheath is leather, made from buffalo (bison), elk or moose hide, and large-size. Seeing an historic Indian knife sheath alone, there is little chance the observer can guess the size or kind of knife it holds. Often the sheath is much larger than needed to hold the knife. The sheath may have loops at the top or back for belt suspension or have simple tying thongs. Usually the back is left plain and flat, with the decoration one-side, on the front.

Early designs on belt-knife sheaths — always a male accoutrement, worn boldly and proudly — were done with natural or dyed porcupine quills. Later, tiny seed-bead designs were used, or the larger "pony" beads for dangles. Whatever decorative measures, these knives were partly utilitarian, partly show pieces, mainly the latter. Sheaths were sometimes so large as to conceal the knife entirely, both blade and handle. For Western examples, the overly large sheath helped hold the blade firmly in place when the owner was on horseback and prevented knife loss.

Sheath decorations may be more than designs done on leather. Some may have tin dangels or cones secured with thread or, on early knives, sinew. Bits of mirror might be used, and short strands of beads were a frequent addition. Feathers or fringes might be added, even the ever-popular brass tacks. All were used to enhance the appearance of this important personal decoration and weapons combination.

Specialized knives

A few Indian knives were very specialized. One example, the crooked knife, had a blade shaped very much like a farrier's hoof-knife, but without the tip curl. It had a straight handle and a curved blade. It contrast to most knives, it could be used with both hands in draw-knife fashion. Strictly for wood-working, the crooked knife was used mainly in northern regions for such tasks as making paddles, shaping canoe ribs and carving wooden bowls.

Some specialized knives were made from large camp knives, with the blades shaped for special tasks. A skinning knife, for instance, might have the blade shortened and the edge swept back into a sharp curve. A knife used for incising a birch tree for bark could have another design, while a fighting knife in pioneer fashion might have both edges sharpened so it could cut in two directions.

When muzzle-loading rifles were obtained, another knife was usually carried in the hunting pouch of Indians and Whites alike. This was the patch knife, used before the days of pre-cut ball patches. The lead ball was seated in a greased patch of thin cloth, usually linen or bed-ticking. This made loading the ball atop the powder charge easier, helped clean the barrel interior and provided a seal that increased velocity. After the ball and fabric were pressed into the muzzle, patch knives cut off excess material. Some blades, straight or curved, were made from straight razors or discarded knife blades. Some of these knives had attached powder measures, serving a double purpose.

Not necessarily specialized knives, but a special knife design were those with a self-contained sheath. These had various names, folding, clasp or pocket. The novelty was several blades and a blade receptacle that became a handle. Many of these knives are quite early, and were made in many styles and sizes. A few with single blades were quite large. These knives have been encountered at a number of historic Indian sites, and were no doubt used for many different purposes. The reduced size when folded meant that they could be carried as personal blades, and were undoubtedly used by men and women alike.

Probably the rarest knife form from historic North America (other than some very important presentation examples) was a giant blade used for many purposes. It originated in Soviet Siberia, and was traded to Alaskan Indians in the AD 1700's. It was several feet long, with a straight backing, an excurvate edge and pointed tip. Of forged iron, it was a heavy-duty multipurpose tool.

Pole-mounted, it was employed as a spear. Unhafted, it was used in a knife-like manner for any number of digging, brush-clearing or wood-chopping tasks. A modern counterpart would be a hefty point-tipped machete. These do not necessarily seem to be individual weapons, but a trail party knife with several being carried with the camp equipment. Sometimes the blade was encased in a wooden scabbard. (Hanson, C. Jr., "The Russian Palma", *The Museum of the Fur Trade Quarterly*, Vol, 16 No. 4, Winter 1980, p. 1-3.)

HISTORIC INDIAN KNIVES

Whatever the type of trade-era knife, there seems to be three main reasons why the Indians accepted them so readily. One was certainly the prestige aspect of an imported item, plus "modern" material as opposed to "old-fashioned" flint or obsidian. Also, iron and steel had strength and were not as brittle (breakable) as chipped examples. Capable of striking sparks, a metal knife could be used as the steel to start a fire with flint-and-steel. Finally, a metal knife could be sharpened hundreds of times instead of only dozens. It is no wonder the ever practical and conservative Indians admired them so much.

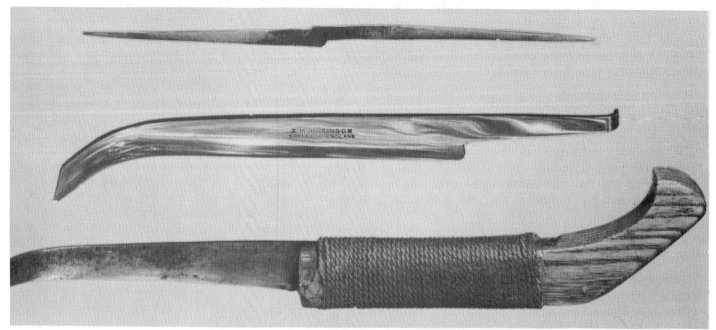

Hudson's Bay Company trade goods.
Top, AWL, with wooden handle at either end.
Center, CROOKED, CURVED, or CANOE KNIFE, with wooden handle to be attached by the person who purchased it.
Bottom, CROOKED KNIFE with the HBC crest and word "Fox" was collected at Moose Factory in 1884.
Photo courtesy Hudson's Bay Company, Winnipeg, Manitoba, Canada; HBC Neg. No. 74-51

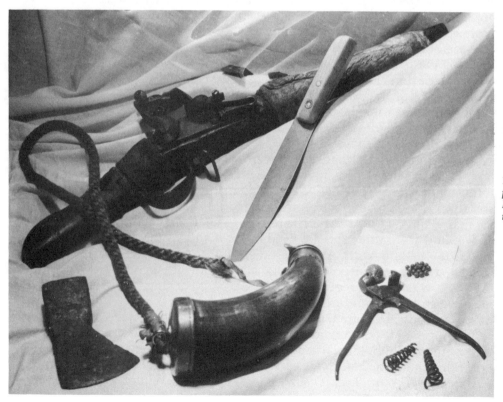

19th Century trade goods, all Hudson's Bay Company. Note the knife with riveted wooden handle. Photo courtesy Hudson's Bay Company, Winnipeg, Manitoba, Canada; HBC Neg. No. 60-96

HISTORIC INDIAN KNIVES

19th Century Hudson's Bay Company trade goods, including the blades for two crooked knives at right center.
Photo courtesy Hudson's Bay Company, Winnipeg, Manitoba, Canada; HBC Neg. No. 60-97

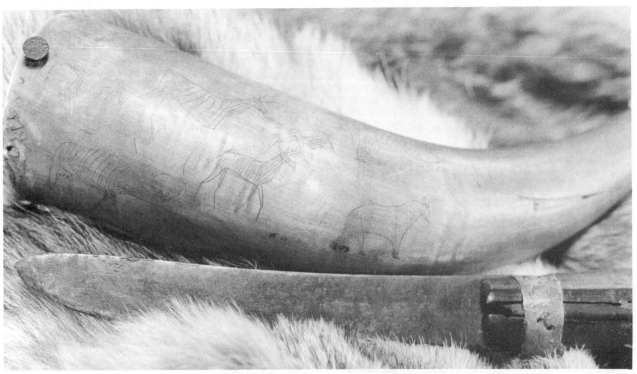

KNIFE AND POWDER HORN of the Potawatomi chief Sauquette. The knife is 9-1/2 in. long, with a 5-1/2 in. blade. It is Sheffield (England), mid-1800's, with rosewood handle and a lead or pewter band poured around the handle, Indian-done. The powder horn decorated with drawings of animals also belonged to chief Sauquette. He was stabbed to death with his own knife for being cooperative with the Whites, this taking place along Mud Creek, near Girod, MI. His Indian slayer was arrested, but traded a pony for freedom.
Historic pieces

Photo courtesy John Alward Collection, Michigan

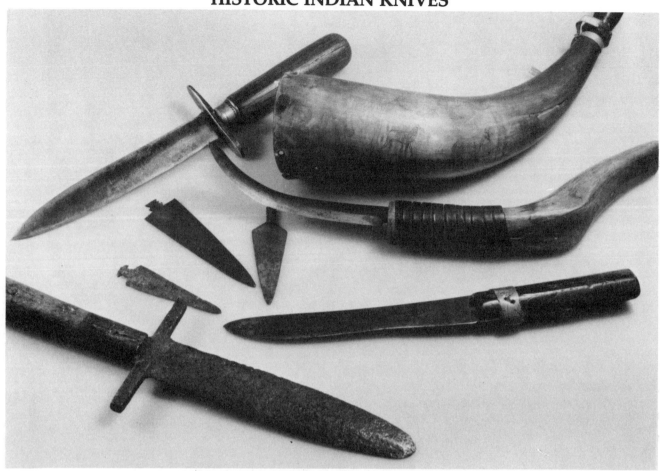

Knives and powder horn mentioned elsewhere, this photo also shows three iron trade arrowheads and a CANADIAN CROOKED KNIFE. The curved blade was made from a file, and the offset handle is also Indian-made; it was held with the right hand, thumb set on the handle back, the blade drawn toward the user. Museum quality
Photo courtesy John Alward Collection, Michigan

Top, PIKE KNIFE, made from an early pike with the blade and guard forged in one piece; converted to a knife by cutting the shaft off. It is 11 in. long. Bottom, KNIFE AND SHEATH, blade made from a file with a loose-fitting iron guard and a ferrule made from a brass-sewing thimble. The sheath is made from a deer-leg skin. It has this notation on the back: "Skelpers knife, Indian Girl. 1875 W.O. Ford". Museum quality Photo courtesy John Alward Collection, Michigan

Top, ESKIMO SNOW KNIFE, walrus oosik, for shaping and trimming snow blocks.
Second down, ESKIMO MAN'S KNIFE, slate blade, fossil-ivory handle.
Third down, ESKIMO SLATE-BLADE KNIFE, rib-bone handle.
Lower center, SLATE BLADES in green and black.
Bottom, all l. to r.: WOMAN'S KNIFE or Ulu, wood handle, steel blade cut from cross-cut saw blade; older style SLATE-BLADE ULU; "FISH-TAILED" SCRAPER, short end scraper blade, whalebone handle to fit palm of hand; TWO-PIECE ESKIMO KNIFE HANDLE to be lashed together with slate blade.   Museum quality
Photo courtesy John Alward collection, Michigan

BOWIE-TYPE KNIFE, classic shape, steel blade and riveted wooden handle.
Ca. 1850-70.   15''
Value...   Museum quality
Photo courtesy Bernard Lueck Collection, California

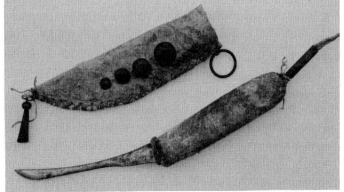

Apache SCALPING KNIFE, with sinew-wrapped handle and sinew-sewn hide sheath. Brass trim, ca. 1870-90.   10''
Value...   Museum quality
Photo courtesy Bernard Lueck Collection, California

HISTORIC INDIAN KNIVES

EARLY TRADE KNIVES
Top, knife type called a Hudson's Bay Camp knife, 13-1/2 in. long.
L. center, two knife types ("Dags") sold to Indians without handles, which
the Indians made.
Bot., two general-purpose butcher knives.
L., double-edged dagger, broken.
R., double-edged dagger made by Indians from an 8-in. bolt.
Most are from Blalock Island, Columbia River, washed out during high floods
in 1948. Values are unknown, but museum-grade.
Photo courtesy Ernest Cowles Collection, Washington

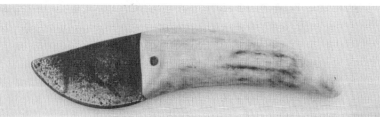

HORN-HANDLED KNIFE, Alaskan Indian, with short, strong metal blade.
A very well-made piece, it is ca. 1870-90.   5"
Value...   Museum quality
Photo courtesy Bernard Lueck Collection, California

VERY EARLY FOLDING KNIFE, 6-1/2 in. closed, 11 in. open. Blade locks
open or closed by pin through a hole in the blade. This knife is of the folding
kind that COULD have been used both by Whites and Indians, but is not
necessarily an Indian artifact. Blade is marked "Geneva Tempered/USA".
Fine historic piece. $150
Photo courtesy David G. Shirley, Michigan

HISTORIC INDIAN KNIVES.
Top, BONE-HANDLED, with single rivet and a silver band around the bone shaft.
Center, ANTLER-HANDLED, very excurvate blade. The guard is Catlinite; this knife has a very Indian appearance.
Bottom, ANTLER-HANDLED, attached with two rivets. Indians often put their own handles on White-made blades. Museum quality
Photo courtesy Jim & Teresa Dresslar, Indiana

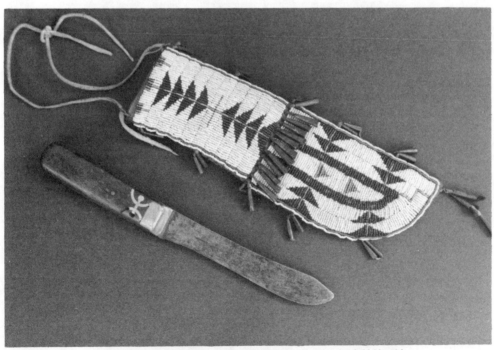

CHEYENNE KNIFE AND SHEATH, ca. 1870. Sheath is beaded hide with green and blue geometric pattern on white background. Attachments are rolled tin cones, overall length, 11 in., superb condition. The trade knife has a pewter-inlaid wooden handle. Museum quality.
Photo courtesy Canfield & Company, Santa Fe, NM

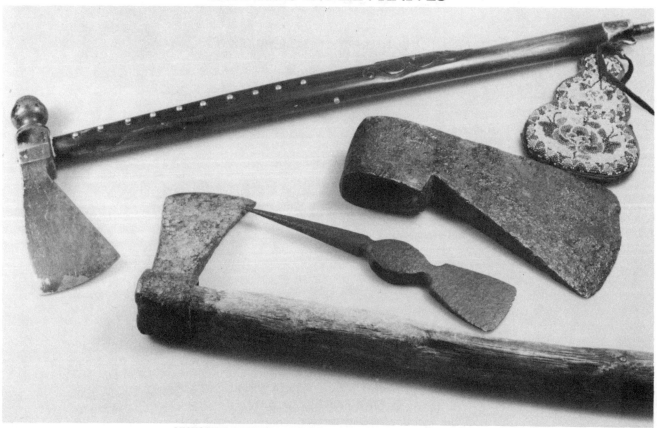

HISTORIC INDIAN TRADE IRON; it should be noted that in an emergency such artifacts could be, and sometimes were, used as knives.
Top, pipe-tomahawk, brass bowl, very ornate ash handle with silver mouthpiece.
Center right, trade axe and Fort Ticondiroga pattern spike tomahawk.
Lower, the so-called ''squaw'' axe or htchet.   Museum quality
Photo courtesy John Alward Collection, Michigan

CHAPTER XVII

KNIVES FROM HISTORIC SITES

A few years ago, according to unconfirmed information, a bulldozer in northern Indiana uncovered the rarest of scarce things: An early fur post's **cache** of trading goods. These supposedly included axes, pipe-tomahawks, silver ornaments, knives, bottles and much more. The author has been unable to locate a report of the discovery in the literature, but the fact is that such finds do occur.

There are two ways trade-era knives are originally found on land. One is the surface find, on or near an historic-period Indian site. These knives are usually picked up in the normal process of cultivation by farmers or surface-hunting collectors. Almost always, scores of years and the elements have pitted the blade and totally destroyed the handle. At times, a maker's mark can be found, a great aid in eventually determining the source and probable age of the blade.

Usually the handle is missing, but not always. Of six trade-era knives shown in the below-cited publication, three are handled and in superb condition, indicating probable contact with their Indian owners, or, pickup or discovery a very few years after loss. One was wood-handled with a leather sheath, and two were antler-hafted. The blade on one of these specimens is worn nearly to awl-like thinness. Here, as with most antler-handled knives, the incurvate contour is on the same side as the "front" blade edge, giving a comfortable fit and good knife-edge control.

Three other examples are without handles, suggesting field-finds, each with a single-edged blade of varying length and thickness. Of interest are the hafts, apparently full-length, including these types: riveted (two holes), tapered-socket, and handle-width tang, flat. Such examples, which seem to be quite early, may have hand-forged blades and seem to be, overall, about 7 to 10 inches. (Kuck, R., **Tomahawks Illustrated,** 1977, p. 108 - 109.)

The second source of trade-knives found recently comes from excavation of historic Indian sites. Unfortunately, some of this digging is uncontrolled, the finds dispersed, the dig unreported. The site is thus destroyed, and scientific value is lost forever. Fortunately, good excavations are done, the results reported, good photos taken, accurate conclusions reached. The very fact that all this is at times done makes part of the following portion of the book possible.

In Illinois, a Kaskaskia Indian village site was excavated. An incredible variety of trade goods was found, including 17 French-made clasp knives, with 12 blades whole and 5 broken. These came from an excavation ca. AD 1900. Three different blade types were found, all categorized according to blade shape. Such knives could have served as general-purpose blades, be belt-carried or cutting tools for household tasks. The French blades are from the AD 1700's. (Good, M., **Guebert Site...** CSAS—Memoir II, 1972, p. 157-162.)

It must be noted that trade knives were used for other purposes than piercing or cutting hand-held tools or weapons. Eastern Woodlands Indians sometimes inserted iron or steel blades (the difference is in the ore and tempering) in fighting clubs. The so-called gunstock club was a favorite, but the blades exist in ball-headed clubs (hardwood, rounded mass at one end) as well. These are early in the historic period, the 1600's to mid-1800's. Some clubs sported one blade, others (possibly ceremonial pieces) as many as three. (Peterson, H., **Amerian Indian Tomahawks,** 1971, p. 88-89, photos 21 and 22.)

Very many North American sites have produced trade-era knives, largely lost to the literature. But surprisingly, some amazing (there is no other word) underwater knife finds have been made. This is not the standard surface-hunting technique of walking the stream nearest an historic site, but an entirely different thing. Underwater explorations have been going on for a number of years in the waterways along the United States - Canada border in the Minnesota region.

Years ago, in the late 1950's, some clear-thinking soul decided that below certain rapids along known trade goods transportation routes, accidents must have happened. Loads of goods or items from such loads would have been lost when freight canoes capsized or struck rocks. And since many of the goods were heavy, they likely sank — and might still be at the site, on the river bottom, unseen but largely intact.

The search began, using SCUBA gear. The Quetico-Superior Underwater Research Project (see also "White Water Yields Relics", *National Geographic*, Sept. 1963, p. 412-435) made important finds. In addition to rare trade-era recoveries — such as a set of 18 tin bowls, ice chisels, trade muskets (some still loaded) and the well-known Horsetail Rapids (Granite River, 1960) find of 17 nested brass kettles, trade beads, etc. — knives were also recovered.

Due to the large variety of shapes and sizes of the knives, it was determined that some were probably the personal property of the **Voyageurs** who manned the large canoes. Others were undoubtedly trade goods, intended for exchange with the Indians, thus historic Indian knives at least in form. French folding knives were found, with wooden handles and blades about 5 in. long. A foot-long fragmentary blade with wooden handle wrapped with flat brass wire may have been a fighting knife.

A dozen wooden knife handles were found, diamond-shaped in cross-section. Butchering knife handles and blades, found separately, were probably trade items. Many knife parts were found, and many others probably not recovered or which remain buried under silt or bottom-tumbled boulders. (*Voices from the Rapids*, Minnesota Historical Archaeology Series No. 3, 1975, p. 1, 65, 83 & 99.)

Trade era knives came to the Indians for centuries from many sources and directions. Only now are we beginning to understand something about them.

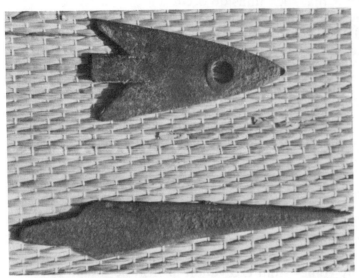

Point, 1 x 2 in., trade-iron, made by early settlers from metal and traded to Indians. Agate Springs, NE. $30
POINT OR KNIFE, 1/2 x 3-1/2 in., tapered haft, very sharp edges. $30
Courtesy Marguerite L. Kernaghan Collection; photo by Stewart W. Kernaghan

POINT OR BLADE, trade-iron, 1 x 5-1/2 in., serrated stem, NE. $70
Courtesy Marguerite L. Kernaghan Collection; photo by Stewart W. Kernaghan

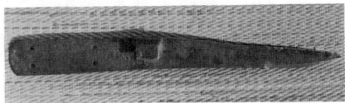

TRADE-IRON KNIFE, 1 x 10-1/4 in., modified by Indians for own use; Agate Springs, NE. $80
Courtesy Marguerite L. Kernaghan Collection; photo by Stewart W. Kernaghan

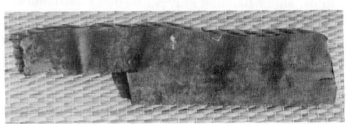

IRON KNIFE, 1-1/4 x 5-1/2, handle haft to left, modified blade; Agate Springs, NE. $15
Courtesy Marguerite L. Kernaghan Collection; photo by Stewart W. Kernaghan

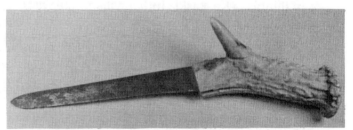

PATCH KNIFE, used with muzzle-loading rifles, blade probably made from an old file. Knives of this type were used by both Indians and Whites alike. Provenance, eastern Midwest.   8¼'' $95
Hothem Collection

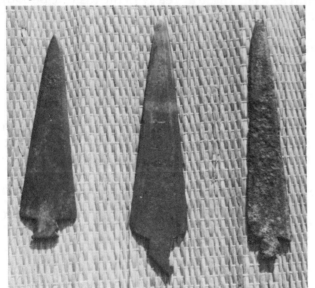

TRADE-IRON POINTS OR KNIVES:
L., 3/4 x 3 in., notched stem, NE. $35
Center, 1 x 3-7/8, straight stem, some basal damage, NE. $25
R., 1 x 3-1/2, notched stem, surface corrosion, NE. $35
Courtesy Marguerite L. Kernaghan Collection; photo by Stewart W. Kernaghan

Staged photo, a man named Kelly and an unidentified Indian warrior. In actual combat of this kind, knives were usually held with the blade projecting between thumb and first finger. Such fighters usually assumed a crouching stance and held the blades much lower.
Morrow photo, courtesy South Dakota State Historical Society

This display illustrates the belief shared by many that the Plevna or dovetail was used as a knife. The first example is only slightly resharpened and the following examples show the degrees of sharpening. (The beveling effect is a result of being worked or chipped from one side only.)

Values:-r. 5''-$300, 4-1/2''-$175, 4''-$150, 3-3/4''-$100, 3''-$40
Courtesy Tom Hendrix, Florence, Alabama

Two unsharpened and one sharpened knives. Far right example shows to what degree the Indian sharpened his knives. 4-3/4, 5-1/4 x 3 in. Lauderdale Co., Ala. $55, $45, $55
Courtesy Tom Hendrix, Florence, Alabama

126

CHAPTER XVIII
GENERAL KNIFE PHOTOS

The photographs that follow are an important part of this book, as they cover knives not generally included in other major chapters. While it is not difficult to categorize Amerind knives — by period or type or material — it is even easier to overlook a whole great class of knife forms that do not easily fit any one description.

There are several reasons for this, one being that any one chipped prehistoric knife may stylistically fall outside an easily recognized type or a known variant of that type. For example, the Hardin of the Midwest has a classic form, and yet there are at least half a dozen sub-types and many other related variants.

Another reason is that a knife form may be a transitional piece, changing form from an earlier type but not yet evolved into a later, firm, widely used type. There are many such examples, for instance, in the Archaic bifurcate-base families, and one piece may have "shared" characteristics of two or more other types.

A third reason is that one-of-a-kind knives do exist. It is usually possible to broadly period-date such curiosities, and even state with some certainty that they may be similar to a type, but identification usually goes no further. It would seem that some knives were experimental, made in strange shapes and styles for whatever valid prehistoric reason.

This then is still another look at ancient Indian knives in all their richness of numbers, beauty of manufacture, their diversity, their mystery.

CURVED-BLADE KNIVES, various types and periods. In most cases, as is typical, the excurvate edge appears to be the primary cutting edge. From MO, IL and, (bot. center), KY. $20-$300
Photo courtesy Ben W. Thompson, Missouri

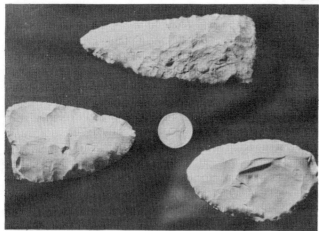

THREE NEW JERSEY KNIVES.
Left and center, material is Pennsylvania jasper. Bot. right, material is a light grey chalcedony. From Monmouth Co., NJ. Top center specimen is 4-3/8 inches, and Woodland period. Unlisted
Photo courtesy Robert Z. Inman, Jr., Collection, New Jersey

Left, KNIFE, *3-5/8 in. long, of unknown flint.*
*Right, "DOG-LEG" or angled knife, made of Pennsylvania jasper.*Unlisted
Photo courtesy Bob Griswold Collection, New Jersey

Top, SEMI-LUNAR KNIFE *or* ULU, *of an unknown yellow-white flint, from Monmouth Co., NJ.*
Bottom, large KNIFE, *4-1/4 in., in grey-blue slate, same origin. May be late Archaic.* Unlisted
Photo courtesy Bob Griswold Collection, New Jersey

CEREMONIAL EFFIGY DAGGER, *Guatemala Central America, figurine 4-1/4 in. high. This human-figure blade has some of the lines put in by string-sawing while others were engraved. This is an early piece, late BC centuries.*
Private collection $400

CEREMONIAL EFFIGY DAGGER, *7/8 x 2-1/4 in., in light green stone. It depicts the human figure with folded arms and string-cut details on reverse depict figurine as if seen from the rear. Dagger tip is at end of the feet and is worn. Guatemala, Central America, late BC centuries.* $300
Private collection

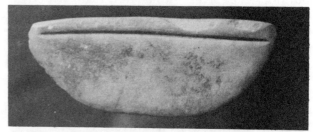

SEMI-LUNAR KNIFE *or* ULU, *5-1/8 in. long. It is made of ground slate, from Monmouth Co., NJ. Late Archaic to early Woodland, the reverse also has an incised upper line to permit hafting.* Unlisted
Photo courtesy Bob Griswold Collection, New Jersey

EFFIGY-PENDANT KNIFE, *1-1/8 x 1-1/2 in., in high-quality dark green jade. Markings depict a stylized face with eyes formed by two narrow lines on edges. Blade edge is on lower side, opposite suspension hole. Some believe the holes were for attaching a handle. This piece is from Costa Rica.*$275
Private collection

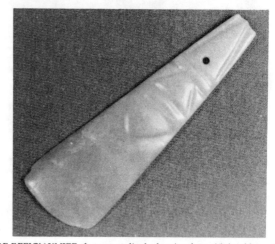

JADE EFFIGY KNIFE, *features stylized, showing face with headdress. Piece is 1 x 3-1/4 in., of mottled translucent high-quality green jade. Back is polished to true mirror gloss and blade edge is the excurvate widest portion at the bottom. Costa Rica, Central America, early AD centuries.* $400
Private collection

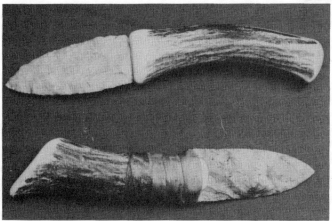

PREHISTORIC BLADES IN RECREATED HANDLES
Top, ADENA stemmed blade hafted in deer antler handle, with center section of antler removed to provide mounting socket for blade stem. Hide glue or pitch is used for binding purposes.
Bottom, HARDIN BARB blade hafted in antler handle, with rawhide lashing. All blades shown are old and authentic.
Photo courtesy Paul Nusbaum, Deer Creek Enterprises, Pandora, OH 45877

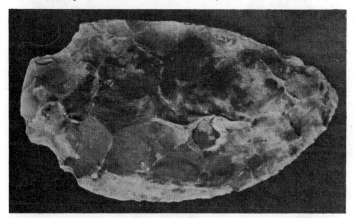

Large Georgia blade, from Calhoun County, 5-1/4 in. long. One shoulder has damage butr there is good edge retouch for the piece. It has white patination with brown-black staining. $30
Photo courtesy Jack M. Hall Collection, Georgia.

MONOLITHIC (artifact in one piece of material, including handle) DAGGER, obsidian, Mexico. It is Aztec, ca. AD 1200, and was found north of Mexico City, DF. Note the full-length serrations on blade edges and the surface encrustation or patina 5''. Value...   Museum quality
Photo courtesy Bernar Lueck Collection, California.

Rare pre-Columbian Mexican artifact, Aztec, an obsidian DOUBLE-ENDED CEREMONIAL DAGGER, about one foot long. It is ca. AD 1200, and the handle center was probably once wrapped with cord, fabric or leather.
11-1/2'' Value   Museum quality
Photo courtesy Bernard Lueck Collection, California

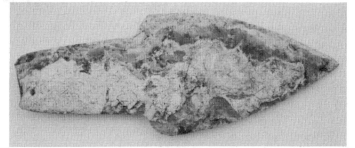

COLIMA MONOLITHIC KNIFE, flint, collected in western Mexico. Note the large and sturdy handle. This is a very early example, ca. 200 BC - AD 300.   7''   Value...   Museum quality
Photo courtesy Bernard Lueck Collection, California

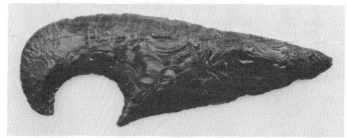

Very rare specimen, a Colima ceremonial MONOLITHIC KNIFE of artistic design. It is of obsidian. Mexico; ca. 750-900 AD. Value...Museum quality
Photo courtesy Bernard Lueck Collection, California   7''

COLIMA BLADE, obsidian, ceremonial. Note the unusual notch/stem hafting design, not seen on North American blades. It is ca. 750-900 AD.
8''   Value...   Museum quality
Photo courtesy Bernard Lueck Collection, California

COLIMA BLADE, ceremonial, done in obsidian. It is ca. AD 750-900. As is obvious, the craftsmen were some of the very best in pre-Columbian Mexico. 12-1/2''   A rare piece. Value...   Museum quality
Photo courtesy Bernard Lueck Collection, California

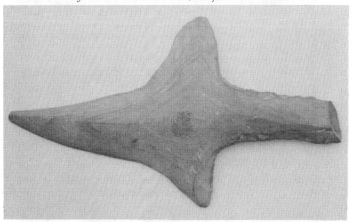

Rare Myan MONOLITHIC DAGGER found in the Yucatan, Mexico. It is made from sandstone that has first been chipped, then shaped by abrasian and polishing. Ca. 750-900 AD.   9''   Value...   Museum quality
Photo courtesy Bernard Lueck Collection, California

Haida Indian DAGGER, found in southeastern Alaska. The blade is bone and the totemic handle is wood. Ca. 1870-90. Value... Museum quality Photo courtesy Bernard Lueck Collection, California 13"

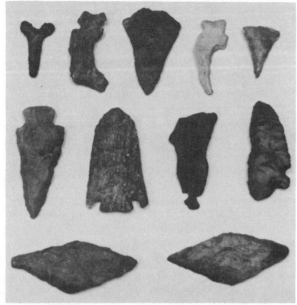

UNUSUAL KNIVES, eastern Midwest. Top, l. to r.: DRILL-SHAPE, from bifurcated blade; HAFTED SHAFT-SCRAPER, early Archaic woodworking knife; PENTAGONAL (?) blade, mild base; SHAFT-SCRAPER; TRIANGULAR blade. Second, HOPEWELL; BASE-NOTCHED (3 in.) in blue Cosh. Co., Archaic; NOTCHED-FLAKE UNIFACE; CORNER-TANG, from KY, with use-edge on tang edge, opposite of SW-U.S. types. Bottom, two 4-bevel (tech. a HARAHEY) blades, l. found in St. Joseph, MI, r. from Williams Co., OH. Such blades suggest both extensive early trade or cultural expansion of flint designs. Values, ea.: $15-$125
Photo courtesy J. B. Geyer Collection, Michigan; photograph by Mark Petrosoff

SHOSHONEAN KNIFE, Late Plains period, AD 1700-1750. It is 1-3/8 x 5-1/4 in., and made of olive quartzite. It is from the Bighorn Mountains, WY. Value unlisted.
Photo courtesy John Byrd, Helena, Montana

Blades, of uncertain time-period, probably Archaic.
Left, pale tan flint or cream, robust construction, well-chipped. $15
Right, finished knife or CACHE-type pre-form, grey and black flint. $10
Hothem collection

KNIFE, percussion shaped, the two sections found at different times. It is of quartzite, 3 x 5-1/2 in. long; this was a surface find near Nucla. CO.$10 Courtesy Marguerite L. Kernaghan Collection; photo by Stewart W. Kernaghan

ARCHAIC or Woodland blade, very fine pressure retouch on all edges. Excurvate (down) edge had the most use, as it is strongly beveled. Material is a quality tan flint, poss. Delaware County. This was a reservoir find.$30 Hothem collection 3-3/4"

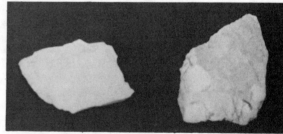

Knives of vein or layer flints, no doubt early but of unknown origin.
Left, bifacially chipped edge is on lower left of piece, plus other working surfaces. $10
Right, unifacially chipped edge is on lower left of artifact. This may well be Paleo as there are several other working edges. $10
Hothem Collection ea. 2-1/2"

Fine knife from Missouri, very thin and delicate, made of high grade chert. Good balanced protruding shoulders go almost to baseline. $20
Hothem Collection 1-7/8"

130

KNIFE, irregular hafting, quartzite, 1-1/2 x 2 in., from Nucla, CO. $2
Courtesy Marguerite L. Kernaghan Collection; photo by Stewart W. Kernaghan

AGATE blade, early shape, 1-1/4 x 3-3/4 in., found near Agate Springs, NE. $30
Courtesy Marguerite L. Kernaghan Collection; photo by Stewart W. Kernaghan

PREHISTORIC BLADES, middle example 2-1/2 in. long.
Left, PALEO LANCEOLATE KNIFE, grey and brown striped flint, with flat-ground basal chipping platform. $30
Center, Archaic leaf-shape, brown chert, unremarkable blade. $8
Right, prob. ARCHAIC in red and cream Flintridge, graver-like tip. $12
Private collection

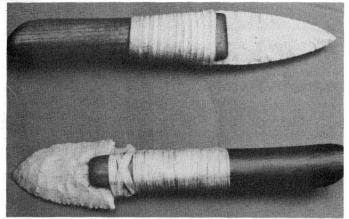

PREHISTORIC BLADES IN RECREATED HANDLES. Top, TRIANGULAR shaped blade hafted in ash handle, with rawhide binding. Bottom, Archaic CORNER-NOTCH blade hafted in hickory handle. Simulated sinew used for lashing. Note: Signs of wear and resharpening are visible on the upper edge of the blade. All handles are facsimiles of museum quality hafted artifacts. All blades are old and authentic.
Photo courtesy Paul Nusbaum, Deer Creek Enterprises, Pandora, OH 45877

PREHISTORIC ABRASION-SHAPED BLADELETS, far-right layer-flint piece 2-1/8 in. long. The main feature of all these dissimilar-appearing pieces is that the major working edge was formed, not by chipping, but by grinding. (Sighting along the edge of the photo will indicate the straightness.) Piece on left has a rounded edge, still produced by abrasion. Values are mainly educational.
Private collection

LOAF-SHAPED KNIVES, San Diego, CA area. Left to right: Basalt, 3-1/2 in.; Felsite, 3 in.' and Chalcedony, 2-3/4 inches. Time period is 2500 BC-AD 500. Each... $40
Photo courtesy Jim Cressey, California

OVOID BLADES, all San Diego area, CA. L. to r.: Felsite, 4-1/2 in.,
Basalt, 3 in., Basalt, 3 inches. These pieces may be quite early. Unlisted
Photo courtesy Jim Cressey, California

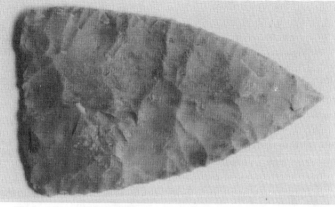

FRIDAY TYPE KNIFE, 4-1/4 in., Edwards Plateau flint, pale tan color.
From Williamson County, TX, a 10-5-81 personal find. $300
Photo courtesy Pat Mahan, Texas

KNIFE, unusual canted tip for graving or slitting use, 3 in. long. Rare
material, petrified coral, was used. It is from Pascoe Co., Florida. $40
Photo courtesy Jim Cressey, California

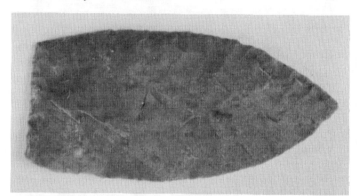

FRIDAY TYPE KNIFE, 4-1/2 in., Edwards Plateau flint, tan-brown col-
or. From Williamson County, TX, a 10-16-81 personal find.
Photo courtesy Pat Mahan, Texas

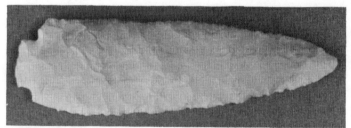

BASE TANG KNIFE, Edwards Plateau flint, Williamson County, TX. It
is 5-3/8 in. long. $300
Photo courtesy Pat Mahan, Texas

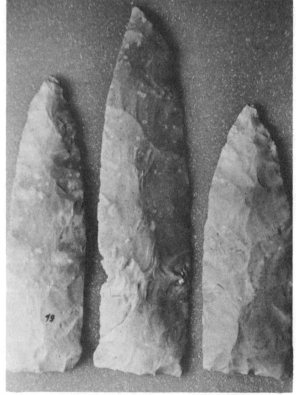

KNIVES, brown flint, longest (center) 6 in., from Texas. These may be in
the late AD centuries. Values, top to bottom, $30, $40, $30.
Photo courtesy Jim Cressey, California

CLEBURNE TYPE KNIFE, 4-3/4 in., Edwards Plateau flint. It is from Ken-
dall County, TX, the Guadalupe River region. $200
Photo courtesy Pat Mahan, Texas

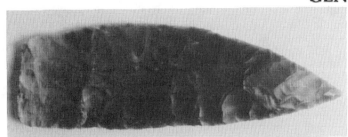

FRIDAY TYPE KNIFE, 5-3/8 in., Georgetown flint. From Travis County, TX, Pedernales River. $300
Photo courtesy Pat Mahan, Texas

PEDERNALES KNIFE, 6-1/16 in., Edwards Plateau flint. A Williamson County, TX, find on 4-25-81, South San Gabriel River. Museum quality
Photo courtesy Pat Mahan, Texas

CURVED-BASE KNIFE, 1-3/4 x 3-7/8 in., made of tan flint. From Vernon Co., WI, this is a well-chipped piece. $35
Courtesy Mert Cowley Collection, WI; by Mohr Photography

BLADE, 2-1/2 x 4-3/8 in., made of Knife River chalcedony. Found in Barron Co., WI, this was a traded-in material. This piece is expertly made and extremely thin, only 1/4 in. thickest part. Due to massive damage to lower corner, this corner-notched knife is mainly of study value.
Courtesy Mert Cowley Collection, WI; by Mohr Photography

Black flint knife, 3-3/4 in., from Northampton County, Pennsylvania. Time period is unknown. $20-25
Photo courtesy Fogelman Collection, Pennsylvania

Top, ovate blade of yellow Pennsylvania jasper, 2-15/16 in. long, unknown period. $20
Bottom, Union County, Pennsylvania, dark brown jasper, 2-7/8 in., fine flaking. $15
Photo courtesy Fogelman Collection, Pennsylvania

Large oval blade in pink flint, 2 x 5-1/2 in. long and very thin. From south-central Johnson County, Missouri. $115
Below, BROWNS VALLEY, Paleo, 1-3/4 x 4-1/4 in., thin and glossy. It is made of honey-colored chalcedony with brown inclusions, and is partially translucent. $200
Photo courtesy Richard L. Warren Collection, Missouri

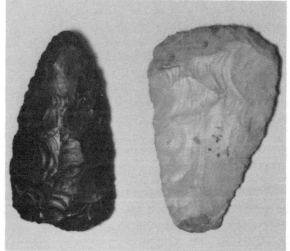

Three triangular blades, each with rounded bases, all found in western Johnson County, Missouri. All bases are heavily edge-ground. Center blade (1-5/8 x 3 in.) has deep patination on base only, indicating it was picked up at later times and resharpened for 3/4 of blade length. Archaic period. Each... $30

Photo courtesy Richard L. Warren Collection, Missouri

Two similar leaf-type knives, one of glossy black flint, second of glossy pink flint.

Black, 1-7/8 x 3-1/2 inches. $25
Pink, 1-5/16 x 3-5/8 inches. $25

They were found a quarter-mile from each other in a drainage ditch.

Photo courtesy Richard L. Warren Collection, Missouri

RECREATED BLADE AND HANDLE, both made by Scott K. Silsby. The material is Western U.S. basalt, and handle is of Virginia black walnut. The recessed binding is double-braided flax and blade is further secured with resin glue. Blade is permanently signed at base.
Photo courtesy Scott K. Silsby, Gulf Branch Nature Center, Arlington, Virginia

RECREATED BLADE AND HANDLE, both made by Scott K. Silsby. The blade is California mahogany obsidian in Virginia black walnut handle. The hafting cordage is wolfsbane, and resin glue secures the blade. The wrist lanyard is of flax. Handle is die-stamped SILSBY with a rectangular border, and blade is permanently marked.
Photo courtesy Scott K. Silsby, Gulf Branch Nature Center, Arlington, Virginia

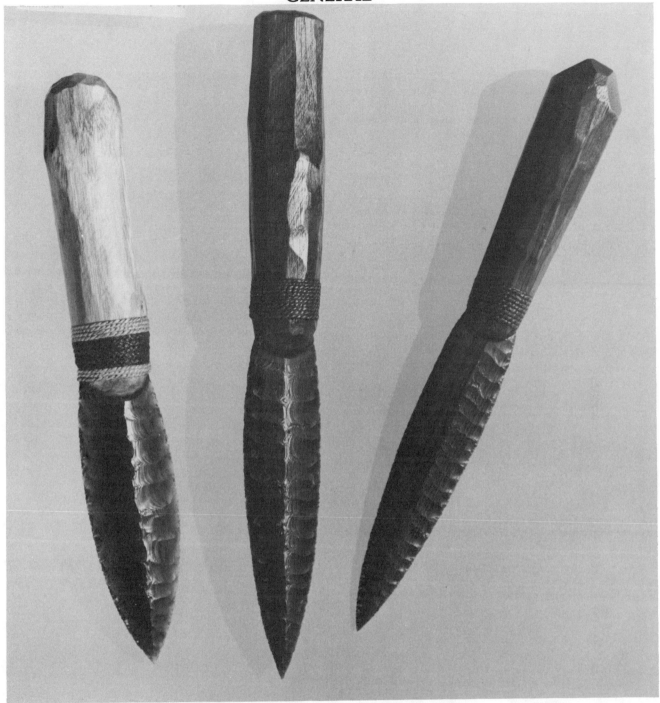

RECREATED BLADES AND HANDLES, all by Scott K. Silsby.
Left, California obsidian in Osage Orange handle, with wisteria and cotton cordage.
Center, Oregon obsidian in black walnut handle, with basswood (linden) cordage.
Right, Nevada obsidian in black walnut handle and with wolfsbane hafting cordage. All knives also have resin glues; blades are deeply engraved with signature.
Photo courtesy Scott K. Silsby, Gulf Branch Nature Center, Arlington, Virginia

Curved-edge blade, one excurvate and "backing" edge straight. It is 1-11/16 and 3-5/8 in. long, and of light brown glossy material. It was found in a drainage ditch in west-central Johnson County, Missouri. $40
Photo courtesy Richard L. Warren Collection, Missouri

Knives with very unusual shapes. Left, 3-1/4 in. long, blade in Alibates flint, mottled. $50
Right, similar shape, agate. $35
Photo courtesy Gerald Riepl Collection, Kansas

Four notched or stemmed blades, longest 2-7/8 inches. Materials, l. to r.: Alibates flint; same; white flint; brown flint. Each ... $15
Photo courtesy Gerald Riepl Collection, Kansas

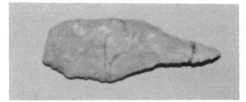

Unhafted knife 3 in. long with narrow tip. It is of yellow flint with thin black lines in the material. $50
Photo courtesy Gerald Riepl Collection, Kansas

Two early blades. Left, 3-1/2 in. long, brown, mottled flint, fine lines.$65
Right, brown flint. $20
Photo courtesy Gerald Riepl Collection, Kansas

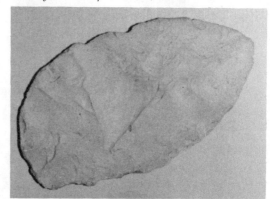

Ovate knife 2-1/2 x 4-3/4 inches. This was possibly a broken corner-tang knife, done in yellow flint. Origin, Kansas. $20
Photo courtesy Gerald Riepl Collecton, Kansas

ULU, with cutting edge the more excurvate. Of flint, is is 2-3/4 x 5 in., poss. late prehistoric. Surface find, Cottonwood Springs and Boars Tooth, near Eden, WY. $35
Courtesy Marguerite L. Kernaghan collection; photo by Stewart W. Kernaghan

Left, KNIFE, 2 in. long, green & cream. $5
Center, KNIFE, chert, surface find. CO. $5
Right, KNIFE, unidentified material, CO. $4
Courtesy Marguerite L. Kernaghan collection; photo by Stewart W. Kernaghan

All L. to r.:
LEAF-SHAPE, 1-1/4 x 2-1/4 in., quartzite, from CO. $5
CIRCULAR knife, quartzite, Naturita, CO. $3
HUMPBACK, 2-1/2 in. long, Nucla, CO. $4
Courtesy Marguerite L. Kernaghan collection; photo by Stewart W. Kernaghun

Triangular KNIFE, 1-1/2 x 2-1/4 in., made from a very rare material, fossilized sea lily stems; from Alabama. $25
Courtesy Marguerite L. Kernaghan collection; photo by Stewart W. Kernaghan

L. "HUMP-BACK" or spoiled knife, yellow jasper, 1-1/4 x 1-1/2 in., CO.$4
Center, KNIFE, chalcedony, CO. $6
R., KNIFE, 7/8 x 2 in., quartzite, CO. $5
Courtesy Marguerite L. Kernaghan collection; photo by Stewart W. Kernaghan

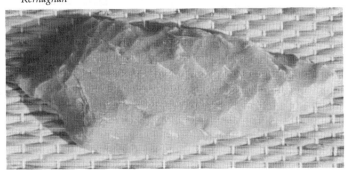

"FLAT-BACK" knife, quartzite, 1 x 3 in. This was a surface find at the Cook Ranch, Agate Springs, NE. It has a hafting nub at the base. $25
Courtesy Marguerite L. Kernaghan collection; photo by Stewart W. Kernaghan

Chert KNIFE or preform, 2 x 3 in., surface find in Berkshire County, MA. Chert does not occur in the area naturally, so must have been traded in.$8
Courtesy Marguerite L. Kernaghan collection; photo by Stewart W. Kernaghan

Large jasper knife from Stafford County, Virginia. It is leaf-shaped with fine secondary flaking on all edges. It is almost crescentic in outline. $45
Photo courtesy Swope Collection, Virginia

Large SAVANNAH RIVER blade from Stafford County, Virginia, made of white quartzite. Note the unusually small (short) stem for this type. $25
Photo courtesy Swope Collection, Virginia 4-1/4"

All knives, l. to r.:
CODY knife, agate, 3/4 x 2-1/2 in., Goshen County, WY. These are
sometimes associated with Folsom points, ca. 8000 BC. $75
KNIFE, red quartzite, 3-1/4 in. long, from Eden WY. $10
KNIFE, obsidian, 1-1/2 in. long, WY. $10
Courtesy Marguerite L. Kernaghan collection; photo by Stewart W.
Kernaghan

All knives, l. to r.:
Chert, 2-1/2 in. long, surface find, NE. $10
Quartzite, 1-1/2 in. long, same provenance. $3
WILLOW-LEAF, unknown banded material, same provenance. $10
Courtesy Marguerite L. Kernaghan collection; photo by Stewart W.
Kernaghan

Circular blade 3 in. across, chipped in a dark semi-transparent flint. Knives
like this may have been hand-held. $35
Photo courtesy Gerald Riepl Collection, Kansas

Attractive knife 4-1/2 in. long, chipped in a grey material. This blade was
found in Kansas. $125
Photo courtesy Gerald Riepl Collection, Kansas

Leaf-shaped blade 2-3/4 in. long, in orange flint, left. $35
Middle, agate blade. $25
Right, Alibates flint stemmed knife. $35
Photo courtesy Gerald Riepl Collection, Kansas

Laurel-leaf shaped blades, 2-3/4 in. long, chipped in brown and yellow flint.
All were found in Kansas. Each... $15
Photo courtesy Gerald Riepl Collection, Kansas

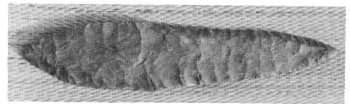

FOUR-WAY BEVEL, (HARAHEY) 2 x 9-1/4 in., of chert, from OK. This
is an extra-long and fine piece, late prehistoric. $600
Courtesy Marguerite L. Kernaghan collection; photo by Stewart W.
Kernaghan

FOUR-WAY BEVEL, (HARAHEY), 7/8 x 2-3/4 in., light-colored quartzite. A surface find at the Cook Ranch, Agate Springs, NE. $25
Courtesy Marguerite L. Kernaghan collection; photo by Stewart W. Kernaghan

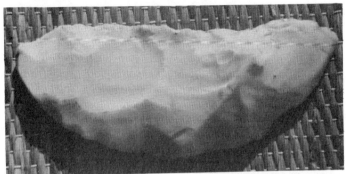

KNIFE, 1-3/8 x 3-1/4 in., from an underwater cave, St. Johnson River, FL. While it has a certain ULA appearance, it is probably much earlier. An interesting example, especially the matter of hafting, if indeed it was. $45
Courtesy Marguerite L. Kernaghan collection; photo by Stewart W. Kernaghan

All blades l. to r.:
KNIFE, pitchstone (traded), Berkshire County, NY. $2
KNIFE, pitchstone 1-1/2 x 2-1/2, same provenance. $4
KNIFE, dark flint, same provenance. $6
Courtesy Marguerite L. Kernaghan collection; photo by Stewart W. Kernaghan

Copper CEREMONIAL KNIFE in rain-god frog effigy, Costa Rica, Central America. It is cast at the top, pounded thin at base with loop at top back for pendant suspension, 1-1/4 x 1-1/4 inches. Base of effigy is in crescentic knife configuration. Rare piece. $100
Private collection

Top row, l. to r.:
HAFTED blade, 3/4 x 1-1/2, Normanskill flint, Staats Farm, NY. $3
TRIANGULAR blade, post-Woodland, NY. $5
RECTANGULAR Paleo, 2 x 2-1/4, traded chalcedony, western NY. $20
Bot. row, l. to r.:
KNIFE, 1-1/4 x 2-3/4, igneous rock, Jefferson County, NY. $15
KNIFE, slate, same provenance. $8
KNIFE, flint, same provenance. $15
Courtesy Marguerite L. Kernaghan collection; photo by Stewart W. Kernaghan

SOUTHERN MEXICAN KNIFE, grey-green striped obsidian, 1-1/2 x 5 inches. It was struck from a specially-prepared natural glass block, and stem base is ground smooth. Stem sides are lightly ground. Fine knife from an early culture, perhaps Olmec. $150
Private collection

TAPER-TIP VARIANT, unhafted, 1-7/8 x 4 in., very good quality dark grey jasper, NE. Unlisted
Photo courtesy W. R. Eckles, Nebraska

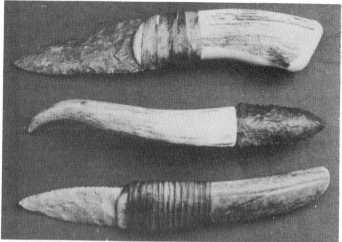

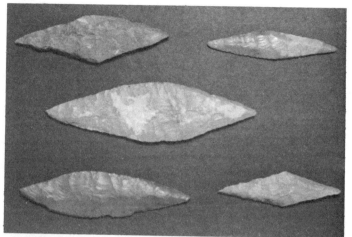

PREHISTORIC BLADES IN RECREATED HANDLES.
Top, LEAF-SHAPED *blade in elk antler handle with rawhide lashing.*
Middle, HEAVY-DUTY *blade hafted in deer antler tine handle, pithy antler center removed to provide socket for blade stem. Hide glue or pitch used to secure blade.*
Bottom, STEMMED LANCEOLATE *with stem portion mounted in deer antler handle, rawhide lashing. All blades shown are old and authentic.*
Photo courtesy Paul Nusbaum, Deer Creek Enterprises, Pandora, OH 45877

HARAHEY KNIVES, *all from Nebraska's W. R. Eckles' collection. Widths vary from 1 to 2 in., and lengths from 4-1/8 to 7-1/4 inches. Material range is from grey cherts to glossy jaspers in tan, brown, yellow and two-tone grey. These four-sided bevel-edged blades are late in the prehistoric period.* Unlisted
Photo courtesy W. R. Eckles, Nebraska

TORTUGAS KNIFE, *3-1/4 in., Edwards Plateau flint. From Williamson County, Texas.* $150
Photo courtesy Pat Mahan, Texas

A fine CANADIAN KNIFE, *in dark flint, 1-1/2 x 5 in. long. It is from the Walker Site in Brant County, East of Brantford, Ontario. The origin is Neutral or Ottawan Iroquois Indians. The site itself was destroyed by opposing Iroquois tribes in AD 1649. The smaller end may have been the hafted region.* $30
Photo courtesy Robert Calvert, London, Ontario, Canada

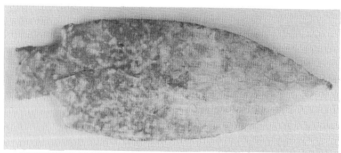

BULVERDE KNIFE, *4-1/4 in., of Edwards Plateau mottled flint. From Williamson County, TX.* $250
Photo courtesy Pat Mahan, Texas

OVATE BLADE, *2-1/2 x 4-1/2 in., in reddish-brown jasper. This piece is remarkably thin for size, with excellent chipping.* Unlisted
Photo courtesy W. R. Eckles, Nebraska

UNKNOWN BLADE, *1-1/2 x 7-1/2 in. long, from Graves Co., KY. It is made from a brown to pinkish-tan flint found in that state. There are low, shallow side-notches and fine percussion flaking with pressure flaking up to the notches. No basal grinding is present. This may be a late prehistoric piece in fine size and good condition.* $600
Photo courtesy J.B. Geyer Collection, Michigan; photograph by Mark Petrosoff

Left, DUO-TIPPED KNIFE, 1-5/8 x 3-1/4 in., in two-tone blue and grey high quality jasper, NE. The shape is unusual. Unlisted
Center, ANGLED-BLADE, 1-1/2 x 4-1/4 in., in medium-grey chert. Note that this form is similar to Paleo general-purpose knives described elsewhere. Unlisted
Right, KNIFE, 1-1/2 x 3-5/8 in., in a light grey and tan mottled jasper, uncommon form. Unlisted
Photo courtesy W. R. Eckles, Nebraska

Fine Texas flint, large and long unhafted blades. They are from Coyrell County and range from 7 to 7-1/2 inches. Material is a tan and grey local chert. For such specimens, values, each... $300
Photo courtesy D. Rogers Collection, Houston, Texas

Wide round-back knives, 4 to 6 in. long, found in Coryell and Medina Counties, Texas. They are made of black and grey cherts. These are fine examples of ancient flintworking. Values, each... $75-150
Photo courtesy D. Rogers Collection, Houston, Texas

Fine Texas blades: SAN SABA base-notched knives, 6 to 8-1/4 inches. They are made from a local tan gravel-deposit chert, and evidence extreme skill in chipping such large pieces. Values for the two smaller specimens, each... $300

The larger example would be worth a great deal more.
Photo courtesy D. Rogers Collection, Houston, Texas

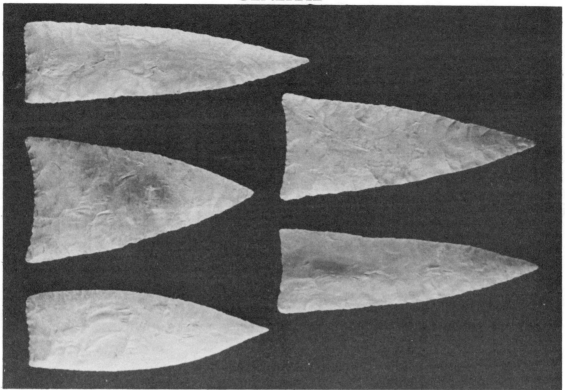

KENNY knives, 5 in. long, made of local tan and grey cherts. All are from Bell and Coryell Counties, Texas. Note the extremely smooth edges of bottom left example. Values, each . . . $75-100
Photo courtesy D. Rogers Collection, Houston, Texas

A fine FRAME OF FLINT, all knives except for smallest point, from a wide range of materials and several cultures. The CORNER-TANG blade at right center is made of grey-white chert and is 4 in. long. The ECCENTRIC at left center is of reddish chert. All artifacts came from a site near Baxter Springs, Kansas. Each . . . $15-250
Courtesy Col. Floyd B. Lyerla Collection, Kansas

FLAKE BLADES, third from left 1-3/8 in., all from the Potomac Valley. Materials, l. to r.: Green prase, brown jasper, green prase, blue chalcedony. Each has the usual median ridge on the obverse (front) left from previous blade strike-offs, and a smooth reverse (back). Such small knives and scrapers were used in all prehistoric time periods. Value - Instructional, or a dollar or two for gem material specimens.
Courtesy Stephen E. Porcelli collection, Virginia; photo by Scott Silsby

Left, BLADE, speckled jasper, from Macon, GA, year 1912. $12
Right, BLADE, 1-3/4 x 4-1/4, fossilized chert, same provenance. $25
Courtesy Marguerite L. Kernaghan Collection, photo by Stewart W. Kernaghan

DOUBLE-NOTCHED blades, found in Michigan, northern IN and n. OH. They may be related to the double-notched TURKEY-TAIL of Indiana hornstone often found in the same area. The presence of heavy basal grinding and fracture-chipped bases on some, however, suggests Archaic affiliation. Materials and origins, top row, l. to r.: FRACTURED-BASE, yellow-cream Flintridge. Bot. row, l. to r.: (All Arthur Abraham coll., Flint, MI, area) Grey, speckled flint; Norton flint, grey and striped; Grey-brown Bay Port chert. All are rare pieces. Each large piece 4-1/2''... $25-125
Photo courtesy J. B. Geyer Collection, Michigan, photograph by Mark Petrosoff

All knives, l. to r.:
Chalcedony, 1 - 1-1/2 in., surface find from NE. $5
Petrified wood knife, Cook Ranch, NE. $8
Chalcedony, 1-3/8 in. long, same provenance. $5
Courtesy Marguerite L. Kernaghan Collection, photo by Stewart W. Kernaghan

OVATE ARTIFACT, 3 x 3-7/8 in., in a glossy cream flint. From Richland Co., WI, the lower sharpened edge suggests possible use as a knife-chopper.$15
Courtesy Mert Cowley Collection, WI; by Mohr Photography

Three knives (center example of rhyolite) from Port Tobacco, Rappahannock River, Virginia. Good style range, with notching, stemming and duo-tipped. (Center, 5'')   Range ... $15-35
Photo courtesy Swope Collection, Virginia

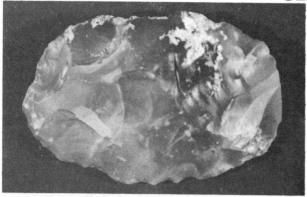

ROUNDED-EDGE BLADE, (#580) 1-1/2 x 2-1/4 in. long. It is in smokey light grey agate, translucent and with intrusions of iron, manganese and carnelian. From Ruby Mtns., Elko County, NV. Ca. AD 1100. $25
Courtesy W. J. Creighton Collection, Arizona

Large quartz knife from Port Tobacco, Virginia, SAVANNAH RIVER type. The edges are extremely well done on this piece.   4-1/4'' $35
Photo courtesy Swope Collection, Virginia

SMALL BLADE, (#1789) 3/4 x 1-1/4 in., done in black rainbow obsidian. Edges are pressure retouched; from Fairview Range, Lincoln County, NV. Ca. AD 1200. $15
Courtesy W. J. Creighton Collection, Arizona

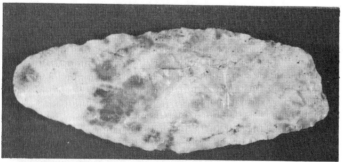

AGATE KNIFE, (#1889) 1-1/8 x 3 in., in mottled tan, medium brown and light grey material. Edges retouched; from Aquarius Mtns., Mohave County, AZ. Ca. AD 1100. $35
Courtesy W. J. Creighton Collection, Arizona

SERRATED KNIFE, (#1984) 7/8 x 1-7/8 in., in dark red-brown agate. It is pressure retouched and the material seems to be jasper-related. From Black Mtns., Mohave County, AZ. Ca. AD 1100. $12
Courtesy W. J. Creighton Collection, Arizona

ELONGATED KNIFE, (#1992) 5/8 x 2 in., in a medium-brown agate. Pressure retouched, it is from the Black Mtns., Mohave County, AZ. Ca. AD 1300. $12
Courtesy W. J. Creighton Collection, Arizona

QUARTZITE KNIFE, 7/8 x 2 in., (#2096), material a brown and tan. It was possibly subjected to erosion because the faceting is not well defined. From the Juniper Mtns., Yavapai County, AZ. Ca. 2000 BC. $8
Courtesy W. J. Creighton Collection, Arizona

SMALL BLADE, (#578) in purple and light grey flint. It is opaque with light gloss, pressure retouched. From Ruby Mtns., Elko County, NV. Ca. AD 1100, 1 x 2 inches. $15
Courtesy W. J. Creighton Collection, Arizona

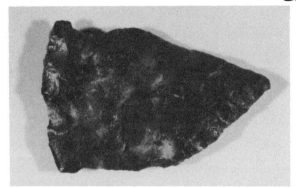

SMALL KNIFE, (#2594) 3/4 x 1-3/16 in., a brown, grey and black agate. Edges finely pressure retouched, from Music Mtns., Mohave County, AZ. Ca. AD 1400. $10
Courtesy W. J. Creighton Collection, Arizona

DOUBLE-POINTED KNIFE, Edwards Plateau Chert, Early Plains Apache site, Crosby Co., TX.   3-1/2'' $100
Photo courtesy Wayne Parker Collection, Texas

TWO-WAY BEVELED KNIFE, Tecovas jasper, found eroding out of a bank in Blanco Canyon. Early Plains Apache, Neo-Indian period, AD 1300 - AD 1700. Crosby County, TX.   2-1/2'' $75
Photo courtesy Wayne Parker Collection, Texas

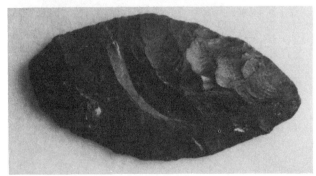

Large gem-quality blade, size 2-1/2 x 5 inches. It is grey flint with white inclusions, from Blalock Island, Columbia River. $75
Photo by Ray Pace Associates; courtesy Cliff Morris Collection

Large gem-quality blade, superbly chipped, 2-1/4 x 6 inches. It is from Sauvies Island, Columbia River. $80
Photo by Ray Pace Associates; courtesy Cliff Morris Collection

Gem blades from the Columbia River area, length range from 2 - 4-1/2 inches. Material is jasper, agate, chalcedony and carnelian, all well-chipped. The crescent knife, a rare type, is carmel and cream agate, lower left. Range, $10-60
Photo by Ray Pace Associates; courtesy Cliff Morris Collection

Gem knives from the Columbia River region, all obsidian, lengths from 1-4 inches. These are some of the finest from the Northwest Coast, and colors are translucent blue and black. Large blade in center is a $225 specimen.
Range, $20-125
Photo by Ray Pace Associates; courtesy Cliff Morris Collection

Obsidian blades from various periods, l - 4 in. long in colors of grey, blue and black. From eastern Oregon desert region, these are not as well chipped as Columbia River artifacts. Range, $15-20
Photo by Ray Pace Associates; courtesy Cliff Morris Collection

UNUSUAL-SHAPED KNIFE, 1-1/8 x 2-1/4 in., (#1471) in a purple and grey flint. This is a flake blade with pressure retouch. From the Ruby Mtns., Elko County, NV. Ca. AD 1000. $15
Courtesy W. J. Creighton Collection, Arizona

EARLY BLADE OR POINT, (#915) in brownish rhyolite with heavy desert varnish. It is 7/8 x 2-1/4 in., from the New Water Mtns., Yuma County, AZ. Ca. 4000 BC. Readers will no doubt notice a great similiarity with this piece and SANDIA II points or blades; if so, actual age would be ca. 18,000 BC. $30
Courtesy W. J. Creighton Collection, Arizona

THREE NEW JERSEY KNIVES.
Top center, 2-5/8 in., PA jasper.
Bot. left, 2-1/2 in., PA jasper.
Bot. right, 2-3/8 in., PA jasper.
All are late Archaic through Woodland sites in Monmouth and Burlington Counties, NJ. Unlisted
Photo courtesy John K. Alexander Collection, New Jersey.

EXCURVATE-EDGE KNIFE, stemmed, 3/4 x 2 in., (#1479). Lower edge serrated, smokey light grey agate, translucent with an inclusion at the 2 o'clock position of silicate iron oxide. From the Ruby Mtns., Elko County, NV. Ca. AD 1300.
Courtesy W. J. Creighton Collection, Arizona

TWO NEW JERSEY KNIVES.
Top, 2-1/4 in., PA jasper, from Ocean Co., NJ.
Bottom, 2-1/2 in., of rhyolite, from Monmouth Co., NJ. Unlisted
Photo courtesy Robert Z. Inman Jr. Collection, New Jersey

FLAKE BLADE, (#1155) 1-1/4 x 4-1/8 in., in a medium brown jasper. It is pressure retouched and has patina. From the Tank Mtns., Yuma County, AZ. Ca. AD 1000, although many such flake knives are from the Paleo era. $50
Courtesy W. J. Creighton Collection, Arizona

HARAHEY KNIFE, four-way bevel, grey Edwards Plateau chert. From Plains Apache site in Blanco Canyon, period AD 1300 - AD 1700. Neo-Indian.   4'' $150
Photo courtesy Wayne Parker Collection, Texas

HARAHEY KNIFE, four-way bevel, dark Edwards Plateau chert, from early Plains Apache site in Blanco Canyon. It is ca. AD 1300 - AD 1700. $175
Photo courtesy Wayne Parker Collection, Texas   5-1/2''

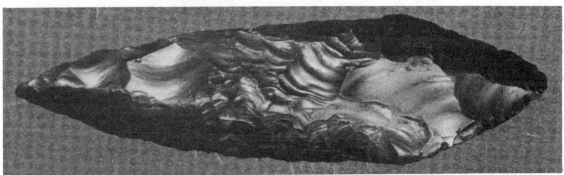

HARAHEY KNIFE, dark Edwards Plateau chert, Robertson site and a surface find. Neo-Indian period.   4'' $100
Photo courtesy Wayne Parker Collection, Texas

OBSIDIAN BLADE, from Northern CA, age or period unknown. It has a heavy patina on one face.   6-1/8'' $250
Photo courtesy Wayne Parker Collection, Texas

DOUBLE-POINTED KNIFE, Edwards Plateau flint, heavy patina on both faces. Surface find, Crosby County, TX, period unknown.   3-1/4'' $75
Photo courtesy Wayne Parker Collection, Texas

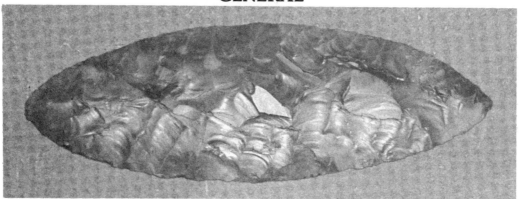

DOUBLE-POINTED KNIFE, dark Edwards Plateau chert. Classic form, age period unknown. Surface find. Crosby Co., TX.   3-1/4'' $200
Photo courtesy Wayne Parker Collection, Texas

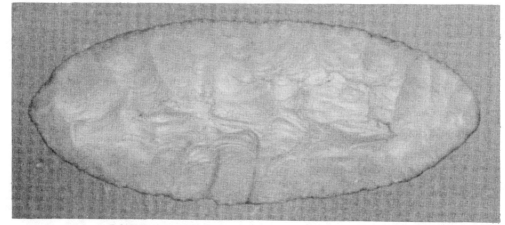

DOUBLE-POINTED KNIFE, light-colored Edwards Plateau chert; surface find in Crosby Co., TX.   4'' $125
Photo courtesy Wayne Parker Collection, Texas

TRIANGULAR KNIFE, dark Edwards Plateau chert, age unknown. Surface find from the Robertson site.   4'' $150
Photo courtesy Wayne Parker Collection, Texas

HARAHEY KNIFE, Alibates flint, Panhandle Plains Aspect site, Neo-Indian period, AD 900- AD 1300.   5-1/4'' $175
Photo courtesy Wayne Parker Collection, Texas

HARAHEY KNIFE, Alibates flint, surface find in Palo Dura Canyon,
Randell Co., TX. Neo-Indian period. 4-1/2'' $175
Photo courtesy Wayne Parker Collection, Texas

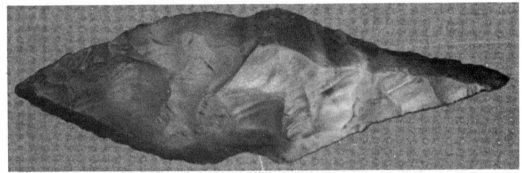

HARAHEY KNIFE, Alibates flint, Panhandle Plains Aspect site, Hutchinson
County, TX. Neo-Indian, AD 900- AD 1300. This is a rare piece because
of the side notches, perhaps for original hafting. 3-3/4'' $150
Photo courtesy Wayne Parker Collection, Texas

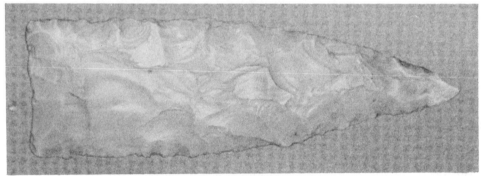

TRIANGULAR KNIFE, light-colored Edwards Plateau chert. Surface find,
Crosby County, TX, of unknown age. 3-3/4'' $35
Photo courtesy Wayne Parker Collection, Texas

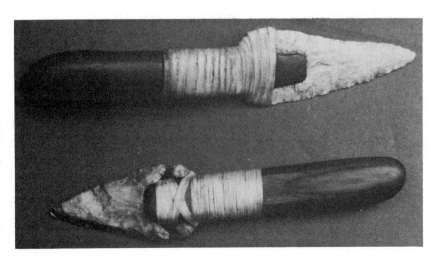

PREHISTORIC BLADES IN RECREATED
HANDLES. Top, large LEAF-SHAPED blade with
hickory handle, rawhide used for lashing. Evidence of wear
and resharpening is visible on the upper edge of blade.
Bottom, Archaic BEVEL blade hafted in ash handle. The
wide and thick stem of this type of blade provided an excellent hafting area. The beveled and serrated edges are
ideal for cutting (PN). Mr. Nusbaum has done considerable research to be sure these handle recreations are
as authentic to the originals as possible. All blades are old
and authentic.
Photo courtesy Paul Nusbaum, Deer Creek Enterprises,
Pandora, OH 45877

CHAPTER XIX

Often it seems that Amerind artifacts — authentic, questionable, or artifake — are more easily available than sound sources of information. Too frequently, the material one reads in professional journals doesn't make much sense to the layman because that person is not familiar with the terminology. Popular accounts, mainly newspapers and television, provide spot attention to the subject, but this is rarely of sufficient depth or clarity to offer understanding.

None of these observations can prevail over the following publications, which have managed to find their audiences. In this day of specialized yet understanding facts, the collector would do well to explore these resources. The author has had some form of direct knowledge of all listings that follow, and does not hesitate to recommend them.

Handbook of North American Indians

Readers will no doubt want to know that some of the listings on knives in Chapters IV and XIV have a common source. This is the book series, *Handbook of North American Indians*, put out by the Smithsonian Institution. Despite the word "Handbook", these are massive, quality clothbound hardbacks packed with innumerable facts and references. This is on glossy paper, with photos, sketches and maps. As with all Smithsonian publications, accuracy is faultless. Of course, information on far more than knives is included in the books. Whole Indian lifeways are covered.

To date (and certainly more when you read this) seven of the twenty volumes have been published, each covering a North American geographic region, including prehistoric, historic and recent. The article writers are all experts in their various fields, and it is probably safe to say that most of what is known about North American Indians will eventually appear in these pages. For examples of size, Vol. 9 (Southwest) has 701 pp., while Vol. 15 (Northeast) has 924 pp. Prices are $23 and $27, respectively. The volumes appear, not in numerical sequence, but as they are completed and printed.

While book prices may seem "steep", the amount of information contained in each book actually makes them a real bargain. Each is the equivalent of several other smaller books. And certainly the series will become collector items in themselves.

By request and via a special printed form, the reader can be put on a mailing list for the announcement of each new volume, and so be assured of getting a copy. This series is highly recommended as **the** foundation for any serious library on Amerind material. For ordering information, write:

Superintendent of Documents
U.S. Government
Printing Office
Washington, DC
20402

Who's Who in Indian Relics

This is a unique series of hardback, high-quality books that covers the spectrum of Amerind artifact collecting today. The approach is direct, and concerns collections across the United States, what owners have acquired. Information is given about pieces picked up in a walk through nearby fields, beginners, to long-term collectors with incredible accumulations that would be the envy of any major museum.

There are several reasons why *Who's Who* is valuable. Collectors are listed, often with address so personal contact is possible, with all the learning and social benefits. Interesting ways of displaying artifacts are demonstrated, from cardboard specimen frames (very popular) to cabinet-maker's examples in fine woods. Some collectors have expansive artifact rooms that simply must be viewed to be appreciated.

A third reason is that *Who's Who* is itself becoming a collector item, a limited-edition book that not only gives pride of ownership but gains in value over the years. Early editions sell at well above the original price, and a complete set (six have now been completed) will one day be very valuable. Still another reason for acquiring some books is that they give a clear idea of Indian artifacts across the country.

Artifacts from all periods (early Paleo into Contact times) can be seen, evaluated, and compared. Each book is a learning session in itself, one that can be obtained only in these pages. Mr. Thompson, by the way, is an advanced collector himself, with many beautiful objects. For information on ordering, write:

Ben W. Thompson
1757 West Adams
Kirkwood, MO
63122

Central States Archaeological Journal

Put out by the Society of the same name, it has eleven member states. As the cover illustration indicates, these are: Illinois, Missouri, Indiana, Arkansas, Kentucky, Tennessee, Iowa, Wisconsin, Georgia, Alabama and Michigan. Persons from these states will be interested, so also those who want to know more about Amerind artifacts from America's "heartland" region. This is a 7 x 10 in. quarterly publication, averaging 50 pages, which covers much American Indian prehistoric activity.

Much that happens in this vital portion of the country is covered eventually in these pages, and the many regional officers and contributions add a far-reaching perspective, and a broad approach. In terms of states involved, this is an important organization that includes the geographic boundaries of some of America's most important early cultures. For information on membership, write:

TCSAS Mgr.
1102 Dougherty Ferry Rd.
St. Louis, MO 63122

Artifact Newspaper

Called "America's First Prehistoric Indian Relic Newspaper", this publication seems to be just that. It is a quarterly (Feb., May, Aug. & Nov.) and the most recent issue received (Winter '85) had 36 pages. A variety of information is presented, all helpful to the collector.

Editorial: A calendar of upcoming events is very worthwhile, including meetings and auctions, mainly Midwest and Southeast. Facts on prehistoric Indians are present, plus brief articles on recent finds, museums, societies, etc. There is $8 worth of free advertising with a paid subscription, which also is $8 per year.

Advertisements: There are many (display and classified) and the reader can learn about artifact buying, selling and trading, auction houses, pottery repair, artifact restoration, books about Indians and artifacts, coverage of leading dealers or collectors, where to obtain display frames, and more. The publication has been in existence for five years. For information write:

Janie Jinks-Weidner
Editor
Indian Relic Trader
P.O. Box 88
Sunbury, OH
43074

U. S. Indian Artifacts

An important book is now being printed. Gregory Perino — columnist, excavator and researcher for over 50 years — is at home in both the library and in the field. He has produced a large volume that will be the final word for years to come. Frankly, the author wished this work had been on the shelf while writing this book.

Entitled *Selected Preforms, Points and Knives Of The North American Indians*, it has typewriter-size pages of highest quality paper, full-size drawings of artifacts, and is hardbound. Reports Mr. Perino (personal communication, 17 Jan 85): "The book will have at least 400 point types illustrated, but I combined some types so that as many as 450 could appear in it".

The book will be 422 pages. Anyone who knows the cost of quality printing will understand that this is a true life's work, done for love of subject matter. The privately published limited-edition book is priced at $40, plus $2 p&h. Oklahoma residents should add $2 sales tax also. The book is available at the below address, and questions and correspondence may be sent to:

Gregory Perino
Archeological Consultant
1509 Cleveland
Idabel, OK
74745

Indian-Artifact Magazine

This is a high-quality quarterly magazine with a new approach — Indian material that is both accurate and understandable. It has it all: Columns; in-depth articles; cartoons; advertisements; drawings; photos; editorials; reports on museums, burial practices, top artifacts, point types, out-standing finds, national parks, historic artifacts, and housing; what's authentic, what's fake; flint, stone and slate artifacts; **plus** the possibility of writing a brief article, seeing it published, and being paid for it.

Subscribers now are at least ten thousand, making it the largest and very likely the most important amateur archeological publication regarding North American Indians.

The magazine is well put-together, and sooner or later has answers for many of the questions collectors ask. Mr. Fogleman, himself a noted writer and collector, has traveled extensively in the Eastern U.S., photographing, interviewing and documenting. He is an authentic citizen archaeologist with many contributions past and future.

IAM, a fairly recent addition to the Amerind publications field, may well be the shape of things to come. For information or ordering, write:

Gary Fogelman
Editor-Publisher
Indian-Artifact Magazine
RR#1 - Box 240
Turbotville, PA
17772

The author occasionally receives letters from collectors desiring to buy or sell artifacts. Specialized (collector-attended) auctions are called for. Requirements are an established record of honesty and fair dealings, the whole run by people who know what they are doing. While many auctions no doubt meet such criteria, two are mentioned here because of personal familiarity. Serious collectors can write to be placed on mailing lists for announcements of upcoming auctions. The sources:

In the East:
Jan Sorgenfrei, Mgr.
Painter Creek Auction Service
RR#1
Pandora, OH
45877

In the West:
Col. Doug Allard
ALLARD AUCTIONS
P.O. Box 464
St. Ignatius, MT
59865

Postcript

This book has explored many different aspects of American Indian knives. The best part is yet to come, this being what the reader can learn by his or her own efforts. Solid information builds knowledge, and knowledge builds good collection. lh